KEEPING FAITH
IN AN AGE OF
REASON

REFUTING
ALLEGED BIBLE
CONTRADICTIONS

—⟨(●)⟩—

JASON LISLE

First printing: October 2017
Second printing: May 2018

Master Books®, P.O. Box 726, Green Forest, AR 72638
Master Books® is a division of the New Leaf Publishing Group, Inc.

ISBN: 978-1-68344-092-5
ISBN: 978-1-61458-605-0 (digital)
Library of Congress Number: 2017954605

Cover by Diana Bogardus

Please consider requesting that a copy of this volume be purchased by your local library system.

Printed in the United States of America

Please visit our website for other great titles:
www.masterbooks.com

For information regarding author interviews,
please contact the publicity department at (870) 438-5288.

Master
Books®
A Division of New Leaf Publishing Group
www.masterbooks.com

Acknowledgments

I am very grateful for the support of family and friends in my life and in my research. I extend a special thanks to Dr. Jim Johnson, and Dr. Ken Gentry for reviewing this book and providing helpful suggestions to improve it. I pray that this book challenges critics to study the Scriptures carefully rather than simply reacting to a cursory or careless reading. I further pray that this book will encourage believers and rekindle an interest in biblical research.

Contents

Introduction

We have all heard the claim "You can't trust the Bible — it's full of contradictions." But when asked specifically which verses supposedly contradict each other, most Bible-deniers can't actually produce any examples. They have *heard* that the Bible contradicts itself, and they have merely repeated that claim in ignorance, without bothering to check. This shows that most Bible critics are not interested in rational scholarship. Instead, they simply don't emotionally like the Bible, so they choose not to believe it. They then uncritically accept any claim they hear that happens to reinforce their uninformed choice. For the Bible critic, there is no need to research claims to see if they are actually *true*. It is enough that they support the critic's preconceived choice.

The Internet is a great place to find examples of such rhetoric. Moreover, the Internet allows the uninformed critic seemingly to support his claim by linking to articles written by other uninformed critics. Some websites include long lists of claims of biblical contradictions, sometimes with several hundred entries. These lists look impressive. And it would seem to prove the critic's point. With *hundreds* of contradictions, how could anyone trust the Bible? Many critics in their Internet debates mindlessly cite these lists as the definitive refutation of Scripture. After all, surely these hundreds of contradictions have been thoroughly researched, deal carefully and fairly with the text, and represent genuine contradictions, right?

As it turns out, this is not the case. When we actually bother to check, we find that *not one* of the hundreds of listed examples is genuinely contradictory at all. In most cases, it is clear that the critic has simply not read the text carefully or in context. In other cases, it is clear that the critic is not reasoning properly — he has made a mistake in logic. And in still other cases, the critic has merely cited a *compatible difference*, which leads me to believe that some critics really don't understand what a contradiction is.

To demonstrate the veracity of Scripture, this book will address *every* alleged Bible contradiction that I have seen posted on the Internet. Whereas there may be a few obscure claims of contradictions that I have not seen, this list covers the most often used examples. It is instructive to go through each of these alleged contradictions and read the text carefully to see what the Bible actually states. This helps us to understand the biblical text better, which is always a blessing. And it increases our confidence in Scripture, showing that even the best of the best Bible critics have not been able to find a single, genuine contradiction in Scripture. It further demonstrates that the Bible critic's choice to reject Scripture is not a rational one but an emotional one driven by the critic's hatred of God. Thus, the critic's lists of hundreds of alleged contradictions shows only his own lack of scholarship and ironically confirms the truth of Romans 1:18–25.

All of the claims below have actually appeared on the Internet. In fact, a common list that critics cite contains every item we address in this book. Before we go through the list in its entirety, let's briefly discuss what a contradiction is *and what it is not*.

What Is a Contradiction?

It is always helpful to define any relevant terms at the outset of the discussion. And since our topic involves the concept of contradiction, we must define this term. Two statements are said to be contradictory when one *asserts* what the other *denies*. The statement "The sky is blue" is contradictory to the statement "It is not the case that the sky is blue." Both statements together form a contradiction: "The sky is blue and it is not the case that the sky is blue." One can turn any statement into its contradictory statement by adding the prefix, "It is not the case that."

In logic, a contradiction is defined as "*A* and not-*A* at the same time and in the same relationship or sense." Here "*A*" is any truth claim, which in logic is called a proposition. Any given proposition is either true or false. And the contradictory proposition will have the opposite truth value. So, if "*A*" is true, then "not-*A*" is false. Conversely, if "*A*" is false, then "not-*A*" is true. Therefore, the combination of *A* and not-*A* must always be false.

The qualifier "at the same time" is very important. It is *not* a contradiction to say "The sky is blue today, and it is not the case that the sky was blue yesterday" because the two claims address two different times. Some things change with time, so "*A*" might be true today while "not-*A*" is true tomorrow. For example, God required circumcision of male children for Israelites during the time of the Old Covenant (Genesis 17:10–13). At a later time, under the New Covenant, God no longer required circumcision (Galatians 5:1–6). There is no contradiction between the claim "God requires circumcision" at one time and the claim "God does not require circumcision" at a *later* time. Yet, this is one of the alleged contradictions that Bible critics have posted online (see #185).

The qualifier "in the same relationship or sense" is also very important. It is not a contradiction to be "unmarried" in the sense of not having a spouse, and yet "married" to one's job. The sense of the word is different in the two cases, and so one claim does not deny what the other asserts. There is no contradiction in the claim "Bear one another's burdens" in the sense of helping those in trouble, and "bear your own burden" in the sense of taking responsibility for your own obligations. Yet, the critics have posted this very claim as addressed in #172. The principle that we should *not* answer a fool according to his folly *in the sense of becoming like him* is perfectly compatible and does not contradict the principle that we *should* answer a fool according to his folly *in the sense of reflecting his absurdity back to him* so that he cannot be wise in his own estimation. The critics make this very mistake as illustrated in #299.

A *compatible difference* is not a contradiction. There is no contradiction between the claim "the car is fast" and the claim "the car is red." The claims are different, but compatible since a car can be both fast and red. The Gospel writers each chose to record different details of what they observed, but the differences are compatible with each other and thus non-contradictory. So, when Matthew states that Joseph of Arimathea buried Jesus this does not contradict John's statement that Joseph *and Nicodemus* buried Jesus. Both statements are true, even though they are different. Now, if Matthew had stated that *only* Joseph *by himself* buried Jesus, then we would have a problem. But that is not what he states. The critic makes this very mistake in example #173.

A distinct but related concept is that of *contrary*. Two statements are contrary to each other if they cannot both be true at the same time. But, unlike contradictory statements, two contrary statements might both be false. Thus, two statements can be *contrary* to each other without necessarily being *contradictory*. For example, the statement "the traffic light is red" is contrary to the statement "the traffic light is green." But it is not in contradiction because both statements might be false: the traffic light might be yellow. However, the statement "the traffic light is red" is *contradictory* to the statement "it is not the case that the traffic light is red." Many times people will mistakenly say that two things are in contradiction when they really mean that the two things are merely *contrary*.

Common Fallacies

A mistake in reasoning is called a *fallacy*. In many of the following cases, we see that the critic has made a mistake in reasoning, leading him to conclude that two verses contradict each other, whereas correct reasoning shows that they do not. For the sake of space, I'd like to discuss here some of the most common mistakes that the critic makes below so that I won't have to repeat them over and over.

The argument from silence is the mistaken assumption that if something is not mentioned then it did not happen. The absurdity of this assumption is quickly revealed when we consider that the Bible never states anywhere that John the Baptist ever had to "use the restroom." But the fact that this is never stated obviously doesn't mean that it never happened! Sometimes one Gospel author will record a detail that another author omits. This is *not* a contradiction! Different authors will make different decisions about what to include and what to omit. But when they omit something, *that doesn't imply that it didn't happen.*

One of the errors frequently committed by Bible critics I will call, for the sake of simplicity, **the subset fallacy.** This is the error of claiming that A and B are contradictory when in fact A is a subset of B, or B is a subset of A, and the two are therefore perfectly consistent. For example, five is a subset of ten — it is not contradictory to ten. So, the statement "I have five fingers" is not contrary or contradictory to the statement "I have ten fingers" since five is a subset of ten. That is, anyone who has ten fingers necessarily has five fingers (and five more).

The subset fallacy is actually one type of argument from silence, because the fact that an author does not include some details or persons in his account does not in any way prove that they did not exist. So, one author may state Jesus healed a demon-possessed man, whereas another states that Jesus healed two. This is not a contradiction because if Jesus healed two people then He necessarily healed one (and one more). The first author didn't mention the other person for whatever reason (perhaps the second healing was less noteworthy), but that doesn't mean he didn't exist. Now, if the first author had written that Jesus healed *only* one man, and the second author stated that He healed two men at the same time and in the same sense, then there would be a problem. But no such problem is found in Scripture.

The bifurcation fallacy is a false-dilemma, also called the "either-or" fallacy. It occurs when a person asserts that there are only two exclusive options, when in fact there is a third possibility. "Either the traffic light is green or it is red" is a bifurcation fallacy because the light might be yellow. "Either a person is justified by faith or by works" is a bifurcation fallacy because a person can be justified by faith before God and justified by works before man. The critic makes this very mistake in #139.

The equivocation fallacy is when a person shifts the meaning of a word within an argument. For example: "James 1:13 teaches that God cannot be tempted, but Hebrews 4:15 teaches that Jesus (God) was tempted in all things — a contradiction." But the word "tempted" is used in two different senses; it can mean to be "tested" (which Jesus was) or it can mean to be "enticed" (which Jesus was *not*). It is no contradiction to affirm that Jesus was tested but never enticed. The critic makes this very mistake in #406.

The semantic range fallacy occurs when a reader determines a word's full semantic range (all the possible meanings that the word might have) and then chooses a definition that *suits* his preconceived *interpretation*, rather than allowing context to constrain the meaning. Context determines the meaning of a word — not the reader's preferences.

The semantic anachronism fallacy occurs when people import a modern meaning of a word into a text where the word did not have such a meaning at the time. For example, suppose someone claimed "The Bible clearly endorses extra-terrestrial life, because many biblical laws have instructions on what to do with the 'alien' (Numbers 9:14, 15:15)." But the biblical word translated "alien" refers to a foreigner — a human being who is not a native or citizen of the land.

The sweeping generalization fallacy is the failure to recognize that some principles are stated as generalizations that have some exceptions. The Book of Proverbs is a collection of such generalizations — things that are generally true in most circumstances, but that have some exceptions. It is the sweeping generalization fallacy to claim that an exception is *contradictory* to the general trend. It is not a contradiction to state "most of the time *A* but occasionally not-*A*." For example, divorce is generally unacceptable — in fact in all cases except infidelity. It is therefore *not* a contradiction to state that divorce is acceptable (not sinful) in cases of infidelity. Yet the critic makes this very mistake in #197.

Failure to do textual transmission analysis is another mistake that critics sometimes make. Textual transmission analysis (sometimes called *textual criticism*) is the science of discovering the wording of the original text of Scripture where minor variations exist. The Christian claim is that the *original* text of Scripture as penned by the authors was infallibly guided by God and thus has no genuine errors or contradictions. We recognize that the process of copying the text of Scripture over the centuries is not perfect, and a few scribal errors exist, causing slight variations in some of the ancient manuscripts. Variations are minor, but they do exist. Sometimes critics will point to a scribal error in a manuscript variation and claim that this contradicts another text where no such error exists. But this is not a genuine contradiction in the actual original text of Scripture. For his claim of a genuine contradiction to be legitimate, the critic needs to show that there is actual manuscript evidence that it is *not* a scribal error and that the contradiction *was in the original.* Bible critics occasionally make this mistake (as in #29 and #74), although it is not as common as one might suspect.

The genre fallacy is the failure to read a text in a way that is consistent with its style of literature. The Bible contains several different styles of literature: history, poetry, prophecy, and parables. And they are not to be interpreted in exactly the same way. Poetry typically contains metaphors and other figures of speech, whereas historical narrative is fairly literal. It would be out-of-context to interpret poetry as history or history as poetry. For example, when the Psalmist asks why God doesn't answer his prayer, why God "sleeps," this "sleep" is not to be taken as a literal loss of consciousness. Yet the critic makes this very mistake in #400.

We will find that many of the errors committed by the critic can be described simply as a **"failure to read the text carefully."** That is, the critic seems to have merely glanced at an isolated text without reading it in context, and has come away with an interpretation that no careful reader would hold. It would be silly to say, "The Bible claims that there is no God in Psalm 14:1," because in context this verse actually says, "The *fool has said* in his heart, 'There is no God.' "

And yet, this is precisely the kind of error the critic commits in #24 and in #420.

Some of the critic's errors I can only describe as a *"bluff."* These are instances where there is not even an *apparent* inconsistency between the verses listed. That is, no rational person would conclude, even from a casual first look, that the verses listed are contradictory. It seems that the critic has merely bluffed, listing verses that are not remotely contradictory, and has hoped that no one would bother to check. Sadly, most people probably did not.

"Specious reasoning" refers to an illogical leap — where the critic's conclusion simply does not rationally follow. Suppose a critic claimed that the statement "Agag was executed" is contradictory to the claim "Agag had many descendants." That would be an example of specious reasoning, because there is no logical reason why Agag couldn't have children and then *later* be executed. His children and grandchildren would not suddenly vanish at his execution. And yet, this is the sort of silly reasoning we see in the critic's example #59.

This covers the more common errors committed by the critic. For a more complete list of logical fallacies and fallacies of interpretation, see my other books *The Ultimate Proof of Creation, Discerning Truth,* and *Understanding Genesis.*

The List: 420 Claims of Contradictions

We will now examine each of the critic's claims of Bible contradictions. I will list the critic's claim in bold and will then state the error made by the critic, followed by a brief explanation. In cases where additional verses would have remedied the critic's confusion, I will display those verses in bold text in my explanation. For the sake of space, I have not written out the text of most of the verses cited. So, the best way to read this book is with a Bible open next to it. For best retention, consider looking up each of the verses listed so that you can see them in context. Some readers will choose to carefully examine each and every example. Others will focus only on those that seem most compelling or interesting and may skim the rest. The list does not need to be read in any particular order.

    The list I used as examples of alleged Bible contradictions can be found here: http://i.imgur.com/8goDAGG.gif, accessed 6/19/2017.

    Note that a number of claimed contradictions in this list are duplicates or repeat the same type of claim. Aside from these duplicates, each of the claims in this list is addressed in this book.

QUANTITATIVE DIFFERENCES

In this chapter, we examine claims that the Bible contradicts itself concerning the number of something. If one verse states that *only* three people were present at a certain time and place, but another verse states that at least four people were present at the same time and place and in the same sense, then the two verses would be in contradiction. The word "only" is an important qualifier because a verse listing three people does *not* contradict the claim that more people were there. To assume that "three" means "only three" without sufficient contextual warrant is the subset fallacy. This is the case with many of the claims below — but not all. If one verse indicates that a king began to reign at age 22, but another verse lists 42, it would make no sense to think that one is merely reporting a subset of another. But are the verses genuinely contradictory?

1. How many men did the chief of David's captains kill? Second Samuel 23:8 says 800, but 1 Chronicles 11:11 says 300.

Subset Fallacy. Jashobeam killed 300 men at one time with a spear (1 Chronicles 11:11). He also killed an additional 500, for a total of 800 men (2 Samuel 23:8). These 500 were apparently killed with a different weapon, and not a spear, so there is no discrepancy. Note that some translations have added the phrase "he lifted up his spear" (against the 800) in 2 Samuel 23:8, but this phrase is not in the original Hebrew text, which is why it is in italics in translations like the KJV and is not included in the NASB, NKJV, ASV, Douay, Geneva, and YLT.

2. How many sons did Abraham have? Hebrews 11:17 and Genesis 22:2 indicate only one. But Genesis 4:22, 16:15, 21:2–3, 25:1–2 teach more than one.

Subset fallacy and failure to distinguish different times. At one time Abraham had no sons. At a later time, he had one son. At a still later time, he had several. The above verses refer to different times — a fact the critic failed to notice. Furthermore, not all of Abraham's sons were legitimate sons of a biblically sanctioned marriage. Abraham's first son, Ishmael, was not born to his wife Sarah but rather to his wife's handmaid — Hagar (Genesis 16:15). Later, Sarah bore him a son, Isaac (Genesis 21:2–3). Abraham then sent away Ishmael (21:14). So, at the time God tested Abraham in Genesis 22:2, Abraham had only one son living within his household. This is the time to which Hebrews 11:17 refers. *At a later time,* Abraham begat six additional sons with his second wife Keturah (Genesis 25:1–2; 1 Chronicles 1:32). None of the passages listed by the critic contradict these facts or each other.

Semantic range fallacy. English translations of Hebrews 11:17 often describe Isaac as Abraham's "only begotten" son. However, the Greek word translated "only begotten" is *monogenes* and has the basic meaning of "one-of-a-kind." An only child would fall into that category but so would a *unique* son. Indeed, the same word is used for Jesus in John 3:16. While God has many adopted sons (Matthew 5:9; Luke 20:36; Romans 8:14; Galatians 3:26), Christ is unique in His sinless and perfect obedience to His Father. Likewise, the Hebrew word translated "only" in Genesis 22:2 means "unique" or "solitary," which certainly applies to Isaac who was — at that time — the only legitimate son from a biblically sanctioned marriage.

3. How long was the Ark of the Covenant at Abinadab's house? First Samuel 7:1-2, 10:24 say 20 years, but 2 Samuel 6:2-3 and Acts 13:21 indicate that it was actually much longer than 20 years.

Subset fallacy and failure to recognize different times. The ark was at Abinadab's house for at least 20 years (1 Samuel 7:2), and apparently another 20 years minimum, since it was there during Saul's reign which lasted 40 years (Acts 13:21), and was retrieved during David's reign (2 Samuel 6:2–3). The 20 years mentioned in 1 Samuel chapter 7 apparently refers to the period of time when the house of Israel lamented after the Lord (1 Samuel 7:2). But there is no verse in Scripture that precludes the ark being at Abinadab's house for an additional 20 or more years before this.

4. How old was Abram when Ishmael was born? Genesis 16:16 contradicts Acts 7:2–4; Genesis 11:26, 32.

Failure to read the text carefully. Abram was 86 years old when Ishmael was born (Genesis 16:16), and no verse says otherwise. Certainly none of the other verses listed by the critic contradict this at all, and it isn't clear why the critic claims that they do. His confusion may stem from a misconception about when Abram left Haran, as addressed in #36.

5. When did Absalom rebel against David? Second Samuel 15:7 says 40 years, but 2 Samuel 5:4 indicates that it must be less than this.

Failure to do textual transmission analysis. Many English translations describe the treachery of Absalom as lasting "40 years" (2 Samuel 15:7). Yet, the text of 2 Samuel 5:4 indicates that David was 30 years old when he began to reign and that he reigned as king for 40 years. It doesn't seem reasonable that Absalom's treachery lasted for David's entire reign or that it began before his reign. However, many ancient manuscripts (the Syriac, the Arabic, and some versions of the Septuagint) list this time of rebellion as "4 years." So, does Josephus (Antiquities 7:196). Many Bible scholars conclude that this "4 years" is what the original text of Scripture records. And David's reign was

40 years (2 Samuel 5:4). So, there is no inconsistency here in the original manuscripts.

6. How many Israelites from each family returned from Babylon? The list recorded in Ezra 2 contradicts the list recorded in Nehemiah 7. For example, Ezra states that 454 sons of Adin returned, but Nehemiah 7:20 states that 655 returned. Which is it?

Failure to distinguish different times or senses. Ezra 2:15 indicates that 454 sons of Adin returned, and Nehemiah 7:20 indicates that 655 returned. This is not a contradiction since 454 is a subset of 655. That is, if 655 people returned, then 454 returned (along with an additional 201). So, technically, the critic has committed the subset fallacy. Nonetheless, we must ask why Ezra does not include the additional 201 in his list. Furthermore, we note that the numbers of several other families also differ between the list in Ezra 2 and that of Nehemiah 7. Why the difference?

Recall that the return from Babylon occurred over a period of time — not in an instant. Over the course of time, additional people would make the journey, while others passed away. And so, depending on the time when the events are reported, differences in the numbers are to be expected. Such differences must occur if the two lists reflect two different dates. So, were Ezra and Nehemiah written at different times? Historians estimate that Ezra was written in the 500s BC. whereas Nehemiah was written in the mid 400s B.C. In a timespan of one hundred years, of course there would be additional people who would make the trip, and some would move out or pass away.

Far from demonstrating a contradiction, the numerical differences demonstrate the authenticity of Ezra and Nehemiah, showing that they were indeed written at different times, during which different numbers of people had made the journey. Recall that Ezra records the census of the people that left for Babylon (Ezra 2:1), whereas Nehemiah records a registry *that he found*, which is apparently an *updated* list (Nehemiah 7:5). Note that the total was not updated in the Nehemiah list, and that neither list records every family that returned. So, the critic's objection is as absurd as claiming that the 2010 national census must be wrong because it contradicts the 2000 national census.

Furthermore, even if the two lists had been recorded at the same time, we might still expect some differences if they each classified family lineage by different *criteria*. (Some have suggested that this is also the case with Christ's genealogies listed in Matthew 1:1–17 and Luke 3:23–38.) For example, the Ezra list might use legal ancestry, while the Nehemiah list uses biological ancestry. That would inevitably lead to numerical differences in cases of remarriage as the following hypothetical scenario illustrates.

Suppose, as one possibility, that Adin adopted a son. This person would be legally the descendent of Adin but biologically the offspring of someone else. If the rest of Adin's children were sired by him, then they and their descendants (454) would belong to Adin both biologically and legally. So, by biological reckoning, 454 of Adin's descendants returned, but by legal reckoning, 655 returned. There are other ways this could occur too. But clearly there is more than one way to classify lineage, and we would expect some numeric differences in terms of which son belongs to which family. So, there is no contradiction, only compatible differences between the two lists that were recorded at different times.

In some lists that circulate on the Internet, the critic lists each and every numerical difference between the Ezra census and the updated Nehemiah census as separate examples of supposed contradictions. Presumably this was done to make the list appear larger than it really is. It would be like claiming that the 2000 U.S. census contradicts the 2010 census for (1) Ohio, (2) Colorado, (3) Michigan, (4) Arizona, and so on, counting it as 50 contradictions. But all numerical differences between these two lists have the same resolution; they are non-contradictory and are in fact expected because the lists were recorded at different times.

7. When did Ahaziah begin to reign? Second Kings 8:25 says this happened in the *12th* year of Joram, whereas 2 Kings 9:29 says this happened in the *11th* year.

Failure to distinguish different senses and semantic range fallacy. In English translations, the text of these two passages indicates that Ahaziah "became king" or "began to reign" in the 11th (9:29) or 12th (8:25) year of Joram respectively. But the Hebrew word used here is "malak" and has a range of meanings. It can mean to "become king" or it can mean to "reign." These are slightly different meanings, and so we might expect a numerical difference depending on which meaning is in play, particularly if the events took place near the end of Joram's 11th year. That is, the ceremony in which Ahaziah was installed as king could have taken place near the end of Joram's 11th year, while Ahaziah did not actually take power until the beginning of the 12th year. Or the reverse: if Ahaziah's father (Jehoram) died unexpectedly near the end of the 11th year, then Ahaziah may have reigned in his father's place for a short time until he was officially installed as king during the 12th year. Similar things takes place in our culture: Donald Trump was elected president in 2016 but began his presidency in 2017. Surely, there is no contradiction here.

8. How old was Ahaziah when he began to reign? Second Kings 8:26 says *22*, but 2 Chronicles 22:2 says *42*.

Failure to do textual transmission analysis and failure to consult the original language. Ahaziah was 22 when he began to reign, according to 2 Kings 8:26. Some ancient manuscripts of 2 Chronicles 22:2 indicate that Ahaziah began to reign at *42*. But does this "42" refer to his age, or the age of Omri's dynasty? The word "was" is not in the Hebrew text. Without it, the text reads "a son of 42 years." The same verse mentions that Ahaziah's mother is the granddaughter of Omri; Omri was a king of Israel whose reign began 42 years before Ahaziah's (1 Kings 16:23; 2 Chronicles 16:13, 20:31, 21:20).

Even if the reference to 42 years is meant to indicate Ahaziah's age, not all ancient manuscripts have this number. Therefore, many Bible scholars, such as John Gill, believe the "42 years" to be an earlier copyist error. Several ancient manuscripts, including the Septuagint, the Syriac, and Arabic texts read "22 years" both in 2 Chronicles and in 2 Kings, as reflected in some modern English translations such as the New American Standard, the ESV, and NIV. In fact, there is only one Hebrew letter that distinguishes "22" from "42." And this letter can easily be confused, particularly since these were handwritten copies. For this passage to be a genuine contradiction, the critic would have to know that it is not an early copyist error and that the number "42" definitely refers to Ahaziah's age — neither of which he has been able to do.

9. When did Baasha die? First Kings 16:6–8 says the 26th year, but 2 Chronicles 16:1 says the 36th year.

Semantic range fallacy. Baasha died during the 26th year of Asa's kingship of Judea (1 Kings 16:6–8, 15:33.) In English translations of 2 Chronicles 16:1 there appears to be an inconsistency because the text indicates that Baasha went to war in the 36th year of Asa's reign. This would seem to be impossible, since it was ten years after Baasha's death.

But the Hebrew word often translated as "reign" in 2 Chronicles 16:1 is most often translated in the KJV as "kingdom." And thus, it was in the 36th year of Asa's kingdom (the Kingdom of Judah) that Baasha went to war. But Judah had already existed as a separate nation for 20 years when Asa became King of Judah. Thus, Baasha went to war in the 16th year of Asa' reign — the 36th year of the Kingdom of Judah. Baasha died ten years later, with no contradiction or inconsistency.

Alternatively, we again note the possibility of a textual transmission problem in modern copies of 2 Chronicles 16:1. Keil and Delitzsch point out that the Hebrew letter denoting "30" is similar to that denoting "10," and thus "16" might be erroneously rendered as "36" by a careless scribe. By either reckoning, Baasha went to war in the 16th year of Asa's reign, which is fully consistent with the passage in 1 Kings 16:6–8.

10. What was the volume of the molten sea in Solomon's temple? First Kings 7:26 says 2,000 baths, but 2 Chronicles 4:5 says 3,000 baths.

Subset fallacy. Neither text gives the exact volume. Rather, the volume was sufficient to hold 2,000 baths (1 Kings 7:26) and 3,000 baths (2 Chronicles 4:5), respectively. Obviously, if the volume is sufficient to hold 3,000 baths, then it is sufficient to hold 2,000 baths. So, there is no contradiction. It could be that the 2,000 baths was the typical volume of water it contained and useful for the priests in washing, but that 3,000 baths was the maximum volume it could contain. In any case, 2,000 is a subset of 3,000, so there is no contradiction or apparent inconsistency.

11. How many believers were there at the time of the ascension? Acts 1:15 says 120, but 1 Corinthians 15:6 says over 500.

Failure to read the text carefully and specious reasoning. The Bible does not say how many believers there were at the time of Christ's ascension. Acts 1:15 refers to one particular gathering of 120 Christians shortly after the ascension — but it does not remotely suggest that these were the only believers on earth at the time. First Corinthians 15:6 reports that Jesus was seen by over 500 people at one time before His ascension — but it does not say how many believers there were who did not see Christ during this period. So, these texts are addressing different events at different times, are perfectly compatible, and have nothing to do with the critic's question. This type of "criticism" shows that the critic is not serious about scholarship or academic integrity.

12. How many blind men were healed near Jericho? Matthew 20:30 indicate that there were two, but Mark 10:46 and Luke 18:35 say one.

Subset fallacy and argument from silence. This is a classic example of the subset fallacy. Jesus healed (at least) two blind men near Jericho (Matthew 20:30). Mark 10 and Luke 18 mention only one of the two, and Mark gives the name as "Bartimaeus." But neither Mark nor

Luke states that there was *only* one blind man. So, there is no contradiction even though only Matthew mentions the other blind man.

13. How long was the Egyptian Captivity? Genesis 15:13 says 400 years, but Exodus 12:40 and Galatians 3:17 say 430 years.

Subset fallacy and failure to read the text carefully. None of the passages listed by the critic specify the length of time of the captivity but rather the length of time that Abraham and/or his descendants would be strangers in a land that they do not possess (only some of that time was in Egypt). But is this length 400 years (Genesis 15:13) or 430 years (Exodus 12:40; Galatians 3:17)? Of course, 400 is a subset of 430, so there is no contradiction. It would be reasonable enough to infer that one text is simply rounding to the nearest hundred, whereas the others round to the nearest ten. That would be perfectly acceptable, and non-contradictory. However, there is more to it than this.

First, the 400 years refers to the time in which Abraham's descendants would be "strangers in a land that is not theirs" (Genesis 15:13) — not merely the subset of that time for which they would be captives in Egypt. Furthermore, a careful reading of Genesis 15:13 shows that this refers to the time that Abraham's *descendants* would be strangers in a land that is not theirs. Thus, the 400 years refers to the time from Isaac — Abraham's son — to the exodus. It excludes the time that Abraham dwelt as a stranger in the land. From Isaac to the Exodus was precisely 405 years, which is rounded quite reasonably to 400 years.

Paul, in Galatians 3:17, refers to 430 years *between the time the promise was given to Abraham* (Galatians 3:16) and the giving of the Law, which occurred around the time of the Exodus. That promise was given 25 years *before* the birth of Isaac (Genesis 12:1–4, 17:21–24). It was at that earlier time that Abraham left his own land and dwelt as a stranger in the land. So, when we include Abraham, we see that the Hebrews dwelt in a land not their own for a total of 430 years. The Exodus 12:40 passage also apparently includes the time that Abraham was a stranger in the land, as the Samaritan version reads. So, unlike the critic, the biblical authors were very meticulous in their attention to detail.

14. How high was the chapiter? Jeremiah 52:22 says five cubits, but 2 Kings 25:17 says three cubits.

Subset fallacy. The capital (*chapiter*) on the pillars was five cubits in height (Jeremiah 52:22), which means it was three cubits in height (2 Kings 25:17) and two more. Why does 2 Kings 25:17 not include the remaining two cubits? One possibility is that only three of the five had the bronze pomegranates and lattice work described in both passages (Jeremiah 52:22; 2 Kings 25:17).

15. How many men did David kill? Second Samuel 10:18 says 700, but 1 Chronicles 19:18 says 7,000.

Subset fallacy and semantic range fallacy. As worded in the original Hebrew, both passages literally say that David killed the *chariots*. This is a figure of speech called *metonymy* in which an object is substituted for the people associated with it. That is, David killed the *people* associated with the chariots. The way in which the people were associated is not stated, and so it may differ between the two passages. Only one person would be the primary driver of the chariot, but several others would have been assigned to the unit. If we suppose that 10 men were associated with a chariot, then the perceived inconsistency disappears. That is, David slew 7,000 men from 700 chariot units.

This is further supported by the choice of the Hebrew word *harag* translated "killed" or "slew." This word also refers to the destruction of inanimate objects, such as the chariots themselves. (The word is used to describe the destruction of vines and trees in Psalm 78:47.) Even modern warfare terminology will refer to the destruction of a tank or a plane as a "kill," regardless of how many people within are killed. Thus, to destroy 700 chariots, or chariot units, is 700 kills and could easily correspond to 7,000 individual deaths.

16. Did Jesus say before the cock crows or before the cock crows twice? Matthew 26:34; Luke 22:34; and John 13:38 all say before the cock crows, but Mark 14:30 says before the cock crows *twice*.

Subset fallacy. If the rooster crows twice, then it necessarily crows once (and then once again). Jesus said that Peter would deny Him three times before the rooster crows *twice* (Mark 14:30). The accounts of Matthew, Luke, and John do not record this detail (that the rooster would crow *twice*) — but they also do not deny or contradict it. That is, neither Matthew, Luke, nor John say that Peter will deny Christ three times "before the rooster crows *only once,*" or "before the *first* crow." You can search all you like, but there is no passage that says the rooster crowed *only* once.

17. Generations from David to the Babylonian Captivity. First Chronicles 3:10–16 disagrees with Matthew 1:6–11.

Subset fallacy and semantic anachronism fallacy. As is well known, the genealogy listed in Matthew 1:1–17 is a summary, and was not intended to be exhaustive. This was a common practice at the time. Recall that in biblical languages the word "son" can also refer to a grandson or a more distant descendant (Luke 19:9; Matthew 1:1). Matthew intentionally did not list every name, so that he could record the lineage of Abraham to Christ in exactly three groups of 14 each (Matthew 1:17). This should be obvious to even the most obstinate critic because Matthew 1:1 gives an even briefer summary — from Abraham to Jesus with only one name in between (David).

The list in 1 Chronicles 3:10–16 does appear to be exhaustive, so it naturally includes some ancestors of Christ that Matthew does not. Matthew 1:6–11 does not list Joash, Amaziah, and Azariah. But neither does it deny their existence or claim that there were no such ancestors of Christ. So, there is no contradiction just because 1 Chronicles records some details that Matthew omits.

18. How many disciples did Jesus appear to in His first post-Resurrection appearance? First Corinthians 15:5 disagrees with Matthew 28:16–17; Mark 16:14; and Luke 24:33–37, which contradict John 20:24.

Failure to read the text carefully. First Corinthians 15:5 does not say how many disciples were present when Jesus *first* appeared after the Resurrection. It says only that Christ appeared to Cephas (Peter), then to the Twelve — referring to the other disciples. Although there were only 11 remaining, the group was still called the "Twelve" (John 20:24) — an example of synecdoche. This verse may imply that Peter saw Christ before the rest of the Twelve, but it does *not* say that Peter was the *first* person to see Christ. Mary Magdalene seems to have been the first (Mark 16:9; John 20:1–18). Matthew 28:16 records Jesus appearing to the remaining 11 disciples, but it does *not* say that this was the *first* appearance — we have good reason to believe it wasn't (see #208, #54, and #115). Likewise, Mark 16:14 records a meeting with the 11 disciples, but it does *not* say that this was the *first* appearance. Luke 24:33–37 also records a meeting of Christ with the 11 disciples, but we know this was not His *first* appearance from verses 13–15. John 20:24 merely states that Thomas was not with the 11 disciples when Jesus had appeared earlier, but it does not say that this was the first appearance. None of the texts listed by the critic even address the issue; thus they cannot contradict each other.

19. Was Enoch the sixth or the seventh from Adam? Genesis 5:3–18; 1 Chronicles 1:1–2; and Luke 3:37–38 contradict Jude 14.

Failure to count properly. Enoch was the seventh generation, and hence the seventh from Adam. Adam was the first generation, Seth was second, Enos was third, Cainan was fourth, Mahalaleel was fifth, Jared was sixth, and Enoch was seventh, as all the biblical texts agree (Genesis 5:3–18; 1 Chronicles 1:1–2; Luke 3:37–38; Jude 14). Perhaps the critic thinks that the "seventh from Adam" means the seventh *after* Adam and not including Adam. But this is not the way genealogies are counted, not in Hebrew, not in Greek, not in English.

For example, "Henry III" or "Henry the third" is the grandson of Henry senior — he is counted as the third, not the second.

20. How many years of famine? Second Samuel 24:13 says seven years, but 1 Chronicles 21:11–12 says three years.

Subset fallacy and failure to read the text in context. God gave David a choice of punishments for the sin of conducting a biblically unsanctioned census (see #180). As one option, the land of Israel would suffer three years of famine (1 Chronicles 21:11). In 2 Samuel 24:13, this option is presented as *seven* years of famine. This is no contradiction because if the land experiences seven years of famine then it logically must experience three years of famine (and four more).

A careful reading of the text shows that the land had *already* experienced three years of famine on account of Saul's sin (2 Samuel 21:1). Three more would be added due to David's sin (if he had chosen that option) for a total of six years. And since the Israelites were not permitted to work the land on the seventh year (Leviticus 25:3–5), there would be a food shortage for a total of seven years — only three of which were due to David's sin. The text in 2 Samuel 24:13 mentions the total number of years of famine, whereas 1 Chronicles 21:11–12 mentions only the three that would be *added* due to David's sin.

21. How long was the Ark afloat? Seven months (Genesis 8:4) or ten (Genesis 8:5)?

Failure to read the text carefully. Genesis 8:4 teaches that the Ark came to rest on the 17th day of the seventh month. At that time, the other mountains still could not be seen from the vantage point of the ark. It was not until the first day of the tenth month that the mountains became visible (Genesis 8:5). There is not even a hint of inconsistency, showing once again that the critic is not engaged in serious scholarship.

22. How long did the Flood last? Forty days and nights (Genesis 7:17), or 150 days (Genesis 7:24, 8:3).

Failure to define terms (equivocation fallacy), and failure to read the text carefully. The Flood occurred in stages: the initial period of rain, the time after the rain when the earth was still globally flooded, the time when the waters steadily receded, the time when the Ark was grounded but other land was not yet visible, the time when the land became visible, the time when the water was no longer upon the land but the land was still muddy, the time when the land became dry, and the time when Noah and those on board the ark disembarked. To which time does the critic refer? He doesn't say, and doesn't seem to have thought through this issue at all, because there is no inconsistency in any of the verses the critic cited:

> The rain fell for 40 days and nights (Genesis 7:17), but the water prevailed (did not subside) for 150 days (Genesis 7:24), after which it began to subside (Genesis 8:3). The tops of the mountains were seen on the 225th day (Genesis 7:11; 8:5). The raven was sent out on day 265 (Genesis 8:6); the dove was sent out on day 272, and again on day 279, and again on day 286 (Genesis 8:6–12). Noah saw that the water was off the surface of the earth by day 315 (Genesis 8:13), and God told Noah to disembark on the 371st day.

Where is there even a *hint* of a contradiction?

23. How many generations from Jesus to Abraham? Matthew 1:17 says 42, but Matthew 1:2–16 says 41.

Failure to read the text carefully and argument from silence. There are 41 *listed* generations from Abraham to Christ — though Matthew does not claim that his list is exhaustive (Matthew 1:2–16). This is actually perfectly consistent with Matthew 1:17, though the critic seems not to have read the latter passage carefully. Verse 17 mentions three groups of 14 people, from which the critic apparently assumes would make 42 people (3 x 14). However, the critic did not read the text carefully, otherwise he would have noticed that David is included *both* in the first group (as the final member) and the second group (as the first member). To be clear, group 1 includes Abraham through David (14 people), group 2 includes David through Josias (14 people), and group 3 includes Jeconiah through Christ (14 people). Since groups 2 and 1 overlap by one person (David), the total number of individuals in all three groups is 41, exactly what Matthew 1:2–16 lists.

24. How many gods are there? *Just the one* according to Deuteronomy 4:35, 39, 6:4, 32:39; 1 Kings 18:39; Isaiah 43:10, 44:8, 45:5–6, 46:9; Mark 12:29, 32; John 17:3; and 1 Corinthians 8:6. *More than one* according to Genesis 1:26, 3:22, 11:7; Exodus 12:12, 15:11, 18:11, 20:3, 5, 22:20, 28, 23:13, 24, 32, 34:14; Numbers 33:4; Deuteronomy 3:24, 6:14–15, 10:17, 28:14; Joshua 24:2, 14; Judges 11:24; 1 Samuel 6:5, 28:13; 1 Chronicles 16:25; Psalm 82:1, 6, 86:8, 96:4, 97:7, 135:5, 136:2; Jeremiah 1:16, 10:11, 25:6, 46:25; Zephaniah 2:11; John 10:33–34; and 1 John 5:7.

Failure to read the text carefully and specious reasoning. The Bible affirms that there is only one God (Deuteronomy 4:35, 39, 6:4, 32:39; 1 Kings 18:39; Isaiah 43:10, 44:8, 45:5–6, 46:9; Mark 12:29, 32; John 17:3; 1 Corinthians 8:6). The Bible also affirms that this one God is three in terms of eternally distinct persons — the Father, Son, and Holy Spirit. This doctrine is commonly called the "Trinity." The Trinity is not contradictory because it does not affirm that God is only one and more than one *in the same sense*. Rather, it affirms that God is one in one sense (in terms of nature or essence) and three in a *different* sense (in terms of persons). Such is true of many things in the world. One molecule may be many in terms of atoms. A church is one group united in fellowship, but it is many in persons. Congress is *one* body but *two* houses and *many* persons. So, obviously there is no logical problem with a triune God.

This one *in one sense* and more-than-one in *another* sense is seen in the first verse of Scripture, where the word translated "God" is plural in the original language, and yet the verb associated with it (created) is singular. It's actually grammatically incorrect, a bit like saying "Gods is good." This formula, a plural noun with a singular verb, is used very consistently in the Old Testament in references to God. These verses demonstrate that the one God is more than one *in persons* (John 8:17–18; Luke 3:22; Genesis 1:26, 3:22, 11:7; John 10:33, 14:16–17; 1 John 5:7; Acts 5:3–4). Sometimes one person of the Trinity speaks to another (Matthew 3:17; 2 Peter 1:17; Hebrews 1:5, 8–9; John 17:1, 5). But notice that none of these verses contradict the others; *none* say that there are multiple true Gods.

Also, note that the Bible acknowledges the existence of *false gods*, which are called "gods" but have no genuine power (Exodus 12:12, 15:11, 18:11, 20:3–5, 22:20, 23:13, 24, 32, 34:14; Numbers 33:4; Deuteronomy 3:24, 6:14–15, 10:17, 28:14; Joshua 24:2, 14; Judges 11:24; 1 Samuel 6:5, 28:13; 1 Chronicles 16:25; Psalm 82:1, 6, 86:8, 96:4, 97:7, 135:5, 136:2; Jeremiah 1:16, 10:11, 25:6, 46:25; Zephaniah 2:11; John 10:34). But since these are not truly gods in any real sense, they do not violate the biblical position of one God. First Corinthians 8:5–6 *explicitly* explains this, so the critic is without excuse for missing this. Having examined all the verses listed by the critic, we find not a single inconsistency.

25. How much gold, silver, and clothing did the people give? Ezra 2:69 disagrees with Nehemiah 7:72.

Subset fallacy and specious reasoning. Ezra lists only the total contributions to the Temple, which amount to 61,000 gold drachmas, 5,000 silver minas, and 100 priestly garments. Nehemiah also lists contributions to the Temple, but breaks them down more exactly, and the totals appear somewhat different: 41,000 gold drachmas, 4,200 silver minas, 530 priestly garments, and 50 basins. There is no contradiction since neither list claims to be exhaustive; if the people gave 61,000 gold drachmas, then they necessarily gave 41,000 (along with 20,000 more). Why Nehemiah does not list the additional 20,000 is not stated in the text, but this isn't required for logical consistency. Nonetheless, we might speculate on the reasons for these differences in the following ways.

Most English translations of Nehemiah 7:70 state that the governor gave 1,000 gold drachmas, 50 basins, and *530* priest's garments. But some scholars have noted that "silver minas" may be implied but not stated in the text in between the 500 and the 30, for the sake of consistency with the verses that follow. If so, then the governor gave 1,000 gold drachmas, 50 basins, *500 silver minas*, and *30* priestly garments. If so, then the Nehemiah list would total 41,000 gold drachmas, 4,700 silver minas, 97 priestly garments, and 50 basins. This resolves two of the three differences: the new list matches Ezra's count of the 5,000 silver minas, and 100 priestly garments when we recognize that Ezra is using round numbers. Ezra's count of 61,000 gold drachmas still doesn't match Nehemiah's 41,000, until we notice that Ezra does not list the 50 basins given by the governor. If these basins have a total value of roughly 20,000 gold drachmas, then both lists match nicely. There are other possibilities of course. But clearly the two texts do not contradict each other, even though they have compatible differences.

26. How many talents of gold did Hiram send Solomon? First Kings 9:27–28 says 420, but 1 Chronicles 8:18 says 450.

Subset fallacy. Hiram sent 450 talents of gold to Solomon (2 Chronicles 8:18), which includes the 420 talents mentioned in 1 Kings 9:27–28. Why the First Kings passage does not include the remaining 30 talents is not mentioned, but it seems very likely that the sailors and other workers were paid for their efforts (1 Timothy 5:18), and thus 30 talents of the 450 may have been used for their wages.

27. How many horsemen did David take? Second Samuel 8:4 says 700, but 1 Chronicles 18:4 says 7,000.

Subset fallacy. David took 1,000 chariots and 7,000 horsemen (1 Chronicles 18:4). These horsemen consisted of 700 ranks with 10 men per rank. Second Samuel 8:4 mentions only the ranks of horsemen (700) and includes the 1,000 chariots in this number, so "1,700 horsemen" is the figure given for the companies of horsemen and chariots, consistent with 1 Chronicles 18:4.

28. How many were in Jacob's family when they came into Egypt? Genesis 46:27 and Exodus 1:5 say 70, but Acts 7:14 says 75.

Subset fallacy and failure to read the text carefully. In Acts 7:14, Stephen says that Joseph invited Jacob and *all his relatives* to come to Egypt, for a total of 75 people. Yet, Genesis 46:26 gives the number as 66 persons. But a more careful reading of Genesis 46:26 says, "All the persons belonging to Jacob . . . *not including the wives of Jacob's sons*, were 66 persons in all." So, the reason the list in Acts is slightly larger than the list in Genesis is because the former *includes the wives,* whereas the latter does not. Each of Joseph's 11 brothers married, so that would be 11 wives. But Judah's wife had died in Canaan before the journey to Egypt (Genesis 38:12). And Genesis 46:10 suggests that Simeon's wife had also died before the journey (and that he later remarried). So, there were 9 living wives who came to Egypt with the 66 descendants of Jacob, for a total of 75 persons.

Why do Genesis 46:27 and Exodus 1:5 list 70 persons? The list from Genesis 46:27 is based on the 66 people mentioned in the previous verse (which excludes the 9 wives), but then *includes* Jacob, and his 3 descendants who were already in Egypt (Joseph and his 2 sons Ephraim and Manassah — see verse 27) — 4 in all. — 66+4 = 70. The numbers are exactly consistent, when the text is read *accurately*. Likewise, Exodus 1:5 either refers to this way of counting or is simply using a round number as the Bible often does.

29. How old was Jehoachin when he began to reign? Second Kings 24:8 says he was 18, but 2 Chronicles 36:9 says that he was 8.

Failure to do textual transmission analysis. Second Kings 24:8 indicates that Jehoachin was 18 years old when he began to reign. Some translations of 2 Chronicles 36:9 state that he was 8 years old but there is evidence that this is a rare transmission error. The ancient Syriac and Arabic translations have 18 years in *both* passages.

So, there seems to be no inconsistency in the original manuscripts. Moreover, the Hebrew language allows for other possibilities as well. We have seen, as with David, that a person can be appointed as king many years before he is officially installed as king.

30. How many sons did Jesse have? First Samuel 16:10–11, 17:12 says 8, but 1 Chronicles 2:13–15 says 7.

Subset fallacy. Jesse had eight sons (1 Samuel 16:10–11). Of these, seven are listed in 1 Chronicles 2:13–15. The eighth is not listed, perhaps having died before being able to start a family of his own.

31. How long did Jotham reign? Second Kings 15:32–33 says 16 years, but 2 Kings 15:30 says at least 20 years.

Failure to read the text carefully. Jotham reigned *as king* of Judah for 16 years (2 Kings 15:32–33), though he had previously reigned for some time *as a representative* of his leprous father King Uzziah/Azariah (2 Chronicles 26:21). No verse contradicts this. Though 2 Kings 15:30 mentions the *20th* year of Jotham, it does *not* say that Jotham was still king at this time; that is, it does *not* refer to the 20th year of Jotham's *reign*. Rather, it describes events that happened in the 20th year since Jotham was installed as king. At that time, Ahaz was king of Judah. But the biblical author had not yet mentioned Ahaz, and therefore marks time from the installment of Jotham as king.

32. What is the human lifespan? Psalm 90:10 says 70 to 80 years, but Genesis 6:3 says 120 years.

Failure to read the text carefully. In Psalm 90:10, Moses gives a *typical* human lifespan *at that time* (hundreds of years after the worldwide Flood) as 70 or 80 years. That does not remotely imply that this has always been the case or that there are no exceptions. Furthermore, Genesis 6:3 is not addressing human lifespans at all. Rather, the 120 years listed there marks the time that wicked humanity had left before God would destroy mankind with the global Flood. That is,

God gave mankind a 120-year period of grace for repentance before carrying out His judgment.

33. How many children did Michal have? Second Samuel 6:23 contradicts 2 Samuel 21:8.

Failure to read the text carefully or to do textual transmission analysis. Michal had no biological children of her own (2 Samuel 6:23). The critic didn't read 2 Samuel 21:8 carefully, because it does not say that Michal birthed any children at all — only that she "brought up" (KJV, translating from the Hebrew), i.e. raised, five children *for Adriel.* Moreover, the critic should have realized his mistake since Michal was not married to Adriel, but to David. Thus, these five children were birthed by Merab (Michal's sister) — Adriel's wife. So, even in the KJV there is no contradiction.

Moreover, the critic failed to recognize (or disclose) any textual transmission analysis, because there is some evidence of transmission confusion in this passage. In a number of the ancient manuscripts, Merab and not Michal is mentioned in 2 Samuel 21:8. (See page 493, BIBLIA HEBRAICA, 1973 Kittel Stuttgart edition, footnote b for 2 Samuel 21:8, identifying text variants.) The critic would have realized this (or at least would have been alerted to the fact that a translation or transmission factor was relevant to the question) if he had bothered to check other English translations, such as the NASB, the NIV, the NLT, or the ESV. The Chaldee manuscript lists both, specifying "the five sons of Merab which Michal the daughter of Saul brought up. . . ."

34. How many people did God kill for "committing whoredom with the daughters of Moab"? First Corinthians 10:8 says 23,000, but Numbers 25:9 says 24,000.

Subset fallacy and failure to read the text carefully. Moses gives the total number who died as a result of the incident — both the leaders that were hanged (Numbers 25:4), and the rest who fell by the sword (Numbers 25:5), a total of 24,000 people (Numbers 25:9). Paul lists only those who "fell" (by the sword) and in one day, 23,000 people. Apparently, 1,000 leaders were executed by hanging, and the remaining 23,000 people fell by the sword. So, both texts agree perfectly.

35. How many officers did Solomon have? First Kings 9:23 says 550, but 2 Chronicles 8:10 says 250.

Subset fallacy and failure to read the text carefully. Solomon had 250 officers to rule over the *people* (2 Chronicles 8:10), and he had an additional 300 who were over the *work*, for a total of 550 officers over the work *and* the people (1 Kings 9:23). So, the texts are perfectly consistent. Incidentally, it appears that there were three ranks of rulers; the lowest rank consisted of 3,300 people (1 Kings 5:16). The next rank consisted of 300 people, and when combined with the lowest rank make 3,600 people (2 Chronicles 2:18). And the highest rank had 250 officers (2 Chronicles 8:10), which when combined with the middle rank make 550 officers (1 Kings 9:23).

36. How old was Abraham when he left Haran? Genesis 12:4 contradicts Acts 7:2–4 and Genesis 11:26, 11:32.

Failure to read the text carefully and semantic anachronism fallacy. Abraham was 75 years old when he left Haran (Genesis 12:4) and no text says otherwise. The other passages listed by the critic do not speak of Abraham's age at the time he left Haran, nor do they give sufficient information to arrive conclusively at such a number. The confusion may stem from the critic's misreading of Acts 7:4. Some English translations seem to imply that Abraham left Haran when his father Terah died at age 205. But Genesis 11:26 suggests that Terah was 70 when Abraham was born. So, wouldn't this mean that Abraham was actually 135 when he left Haran? No, for the following reason.

The referent of the words "he" and "him" in the last part of Acts 7:4 is left ambiguous. Many people suppose that the "he" refers to God and "him" to Abraham — that God removed Abraham from Haran at the time of Terah's death. But more naturally, the referent of "he" is Abraham and "him" refers to Terah. That is, at the time of Terah's death, Abraham removed Terah's deceased body from Haran and buried the body in Canaan where Abraham had moved decades earlier. So, there is perfect harmony between all the texts.

37. How many overseers did Solomon have? First Kings 5:16 says 3,000, but 2 Chronicles 2:18 says 3,600.

Subset fallacy (see #35). Solomon had 3,300 rulers of the lowest rank (1 Kings 5:16) and 300 of the middle rank, adding up to 3,600 rulers in these two ranks (2 Chronicles 2:18). He also had 250 rulers of the highest rank (2 Chronicles 8:10). The verses agree very consistently.

38. How many days is unleavened bread to be eaten during the Passover? Deuteronomy 16:8 says *six* days, but Deuteronomy 16:3 and Exodus 12:15, 23:15 say *seven*.

Subset fallacy and fallacy of argument from silence. The answer is: seven days. No text contradicts this. Six of these days were ordinary work days in which unleavened bread was to be eaten. The seventh day was a day of rest and no work was to be done on it. Deuteronomy 16:8 does not specifically say whether unleavened bread was also to be eaten on the seventh day, but neither does it deny this. Hence, the critic has committed the error of the faulty argument from silence (assuming the absence of something on the basis that it is not mentioned). From Deuteronomy 16:3 and Exodus 12:15, 23:15, we read that the unleavened bread was also to be eaten at the assembly on the seventh day. So, where is any inconsistency?

39. How high were the pillars? First Kings 7:15 contradicts 2 Chronicles 3:15.

Failure to read the text carefully. The height of *one* pillar was 18 cubits (1 Kings 7:15). The (combined) height of both pillars was 35 cubits (2 Chronicles 3:15). There is no inconsistency. Either the second pillar was 17 cubits tall, or more likely both pillars were just over

17.5 cubits, which rounded gives 18 cubits, with a total combined height of 35 cubits. The passages show no contradiction, but indicate that the Israelites understood arithmetic.

40. How many men were possessed with devils? Mark 5:1–2 and Luke 8:26–27 say *one*, but Matthew 8:28 says *two*.

Subset fallacy. Two men were demon-possessed (Matthew 8:28). Mark and Luke mention only one of the two. This is perfectly consistent because, obviously, if two men were demon-possessed then one man was demon-possessed (and one more). Mark and Luke chose to mention only one of the two, probably because only the one was seen later and continues the narrative (Mark 5:14–20; Luke 8:36–39), as the critic might have realized if he had read just a few verses more.

41. On what day of the month was Jehoiachin released from prison? Second Kings 25:27 says on the 27th day, but Jeremiah 52:31 says it was the 25th day.

Failure to read the text carefully. Jeremiah 52:31 states that the King of Babylon *showed favor* to Jehoiachin on the 25th of the month and that he (subsequently) brought him out of prison. Note that the text does not say that both events happened on the same day. Favor was shown on the 25th, but the text does *not* say that he was released the same day. The implication is that Jehoiachin's release was as a result of, and therefore sometime *after*, the showing of favor. Thus it would be on or after the 25th day. Second Kings 25:27 confirms that Jehoiachin was released from prison on the 27th day, which indeed is after the king showed him favor, and thus consistent with Jeremiah 52:31.

42. Was Jesus a ransom for many or for all? Matthew 20:28 and Mark 10:45 say "many," but 1 Timothy 2:6 says "all."

Bifurcation fallacy and equivocation fallacy. Christ was ransomed for *all* who receive him, which are *many* (Matthew 20:28; Mark 10:45; 1

Timothy 2:6). Universal terms like "all" are sometimes restrained by context, as is the case in 1 Timothy 2:6. For example, "All people are required to present a birth certificate in order to obtain a passport." Clearly, this doesn't mean all people on earth are required; rather "all" refers to those who are going to get a passport. Likewise, Christ was a ransom for all people *who are to be saved,* as context indicates (1 Timothy 2:4–6). Christ's payment on the Cross is certainly sufficient for anyone to be saved. But people are actually saved only if they receive God's grace through faith in Christ.

43. How many soldiers? There were 800,000 according to 2 Samuel 24:9, but there were 1,100,000, according to 1 Chronicles 21:5.

Subset fallacy. If there were 1,100,000 men from Israel (1 Chronicles 21:5) then there were necessarily 800,000 men (2 Samuel 24:9) along with 300,000 more. Second Samuel 24:9 apparently does not include the king's militia, which consisted of 24,000 each month (1 Chronicles 27:1–2), which over one year would be 288,000 men. Including the officers, this would be about 300,000 men, which only the 1 Chronicles passage includes. So, there is no inconsistency. Moreover, the 2 Samuel account seems to round numbers to the nearest 100,000, whereas the parallel account in 1 Chronicles rounds to the nearest 10,000. Hence the men of Judah are reported either as 470,000 or rounded to 500,000 respectively.

44. Was Solomon David's second or fourth son by Bathsheba? He was the second son according to 2 Samuel 12:15, 24, but he was fourth according to 1 Chronicles 3:5.

Fallacy of argument from silence. *Neither passage* specifies when Solomon was born relative to his brothers. Second Samuel 12:15 does *not* say anything whatsoever about Solomon's brothers. First Chronicles 3:5 has Solomon as the fourth name in a list of his brothers. But that doesn't necessarily mean he was born fourth — only that he was *listed* fourth. Neither passage gives the order; hence, they cannot possibly contradict each other on a topic which neither addresses.

45. What was Solomon's gift to Hiram? First Kings 5:11 contradicts 2 Chronicles 2:10.

Failure to read the text carefully. Solomon gave Hiram 20,000 kors of wheat as food *for Hiram's household* and 20 kors of beaten oil (1 Kings 5:11). In addition, Solomon also gave to Hiram's *servants* 20,000 kors of barley, 20,000 baths of wine, and 20,000 baths of oil (2 Chronicles 2:10). Where is there any contradiction in Solomon giving different gifts to different people?

46. When did Solomon's reign begin? First Kings 6:1 contradicts Acts 13:17–18, 20–22 and 1 Chronicles 29:26–27.

Failure to read the text carefully and failure to check the original language. Solomon's reign began 477 years after the exodus from Egypt, because the fourth year of his reign corresponds to the 480th year after the exodus (1 Kings 6:1). Acts 13:19–20 mentions a period of 450 years, but it is not obvious what this period refers to. Some English translations imply that this period corresponds entirely to the time of judges — the time between Joshua and Samuel. But if that were so, then adding 450 to the 40 years of wandering in the wilderness, plus the 40 years of the reign of Saul, plus the 40 years of the reign of David, would yield a date for the start of Solomon's reign at 570 years or more after the exodus. Presumably, this is how the critic interpreted the passage.

But, had he bothered to check the original Greek text or had he consulted a few other English translations, the critic would have found some other renderings. For example, in Young's Literal Translation, Acts 13:19–20 states, "and having destroyed seven nations in the land of Canaan, He did divide by lot to them their land. And after these things, about four hundred and fifty years, He gave judges — till Samuel the prophet." On this translation, the 450 years refers to the time between the choosing of the people of Israel and their taking the land of Canaan — *not* the time of the judges. So, it is not addressing the same time period at all. The critic was very careless in his analysis.

47. How many stalls did Solomon have? First Kings 4:26 says 40,000. However, 2 Chronicles 9:25 says 4,000.

Fallacy of equivocation. Note that Chronicles uses a slightly different Hebrew word for "stalls" than does Kings, and so we might expect that one refers to the entire stable, while the other refers to the number of individual compartments. Solomon had 4,000 stalls or "stables" (2 Chronicles 9:25), each of which apparently had ten partitions, such that the total number of stalls is 40,000 (1 Kings 4:26).

48. How old was Terah when he died? Genesis 11:26, 12:4 contradicts Genesis 11:32.

Failure to read the text carefully or properly do arithmetic. Terah died at the age of 205 years (Genesis 11:32). No Scripture contradicts this. Genesis 11:26 and Genesis 12:4 do not provide enough information to give the age of Terah when he died. They only state that Terah was 70 when he fathered (the first of) Abram, Nahor, and Haran, and that Abraham left Ur when he (Abraham) was 75. The critic may be confused due to a misunderstanding of Acts 7:4, as covered in #36. But there is no inconsistency in the text.

49. For how much did David buy the threshing floor? Second Samuel 24:24 says 50 shekels of silver, but 1 Chronicles 21:25 says 600 shekels of gold.

Failure to read the text carefully. Again we see that the critic is simply not reading the text with any diligence whatsoever, for there is no inconsistency. David bought the *threshing floor and oxen* for 50 shekels of silver (2 Samuel 24:24). He also bought *the site* for 600 shekels of gold (1 Chronicles 21:25). The site would be the entirety of the land, of which the threshing floor was merely a small part.

50. When did the transfiguration occur? Six days later (Matthew 16:28–17:2; Mark 9:1–2) or eight days later (Luke 9:27–28)?

Subset fallacy and failure to read the text carefully. Both Matthew and Mark indicate that Jesus told of His coming and that the transfiguration occurred six days later. Luke, however, says "about eight days after these sayings." The critic seems to have missed that important word: "about." It seems that Matthew and Mark started counting from the day after Jesus had mentioned His coming kingdom, but Luke includes the day itself. Moreover, Luke's use of the word "about" indicates that eight days is not exact, but rounded. This would make sense if the transfiguration took place very late on the seventh day, such that it was almost the eighth day and rounding up would be called the "eighth day," whereas Mark and Luke only record the six days *in between* these events. Even in our modern language we refer to the *1900s* as the *20th* century with no contradiction.

51. How many animals of each kind did Noah take into the Ark? Two of each kind (Genesis 6:19, 7:8–9, 15) or seven (Genesis 7:2)?

Subset fallacy. Two of each kind of air-breathing land animal were to be brought into the ark (Genesis 6:19, 7:8–9, 15). In addition to this, a greater quantity of animals that were classified as ceremonially "clean" was also included, though only a small fraction of animals were ceremonially clean. Namely, seven of the clean kinds were brought aboard (Genesis 7:2). Of course, if seven were brought onboard, then two were necessarily brought onboard (and five more). So, there is no contradiction. Not all texts in Genesis 6–8 mention the qualification that an additional number of clean animals was to be included. But no text contradicts it.

52. How many men were in the king's presence? Second Kings 25:18–19 contradicts Jeremiah 52:24–25.

Subset fallacy. All the numbers agree between the two passages except the number of advisors to the king. Second Kings 25:19 indicates that five were taken, whereas Jeremiah 52:25 indicates that seven were taken. There is no contradiction of course, because if seven were taken then necessarily five were taken (and two more). We might speculate as to why the account in Kings does not mention the additional two. Perhaps they were less conspicuous, or were immediately dismissed. But regardless of the reason, there is no contradiction.

53. Who did the women see at the tomb? One angel (Matthew 28:2; Mark 16:5; and John 20:12), or two angels (Luke 24:4)?

Subset fallacy and failure to distinguish different times and different persons. The women saw two angels (Luke 24:4), though only one of the two angels is specifically mentioned in Matthew 28:1–8 and Mark 16:5. Mary Magdalene, who arrived before the others (John 20:1), saw an empty tomb, but on her second visit she saw two angels (John 20:11–13). She then saw Jesus (John 20:14). Later, all the women saw Jesus (Matthew 28:9; Mark 16:9). So, where is the supposed contradiction?

54. How many women came to the sepulcher? John 20:1 contradicts Matthew 28:1, which contradicts Mark 16:1, which contradicts Luke 24:1, 10.

Fallacy of argument from silence. None of the passages listed by the critic state how many women came to the tomb. But they do provide enough information for us to conclude that there were at least four: Mary Magdalene, Mary the mother of James, Salome, and Joanna. But there may have been others too, as suggested by Luke 24:10. Each Gospel mentions only some of the women by name, but none deny that the others were there as well. Thus, there is no inconsistency.

John 20:1 mentions only Mary Magdalene, presumably because she arrived first. Matthew 28:1 mentions Mary Magdalene and the other Mary (the mother of James). So, does Mark 16:1, which also mentions Salome. Luke 24:10 mentions Mary Magdalene, Mary the mother of James, and Joanna by name, but also mentions that others were present. Where is the supposed contradiction?

NAMES, PLACES,
AND GENEALOGIES

In this section, we examine claims that the Bible confuses names of people or places or that it incorrectly reports the genealogical relationship between particular persons. The Bible is a history book and therefore often reports the location of important events as well as the names of the people involved. It often records detailed genealogies as well. Does it ever contradict itself in this regard?

55. Was Abiathar the father or the son of Ahimelech? First Samuel 22:20, 23:6 teach that Abiathar was the son of Ahimelech. But 2 Samuel 8:17 and 1 Chronicles 18:16, 24:6 teach that Abiathar was the father.

Equivocation fallacy. Abiathar's father was named Ahimelech, and Abiathar's son was also named Ahimelech. That is, Abiathar named one of his sons after his own father, perhaps to honor the latter's martyrdom. That the text refers to two different people, each named "Ahimelech" is obvious because *they lived at different times*. Namely, Ahimelech the son of *Ahitub* (1 Samuel 22:11) lived during the reign of King Saul and was killed by Saul *before* David became king of

Israel (1 Samuel 22:16–19). However, Ahimelech the *son* of Abiathar, served as priest *during* the time that David was king over Israel (2 Samuel 8:15, 17).

56. Who was Abijam's mother? First Kings 15:1–2 says "Maacah," but 2 Chronicles 13:1–2 says "Micaiah."

Bifurcation fallacy. The critic has made the opposite mistake as his previous error, where the critic had made the ludicrous assumption that two different people could never have the same name. Here the critic has assumed that one person cannot ever be called by more than one name: "Either a person is called A or B." But the Bible often uses more than one name for one person, such as Saul/Paul, Jacob/Israel (Genesis 32:32, 42:6), or Simon/Peter (Matthew 4:18). Abijam's mother is called "Micaiah" in 2 Chronicles 13:2 and "Maachah" in 1 Kings 15:2 — a very minor spelling difference, but there is no contradiction. In fact, spelling differences are to be expected from two books that were written hundreds of years apart, since spelling changes with time. Consider how the spelling of many English words has changed in just the last 400 years and then consider that 2 Chronicles was written about a *thousand* years after Genesis. Moreover, even today people often have a formal version of their name, plus a familiar version: Thomas/Tom/Tommy, Andrew/Andy/Drew, or James/Jim. That hardly constitutes a contradiction!

57. How were Abijam and Asa related? First Kings 15:8 says that Asa is Abijam's son, but 1 Kings 15:1–2, 9–10 imply that they are brothers because they had the same mother.

Semantic range fallacy. Asa is the son of Abijam (1 Kings 15:8), and no verse says otherwise. Perhaps the critic is confused because Maachah is called the "mother" of Asa (1 Kings 15:10, 13), yet we know she is the mother of Abijam (1 Kings 15:1) and is therefore actually Asa's grandmother. But of course, the Hebrew word for "mother" is "em" and literally means "female ancestor." Its range of meanings includes "mother," "grandmother," or even a more distant ancestor.

58. Who was Achan's father? Joshua 7:1 says that his father was "Carmi," but Joshua 7:24, 22:20 say "Zerah."

Bifurcation fallacy and semantic range fallacy. Achan's immediate father was Carmi (Joshua 7:1) and his more distant father (his great grandfather) was Zerah (Joshua 7:1 *and* Joshua 7:24, 22:20). The Hebrew word translated "father" literally means "male ancestor." That certainly includes a "father," but a more distant ancestor would also be included, as in "father Abraham" (Genesis 28:13, 32:9; Joshua 24:3). The Greek word translated "father" also allows for a more distant ancestor (Luke 16:24; John 8:56; Acts 7:2). So, there is simply no excuse for this critic's blunder.

59. Was Haman an Agagite? Esther 3:1 says *yes*, but 1 Samuel 15:2–3, 7–8, 32–33 say *no*.

Specious reasoning. Haman was indeed an Agagite (Esther 3:1) and no verse in Scripture contradicts this. The verses in 1 Samuel 15 describe Agag, a king of Amalek who was executed by Samuel. But nowhere do the Scriptures hint that Agag did not have any surviving descendants. Moreover, Agag is not a proper name, but the general term used for the King of Amalek — of which there were many. So, the critic has made at least two mistakes here.

60. What tribe was Aijalon from? Joshua 21:23–24 says "Dan," but 1 Chronicles 6:66, 69 says "Ephraim."

Failure to read the text carefully and failure to distinguish different times. Aijalon was a *place*, not a person. It was a frontier city allotted to the priests who were sons of Kohath. Aijalon was originally part of the territory that the tribe of Dan was to conquer (Joshua 21:23–24); however, Dan failed to take the city from the Amorites (Judges 1:34–35). The tribe of Ephraim held it for some time (1 Chronicles 6:66, 69), and it was at another time held by Benjamin (1 Chronicles 8:13) and by Judah (2 Chronicles 28:18). Apparently, the critic does not know that national or tribal boundaries can change from time to time. But where is there any contradiction or inconsistency about a city being held by different tribes *at different times*?

61. Who was Amasa's father? Second Samuel 17:25 says "Ithra," but 1 Chronicles 2:17 says "Jether."

Bifurcation fallacy. Some people have more than one name. Amasa's father was called "Jether" (1 Kings 2:5, 32; 1 chronicles 2:17) and also "Ithra" (2 Samuel 17:25). He may have been an Ishmaelite by birth but then became a part of Israel.

62. Who was Anah? Genesis 36:2, 14 contradicts Genesis 36:20 and 1 Chronicles 1:38, which contradict Genesis 36:24 and 1 Chronicles 1:40.

Failure to read the text carefully and semantic range fallacy. Anah was the Father of Oholibamah (one of Esau's wives), the son of Zibeon (Genesis 36:2, 14) and the grandson of Seir (Genesis 36:20, 24; 1 Chronicles 1:38, 40). Where is any supposed contradiction? Perhaps the critic is unaware that "sons" can refer to a grandson or more distant descendent, as in "the sons of Israel" (Exodus 3:9, 12:50; Leviticus 7:29; etc.).

63. What were the names of the Apostles? Matthew 10:2-4 disagrees with Mark 3:16–19, which disagrees with Luke 6:14–16, which contradicts Acts 1:13.

Failure to read the text carefully and bifurcation fallacy (in failing to realize that some people have more than one name). The Apostles are Peter (also named Simon), Andrew (Peter's brother), James the son of Zebedee, John (brother of James), Philip, Bartholomew, Matthew (also known as Levi), Thomas, James the son of Alphaeus, Thaddaeus (also called Judas Lebbaeus), Simon the Canaanite (also called Zelotes), and Judas Iscariot. Note that Matthew, Mark, and Luke all agree with this list, contrary to the critic's claim. Acts 1:13 also lists all these except Judas Iscariot, who was understandably omitted since

Acts records the events *after* Judas' betrayal and suicide (Mark 3:19; Matthew 27:5).

64. Who was Bashemath's father? Genesis 26:34 says "Alon," but Genesis 36:2–3 says "Ishmael."

Equivocation fallacy. These two texts speak of two different women, although they were both married to Esau. That two different persons are addressed is obvious because they have different fathers, and different *second* names. The Basemath who was also named "Adah" was a daughter of Alon the Hittite (Genesis 26:34, 36:2). The Basemath who was also named "Mahalath" was a daughter of Ishmael and a brother of Nebaioth/Nebajoth (Genesis 28:9, 36:3).

65. Who named Beersheba? Genesis 21:31 indicates that it was Abraham and Abimelech, but Genesis 26:33 says it was Isaac.

Bifurcation fallacy. Abraham and Abimelech first dug the well and named the location "Beersheba" (meaning "well of oath"). When Isaac reopened the well, he rechristened it with the same name.

66. Where did Joseph and Mary live before the birth of Jesus? Luke 2:1–7 contradicts Matthew 2:1–2, 11, 22–23.

Failure to read the text carefully. Joseph and Mary may have lived separately in several different places before the birth of Christ. The text doesn't say. It only says that they came out of Nazareth, a city in Galilee (Luke 2:1–7). They traveled to Bethlehem for the census since Joseph was descended from David (Luke 2:4–6), and that is where Christ was born. Sometime later, they lived in a house in or near Bethlehem, and this is when the magi visited them (Matthew 2:1–2, 11). This could have been up to two years after Christ's birth (Matthew 2:16). Joseph, Mary, and Jesus then briefly lived in Egypt and finally settled back in Nazareth (Matthew 2:14–15, 23). Where is there any supposed contradiction?

67. Who were the sons of Benjamin? Genesis 46:21 disagrees with Numbers 26:38–40, which disagrees with 1 Chronicles 7:6, which contradicts 1 Chronicles 8:1–2.

Subset fallacy and specious reasoning (failure to recognize spelling changes). Genesis 46:21 records the names of ten of Benjamin's sons. Numbers 26:38–40 lists five of these sons. There are minor changes in the Hebrew spelling for three of them: "Ehi" becomes "Ahiram," Muppim" becomes "Shephupham," and "Huppim" becomes "Hupham," but that hardly constitutes a contradiction. Our own English language shows that words change spellings over a few hundred years.

Additionally, we learn from Numbers 26:40 that Ard and Naman are sons of Bela and, thus, *grandsons* of Benjamin. These could be the same Naman and Bela listed as sons of Benjamin in Genesis 46:21 when we remember that the Hebrew word for "son" can include grandsons or even more distant descendants. Alternatively, the sons of Bela may have been named after two of their uncles. Either way, there is no contradiction.

And what of the other three sons of Benjamin listed in Genesis 46:21 (Becher, Gera, and Rosh) who are not listed in Numbers 26? It's possible (at least for Gera and Rosh) that they died without having sons of their own. After all, Numbers 26:38 lists only the "sons of Benjamin *according to their families*" and so naturally those that died without an heir would not have a family tree to trace through the time of the writing of Numbers. Although Becher has many sons listed in 1 Chronicles 7:8, these may have been adopted rather than biological, which might explain why he and his line are not included in the Numbers passage (e.g., see #6 and #109). In any case, we see that there is no contradiction whatsoever between Genesis 46:21 and Numbers 26:38–40; neither list claims to be complete.

Likewise, in 1 Chronicles 7:6 and 8:1–2, we have additional spelling changes that have accumulated over the centuries: "Ahiram" becomes "Aharah," "Ashbel" becomes "Jediael," and "Rosh" becomes "Rapha." So, we have some descendants listed in one account whereas others are included in another account. *But we see no contradictions.*

68. Were Naaman and Ard the sons or the grandsons of Benjamin? Genesis 46:21 says "sons," but Numbers 26:38–40 indicates grandsons.

Bifurcation fallacy and semantic range fallacy. In Hebrew, the term "son" can include a grandson or more distant descendant. So, Naaman and Ard are grandsons of Benjamin, perhaps the very ones mentioned in Genesis 46:21. Alternatively, Naaman and Ard, the grandsons of Benjamin, may have been named after their uncles — who were direct sons of Benjamin. Either way, there is no obvious contradiction or inconsistency.

69. Who asked for the best seats in heaven? Mark 10:35–37 says James and John. But Matthew 20:20–21 says it was the *mother* of James and John.

Bifurcation fallacy. James and John asked to sit on either side of Christ in glory (Mark 10:35–37), *and* their mother also asked Christ on their behalf (Matthew 20:20–21). There is no logical reason why both the sons and their mother couldn't make this request of Jesus. Their mother seems to have spoken on their behalf; they asked Jesus using their mother as the intermediary.

70. Where did Jesus cure the blind man? Mark 8:22–25 says he was healed in Bethsaida, whereas John 8:59–9:1-6 indicate that it was at the pool of Siloam.

Bifurcation fallacy. Jesus healed *many* blind people in various locations (Matthew 9:27–30, 11:4–5, 12:22, 15:30–31, 20:30–34, 21:14; Mark 8:22–25, 10:46–52; Luke 4:18, 7:21–22, 18:35–43; John 9:1–7). Mark 8:22–25 and John 8:59–9:1–6 clearly describe two different blind men that Jesus healed in two different ways. One was brought to Jesus by others and given sight directly by Jesus in two stages (Mark 8:22–25). The other was told to go and wash in the pool of Siloam in order to receive his sight, which he did. The critic must be blind to think that these two different events are somehow contradictory.

71. Which sons of David were born in Hebron. Second Samuel 3:2–5 lists "Chileab," but 1 Chronicles 3:1–4 lists "Daniel."

Bifurcation fallacy. David had six sons in Hebron. In order of birth, they were Amnon, Daniel (also called "Chileab"), Absalom, Adonijah, Shephatiah, and Ithream. Both 2 Samuel 3:2–5 and 1 Chronicles 3:1–4 list these in this order and list the same birth mother for them all. Perhaps the critic is bothered by the fact that 1 Chronicles refers to Daniel by his given name, whereas 2 Samuel refers to him as "Chileab." Some people have more than one name. And there is no doubt that both passages refer to the same person, as both list him as the second son of David in Hebron, whose mother was Abigail the Carmelite.

72. Which sons of David were born in Jerusalem? Second Samuel 5:14–16 contradicts 1 Chronicles 3:5–8, which disagrees with 1 Chronicles 14:3–7.

Subset fallacy. Both 1 Chronicles 3:5–8 and 1 Chronicles 14:3–7 list 13 sons of David born in Jerusalem. And despite the critic's claim, there is no inconsistency at all between these two lists. The names are *identical* apart from minor spelling differences: "Shimea" becomes "Shammua," "Elishama" becomes "Elishua," "Eliphelet" becomes "Elpelet," and "Eliada" gets a prefix to become "Beeliada." But there is no contradiction in having alternate spellings for a name.

Likewise, the list given in 2 Samuel 5:14–16 has a few minor spelling differences. Also, it lists only 11 sons. Nogah and (the first) Eliphelet are not included. But the remaining names are the same, aside from spelling. Why were Nogah and Eliphelet not included in the 2 Samuel list? Perhaps they died before having any children of their own, or perhaps they were not noteworthy. In any case, 2 Samuel 5:14–16 does not claim that it is an exhaustive list; it does not claim that these 11 were the *only* sons born to David in Jerusalem. So, where is there any contradiction or inconsistency?

73. From which of David's sons was Jesus descended? Matthew 1:6–7 says Solomon, but Luke 3:31 says Nathan.

Bifurcation fallacy. The critic's question is as silly as this: "Are you descended from your mother or from your father?" Except for Adam and Eve, all people have at least two lineages — one through their mother and one through their father. So, it's hardly surprising that Jesus had two lineages as well. The Bible acknowledges that Jesus had no biological father, but is nonetheless considered the son of Joseph (Luke 3:23). Some people have *more* than two lineages because they have a biological father and in addition a legal father, as in the case of an adopted child or a stepchild.

So, Jesus is descended both from Solomon (Matthew 1:6–16) and from Nathan (Luke 3:23–31). It could be that Luke is describing the line through Mary (Joseph being the son-in-law of Heli), while Matthew records the lineage through Joseph, the son of Jacob. Alternatively, Matthew may record the biological ancestry of Joseph, while Luke records the legal ancestry. In this case, Jacob would be Joseph's biological father, while Heli would be his legal father. If Jacob died when Joseph was very young and Joseph's mother remarried to Heli, then Heli would be Joseph's legal father. In any case, it's hardly a contradiction to have two lineages, since this is true for everyone living today.

74. Who did Elhanan kill? Second Samuel 21:19 says Goliath, but 1 Chronicles 20:5 says Lahmi (Goliath's brother).

Failure to do textual transmission analysis. Elhanan killed Lahmi, the brother of Goliath the Gittite (1 Chronicles 20:5). In 2 Samuel 21:19, some English translations state that Elhanan killed Goliath, but there is evidence of transmission errors in this passage. First, Elhanan, the son of Jair, is said to be the son of "Jaare-oregim," in 2 Samuel 21:19, where the "oregim" is the Hebrew word for "weaver," apparently duplicated from the line below it. Also, the word "Bethlehemite" is the compound of "Beythhal" and "lehemite" — where "lehemite" is exactly the word used in 1 Chronicles 20:5 for the name of the man that Elhanan killed — "Lahmi" in modern English. That is, if we presume that "Beythhal" was added to 2 Samuel 21:19, then both texts fully agree that Elhanan killed Lahmi. Second Samuel 21:19 does not use the word "brother," but instead connects Lahmi and Goliath with the Hebrew word "eth," which can mean "with" (e.g., Genesis 5:22: "Enoch walked with God . . ."). That is, Elhanan killed Lahmi (who was) *with* Goliath the Gittite. Of course Lahmi was with Goliath because he was his brother. So, there appears to be no inconsistency in the original texts.

75. Genealogy of Jesus (1) Matthew 1:6–16 contradicts Luke 3:21–31.

Bifurcation fallacy (see #89). All people have at least two genealogies — one through their mother, the other through their father. Some people have more than this because they may be physically descended from one father but then legally adopted by another. So, we shouldn't be surprised that Jesus also has two genealogies, the one through Jacob is recorded in Matthew and the one through Eli is recorded in Luke.

76. Genealogy of Jesus (2) Matthew 1:6–16 disagrees with 1 Chronicles 3:10–16.

Subset fallacy and semantic anachronism fallacy (see #17, #58). Matthew does not claim that his list is exhaustive, but rather abbreviated. (The Greek word translated "beget" can refer to a son/daughter *or* a more distant descendent.) As was common at the time, some generations in the genealogy are intentionally omitted; Matthew did this so that Christ's ancestors from Abraham could be grouped into three groups of 14 (Matthew 1:17). Moreover, some names have more than one spelling ("Ahaziah" is also spelled "Uzziah") but no contradictions. Matthew simply omits Joash, Amaziah, Azariah, and Jehoiakim.

77. Who killed Goliath? It was David according to 1 Samuel 17:49–51, 21:8–9, but it was Elhanan according to 2 Samuel 21:19.

Failure to do textual transmission analysis (see #74). David slew Goliath (1 Samuel 17:49–51). Second Samuel 21:19 in the original text confirms that Elhanan killed Lahmi the *brother* of Goliath.

78. Who was Heman's father? First Kings 4:31 says Mahol, but 1 Chronicles 2:6 says Zerah, and 1 Chronicles 6:33, 15:17 says Joel.

Failure to read the text carefully and specious reasoning. Zerah was the father of Heman mentioned in 1 Chronicles 2:6. This seems to be the same Heman mentioned in 1 Kings 4:31, which describes his brothers (Calcol and Darda) as being "sons of Mahol." The critic might have concluded that this means that Heman's father is named Mahol; this is possible and non-contradictory since people sometimes have more than one name, and Zerah may have also been named "Mahol." But more likely, "Mahol" is not a proper name at all, being the Hebrew word for "dance", in which case Calcol and Darda are figuratively called the "sons of the dance" much like the "daughters of song" mentioned in Ecclesiastes 12:4.

First Chronicles 6:33 mentions a *different* Heman whose father was Joel. It is obvious that this Heman is different from Heman, son of Zerah, because they lived at very different times. Heman, son of Zerah, is the grandson of Judah, and therefore lived long before King David (1 Chronicles 2:3–6). But Heman, son of Joel, was the grandson of Samuel (1 Chronicles 6:33), and therefore contemporaneous with King David.

79. Where did Aaron die? Was it Mount Hor according to Numbers 20:27–28, 33:38, or Moserah according to Deuteronomy 10:6?

Bifurcation fallacy. Numbers 20:27–28 and 33:38 state that Aaron died on Mount Hor. Deuteronomy 10:6 indicates that Aaron died and was buried in Moserah. Which is true? Both. Mount Hor is in the region of Moserah.

80. Which tribe was Hyram from? First Kings 7:13–14 says Naphtali, but 2 Chronicles 2:13–14 says Dan.

Failure to read the text carefully and specious reasoning. Hiram was from the tribe of Naphtali (1 Kings 7:13–14), and no verse denies this. In 2 Chronicles 2:13–14, the Bible infallibly records the words of the king of Tyre, who claimed that Hiram's mother was "of the daughters of Dan" — indicating Hiram's mother was of Dan — either the tribe of Dan or the city of Dan in Naphtali. If she had previously been married to a Naphtalite or if she was a Naphtalite and lived in the city of Dan, then her son would be of Naphtali.

81. Was Zechariah Iddo's son or grandson? Ezra 5:1, 6:14 says son, but Zechariah 1:1 says grandson.

Semantic range fallacy and bifurcation fallacy (see #17, #58). In Hebrew, "son" can refer to a direct son, a grandson, or a more distant descendent (e.g., Exodus 6:9, 11; Leviticus 1:2). Zechariah is the son of Berechiah and the grandson of Iddo (Zechariah 1:1, 7) and is, therefore, necessarily a son (descendent) of Iddo (Ezra 5:1, 6:14).

82. Who bought the sepulchre in Sechem from the sons of Hamor? Joshua 24:32 says Jacob, but Acts 7:16 says Abraham.

Failure to read the text carefully. *Jacob* bought a parcel of land in Shechem from the sons of Hamor in which he was later buried (Joshua 24:32). Abraham had previously bought a *different* field from Ephron the Hittite. This field was near Mamre. A cave in that field would be used as a tomb in which Abraham, Sarah, Isaac, Rebekah, and Jacob were buried (Genesis 49:29–31, 50:13–14).

The apparent difficulty lies in Acts 7:16, in which Stephen seems to attribute the purchase of the land in Shechem to Abraham rather than Jacob. If so, has the Bible contradicted itself? Not at all. It is not a contradiction to say "X *and* Stephen says 'not-X.' " The Bible nowhere asserts that Jacob did not buy the parcel of land in Shechem. Rather, it infallibly records what *Stephen said* (Acts 6:8, 7:2, 16).

This being said, it is highly unlikely that Stephen was mistaken — he was very knowledgeable of Old Testament history. Furthermore, the record of Stephen's speech is likely abbreviated. That is, the Scriptures record only the highlights, not every word. With this in mind, we see in verse 15 that Stephen is addressing all of the patriarchs that went down to Egypt — not just Joseph. And whereas Joseph was buried in Schechem in the land purchased by Jacob, Jacob was not. Where was Jacob buried? He was buried in the field of Machpelah near Mamre that had been purchased by *Abraham* (Genesis 49:29–31, 50:13–14). Since Acts 7:16 refers to the burials of *both* Jacob and Joseph (see verse 15), and since they were buried in different locations, it seems likely that this verse is compactly referring to both locations. Namely, Jacob and his sons were "laid in the tomb which Abraham had purchased [and in the tomb Jacob had purchased] for a sum of money from the sons of Hamor in Shechem." This understanding removes any apparent difficulty.

83. Where was Jacob buried? Genesis 50:13 says in Machpelah, but Acts 7:15–16 says in Shechem.

Failure to read the text carefully. Jacob was buried in a cave in Machpelah, in Hebron, near Mamre (Genesis 50:13). No verse says otherwise. In Acts 7:15–16, Stephen states that "our fathers" — *not Jacob* — were buried in Shechem. In the original Greek text, the verb "died" is in the singular and therefore refers to Jacob, although the fathers of each tribe also died. But the verb "were carried" is in the plural, and thus refers to "the fathers" (Joseph and his brothers) and does not necessarily include Jacob.

84. Was Jechoniah the son or the grandson of Josiah? Matthew 1:11 says son, but 1 Chronicles 3:15–16 says grandson.

Bifurcation fallacy and semantic range fallacy. Jechoniah is the grandson of Josiah (1 Chronicles 3:15–16), and, thus, is rightly called the son (offspring) of Josiah (Matthew 1:11), just as Jesus is the son of

David (Matthew 1:1). The Hebrew word *ben* used in these passages literally means "male descendant," so it can refer to a son, grandson, great-grandson, and so on, depending on context. Likewise, the Greek word translated "beget" can also refer to more distant relations than father and son.

85. Who succeeded Jehoiakim as king? Second Kings 24:6 says Johoiachin did, but Jeremiah 36:30 indicates that no one would succeed Johoiakim.

Failure to read the text carefully. Jehoiachin succeeded Jehoiakim as king (2 Kings 24:6). Jeremiah 36:30 does not deny or contradict this. Rather, God promised that there would come a time when Jehoiakim would have no descendant to sit on the throne of David. This of course happened. The reign of Jehoiachin *in Jerusalem* was very short, lasting only three months, and then his royal line was ended with none of his biological descendants ever ascending to the throne. No verse says otherwise. Jeremiah 36:30 does not deny that Jehoiakim would have no descendants, but rather that there would come a time (soon) when "he will have no one [a descendant] *to sit on the throne of David*" — marking the end of his dynasty. This prophecy was fulfilled three months and ten days into Jehoiachin's reign, at which point Jerusalem was sieged and captured by Babylon, and Jehoiakim's dynasty was ended forever.

86. Did Jehoiakim die in Babylon or near Jerusalem? Second Chronicles 36:5–6 contradicts Jeremiah 22:18–19.

Failure to read the text carefully. *Neither* text states where Jehoiakim died, so obviously they cannot contradict each other on that issue. Jeremiah 22:18–19 infallibly prophesies that Jehoiakim would be "dragged off and thrown out beyond the gates of Jerusalem," which may suggest that his dead body was discarded near Jerusalem — though where he died the text does not say. Second Chronicles 36:5–6 indicates that Nebuchadnezzar had Jehoiakim bound with chains in order to "to take him to Babylon." But the text does not say whether this journey actually occurred; no text indicates that Jehoiakim ever made it to Babylon. Although many details are left to the imagination, there is no inconsistency to be found in the actual text.

87. Was Jehu the son or grandson of Nimshi? First Kings 19:16 says son, but 2 Kings 9:2 says grandson.

Bifurcation fallacy and semantic range fallacy. In Hebrew (and Greek, and even in English), the term "son" (Hebrew: *ben*, literally "male descendant") can refer to a grandson or a more distant descendent, which is why Christ can be called the son of David (Matthew 1:1). Jehu was the grandson of Nimshi (2 Kings 9:2), and was therefore the son (descendent) of Nimshi (1 Kings 19:16).

88. Where did John baptize? Matthew 3:4–6 and Mark 1:9 disagree with John 1:28.

Bluff and failure to read the text carefully. Matthew 3:4–6; Mark 1:9; and John 1:28 all confirm that John was baptizing in the Jordan River, with no apparent inconsistency. John 1:28 refers to John's previous conversations with the Pharisees in "Bethany beyond the Jordan" (the "Jordan where John was baptizing"). This seems to be a different Bethany than the one near Jerusalem, which is why the author attaches the qualifier. But the three accounts all agree that John baptized in the Jordan River, and no text contradicts this. Furthermore, John may have baptized in other places at different times.

89. Who was Jesus' grandfather on His father's side? Matthew 1:16 says Jacob, but Luke 3:23 says Eli.

Bifurcation fallacy and semantic range fallacy. As in English, in Greek, a son-in-law can rightly be called a son. Moreover, an adopted son is also rightly called a son. Like all of us, Jesus had (at least) two grandfathers. One was named Jacob (Matthew 1:16), and the other was Eli — sometimes spelled "Heli" (Luke 3:23). Neither text explicitly states which is Christ's paternal grandfather, since the words "father" and "son" can be used of in-laws or of more distant relationships (grandfather, grandson, etc.). However, Matthew 1:16 seems to imply that Jacob was the biological father of Joseph and, thus, Jesus' paternal grandfather.

Luke says only that Jesus was, as supposed, the son of Joseph, the son of Eli (or Heli). But if Eli is Mary's father, then Joseph is indeed his son, in that he is the son-in-law. This would make Eli the maternal grandfather of Jesus, though the line is listed through Joseph since women were seldom included in genealogies. Moreover, considering that "son" can imply a more distant descendent, Jesus might be the subject for all the ancestors listed in Luke 3. In other words, Jesus is the son of Joseph, *Jesus* is the son (descendant) of Eli, *Jesus* is the son of Matthat, and so on, culminating with Jesus is the son of Adam, and Jesus is the Son of God (Luke 3:23–38).

Alternatively, Eli could be the adopted father of Joseph, rather than the father-in-law. If Jacob had died while Joseph was very young, and if Joseph's mother then married Eli, then no doubt Joseph would be the son of Eli, although Joseph's biological father is Jacob. In any case, there is no inconsistency in having two genealogies, and that is indeed the case with all of us.

90. Where did Josiah die? Megiddo (2 Kings 23:29–30) or Jerusalem (2 Chronicles 35:23–24)?

Semantic range fallacy. Neither passage gives the exact moment of death. Josiah was mortally wounded in the battle at Megiddo (2 Kings 23:29; 2 Chronicles 35:23). But we know that his death was not instantaneous, since he had time to express how badly hurt he was (2 Chronicles 35:23). His servants transported him while he was dying, or perhaps while he was already dead, back to Jerusalem. Some English translations of 2 Chronicles 35:24 seem to imply that the moment of death occurred in Jerusalem, but this isn't required in the original text. We know only that Josiah was mortally wounded at Megiddo and was buried in Jerusalem. Neither text explicitly says where the death occurred, and thus cannot contradict each other on the issue.

91. Who was the father of Kish? First Samuel 9:1 says Abiel, but 1 Chronicles 8:33; 9:39 says Ner.

Bifurcation fallacy and equivocation fallacy. The word "father" (Hebrew *ab*, literally meaning "male ancestor") can mean the direct father or a more distance ancestor, just as "son" can mean a grandson or more distant descendent. Ner was the direct father of Kish (1 Chronicles 8:33, 9:39), and Abiel was a more distant father (male ancestor), specifically, his grandfather (1 Samuel 9:1, 14:51).

92. Who was Korah's father? Genesis 36:14 says Esau, but Genesis 36:15–16 says Eliphaz.

Bifurcation fallacy and equivocation fallacy. Which Korah? There are several in Scripture. Esau had a son named Korah (Genesis 36:5, 14), and Esau's son Eliphaz had a son named Korah (Genesis 36:15–16). For that matter, there is a third Korah mentioned in Scripture who was a cousin of Moses; this Korah's father was Izhar (Exodus 6:18–21). A fourth person named Korah was the son of Hebron (1 Chronicles 2:43). So, the answer to the critic's question is: Esau, Eliphaz, Izhar, or Hebron — depending on which Korah he has in mind. It's just silly to suppose that no two people have ever had the same first name.

93. Who was Laban's father? Genesis 28:5 says Bethuel, but Genesis 29:5 says Nahor.

Bifurcation fallacy and equivocation fallacy (same error as #91). Laban's immediate father was Bethuel (Genesis 25:20, 28:2, 5). His more distant father, specifically his grandfather, was Nahor (Genesis 22:20–23, 29:5).

94. Was Mahli the son of Levi? Ezra 8:18 contradicts Genesis 46:11 and 1 Chronicles 6:1, 16:16, 23:6.

Equivocation fallacy and semantic range fallacy. Mahli was indeed the son — the descendent — of Levi (Ezra 8:18). Specifically, the grandson of Levi was named Mahli, the son of Merari (1 Chronicles 6:16, 19, 29, 23:6, 21, 29; Exodus 6:16, 19; Numbers 3:17, 20). Also, one of Levi's *great* grandsons was named Mahli; he was the son of Mushi, the son of Merari (1 Chronicles 6:47, 23:21, 23, 24:26, 30). The Bible frequently uses "son" to refer to a more distant descendant, as in the "sons of Israel" (e.g., Exodus 12:50–51, 13:2, 18, 14:2–3, 16:35; Leviticus 25:25, 26:46, etc.). So, this again shows that the critic is not serious about careful scholarship.

95. Who was Moses' father-in-law? Exodus 3:1, 4:18, 18:1, 5 says Jethro, but Judges 4:11 and Numbers 10:29 say Hobab, whereas Exodus 2:18–21 says Reuel.

Bifurcation fallacy. Moses' father-in-law was called by two names: Hobab and Jethro (Exodus 3:1, 4:18, 18:1, 5–6; Judges 4:11; Numbers 10:29). The name "Jethro" means "excellency" and may have been a title rather than a proper name. The father of Hobab was Reuel (Numbers 10:29). Hence, since "father" and "daughter" can refer to more distant relations (grandfather / granddaughter), Reuel is rightly said to be the father of Moses's wife Zipporah (Exodus 2:18–21). Perhaps the critic has forgotten that many important persons in Scripture went by two names, e.g., Woman/Eve, Abram/ Abraham, Sarai/Sarah, Jacob/Israel, Esau/Edom, Saul/Paul, Simon/ Peter, etc. (See also #56.)

96. Where was the home of Peter and Andrew? Capernaum according to Mark 1:21, 27 but Bethsaida according to John 1:44.

Specious reasoning. Peter and Andrew were originally from the city of Bethsaida (John 1:44). No passage contradicts this. Mark 1:21–27 says nothing about where Peter and Andrew were originally from. It only says that Christ went into Capernaum and taught in the synagogue there. Mark 1:29 indicates that after teaching there, Christ went straightaway to the home of Peter and Andrew. It may have been that their home was in Capernaum at that time. Or, since Capernaum was right next to Bethsaida, the latter might be considered part of the former — a suburb. Geographical boundaries were less exact during this time, nearly 2,000 years before GPS. Either way, there is no inconsistency in a person being originally from one place and later living in a different place.

97. Who was the father of Salah? Arphaxad, according to Genesis 10:24, 11:12, but Cainan according to Luke 3:35–36.

Failure to do textual transmission analysis. Arphaxad was the father of Shelah (Genesis 10:24, 11:12). Some translations of Luke 3:35–36 seem to indicate that Arphaxad was the grandfather of Shelah, with Cainan being Shelah's immediate father. Even if this were so, it would not be a contradiction, since in Hebrew custom a grandfather or more distant ancestor may be called a "father" (Luke 1:73, 3:8, 16:24; Acts 7:2). However, this "Cainan" appears to be an early transmission error — accidentally duplicated from the next verse (Luke 3:37) where we read of Cainan the father of Enosh. The most ancient manuscripts do not have this extra Cainan; thus Luke 3:35–36 in the original text confirms that Arphaxad was the father of Shelah. (See Jason Lisle and Tim Chaffey, "Are There Gaps in the Genesis Genealogies?" posted at https://answersingenesis.org/bible-timeline/genealogy/are-there-gaps-in-the-genesis-genealogies/. See also Paul F. Taylor, "An Extra Cainan?" posted at https://answersingenesis.org/bible-timeline/genealogy/an-extra-cainan/.)

98. Who was Samuel's firstborn son? Joel (1 Samuel 8:2) or Vashni (1 Chronicles 6:28)?

Failure to do textual transmission analysis. Samuel's firstborn son was named "Joel" (1 Samuel 8:2). First Chronicles 6:28 in the Syric and Arabic text also confirms that Joel was Samuel's firstborn son. In some manuscripts, the name was dropped from 1 Chronicles 6:28 due to a copyist error, and the Hebrew word denoting "the second" (son) was taken as the proper name "Vashni" as rendered in KJV translation. But there is full agreement between these two verses in the original manuscripts.

99. Was Samuel an Ephraimite or a Levite? He was an Ephraimite according to 1 Samuel 1:1–2, 20 but a Levite according to 1 Chronicles 6:27–28, 36–38.

Bifurcation fallacy. Both. Samuel was a Levite by paternal bloodline (1 Chronicles 6:27–28, 33–38) and an Ephraimite by country (geographic region) of origin (1 Samuel 1:1–2, 20). Indeed, 1 Chronicles 6:33–38 lists all of Samuel's paternal ancestors back to Levi. And 1 Samuel 1:1 states that Elkanah (Samuel's father) was "from the hill country of Ephraim" and hence an "Ephraimite." Notice that, like the words "Israel" and "Edom," "Ephraim" can refer to either an ethnic people-group or to a geographic region often dominated primarily by the people-group of the same name.

100. Where did Moses receive the Ten Commandments? On Mount *Sinai* according to Exodus 31:18, 34:4, 32; Leviticus 26:46, 27:34; and Nehemiah 9:13. On Mount *Horeb* according to 1 Kings 8:9; 2 Chronicles 5:10; and Malachi 4:4.

Bifurcation fallacy — and a very obvious one. Presumably, the critic thinks that either (1) Moses received the Ten Commandments on Mount Sinai, or (2) Moses received them on Mount Horeb. But of course, Mount Horeb *is* Mount Sinai. Just like people, some mountains can have more than one name. Specifically, Sanai seems to refer more specifically to the summit. In any case, the Scriptures use Horeb and Sinai virtually interchangeably (Exodus 3:1, 17:6, 19:1, 20, 31:18, 33:6, 34:32).

101. Who were the sons of Heman? First Chronicles 25:4 contradicts 2 Chronicles 29:14.

Bifurcation fallacy, equivocation fallacy, and semantic range fallacy. Recall that in Hebrew (as well as English) the word "son" can refer to an immediate son or a more distant descendant. First Chronicles 25:4 records the sons of Heman living at the time of David (1 Chronicles 25:1). The passage in 2 Chronicles takes place during the reign of Hezekiah, over 200 years *after* David, as the critic would have realized if he had bothered to read the beginning of the chapter (2 Chronicles 29:1). Thus, 2 Chronicles 29:14 lists two of the sons (descendants) of Heman alive at that time. These would obviously not be the same as the sons that lived two centuries earlier. This appears to be yet another example of the critic utterly failing to actually read the text.

102. What were the 12 tribes of Israel? Genesis 49 contradicts Numbers 1, which contradicts Numbers 13, which contradicts Deuteronomy 33, which contradicts Ezekiel 48, which contradicts Revelation 7.

Failure to distinguish different times, genre fallacy, and specious reasoning. First of all, the critic failed to distinguish different times in history; and this is crucial since the 12 tribes changed over time. Although there were *initially* 12 tribes of Israel, each one stemming from one of the sons of Jacob (as recorded in Genesis 49), the tribe of Joseph would eventually branch into *2* tribes each stemming from Joseph's two sons: Ephraim and Manasseh. So, *at a later time*, there were actually 13 tribes of Israel (as shown in Numbers 1). Also, we note that the tribe of Levi is sometimes omitted from the list of tribes because the Levites were priests and were not given a portion of the land (Deuteronomy 10:9; 18:1). So, there are 12 tribes of Israel *that inherited the land of Canaan.*

Note that since both the tribes of Ephraim and Manasseh belong to the tribe of Joseph, either Ephraim or Manasseh can be referred to as the tribe of "Joseph" by synecdoche. This is obvious in Numbers 1:32 and Numbers 13:11. Also, Deuteronomy 33:13–17 makes clear that the tribe of Joseph consists of the 2 tribes of Ephraim and Manasseh.

With these facts in mind, we see that there is no inconsistency whatsoever in the Old Testament texts listed by the critic. The 12 tribes of Israel that inherited the land of Canaan were: Reuben, Simeon, Gad, Judah, Issachar, Zebulun, Ephraim (of Joseph), Manasseh (of Joseph), Benjamin, Dan, Asher, and Naphtali. And Levi was the priestly tribe.

Genesis 49 records the original 12 tribes, before the split of Joseph. Numbers 1 takes place at a later time and records all 13 tribes, including the split of Joseph into Ephraim and Manasseh. So, does Ezekiel 48. Numbers 13 lists the tribes of Israel that were to spy out the land of Canaan in preparation for taking the land (verse 2). So, this list appropriately does not include Levi but includes all the tribes that had a portion of the land.

Deuteronomy 33 is *not* a list of the 12 tribes, as the critic falsely implied, but rather records Moses's blessing to many of the tribes of Israel (verse 1). Notice that the text does *not* say that this list includes *all* the tribes of Israel. God, through Moses, chose not to bless the tribe of Simeon. The reason is not stated, though it may be on account of the sinful actions of the tribe's forefather (Genesis 34:25–29, 49:5–7). In any event, there is no contradiction; all these Old Testament passages are perfectly consistent.

And what of Revelation 7? Here the critic has committed the genre fallacy, in failing to recognize that the Book of Revelation is prophetic literature and uses dramatic imagery rather than a literal retelling of history. In the New Testament, the term "Israel" is often used symbolically of the people of God, rather than the physical nation (Romans 2:28–29, 9:6–8, 11:26). In penning the Book of Revelation, the Apostle John specifically and deliberately used a slight variation of the names of the tribes of Israel, in order to emphasize that this is spiritual Israel — the people of God, not the land of Canaan. For this reason, John includes the tribe of Levi (though they had no land of their own) and uses "Joseph" as synecdoche for "Ephraim." Of course, this is fully consistent with the Old Testament. The strange thing is that John omits the tribe of Dan. Why? He had a great reason. The tribe of Dan had fallen into idolatry (Judges 18:30; 1 Kings 12:28–30) and therefore was not counted as a part of spiritual Israel (God's people).

103. Where did God kill Uzza? Second Samuel 6:6 contradicts 1 Chronicles 13:9.

Bifurcation fallacy. Uzza was killed by the Ark of the Covenant at the threshing flood (2 Samuel 6:6; 1 Chronicles 13:9). Both texts are in explicit agreement. Perhaps the critic is confused because the threshing floor is said to be "of Nacon" in 2 Samuel and of "Chidon" in 1 Chronicles. But people and places often have more than one name. So, there is no inconsistency here.

104. Where did Moses get water from a rock? At Rephidim (Exodus 17:1–7) or at Kadesh (Numbers 20:1–8, 27:14; Deuteronomy 32:51)?

Bifurcation fallacy and failure to read the text carefully. At two different times in history, the Lord gave the Israelites water from a rock. The first was at Rephidim (Exodus 17:1). The second time was at Kadesh (Numbers 20:1, 27:14; Deuteronomy 32:51).

It is very obvious from the text that these are two different events; not only was the location different, but God's instructions to Moses were also different. At Rephidim God instructed Moses to *strike* the rock (Exodus 17:6). Moses obeyed and water came forth. However, at Kadesh, God commanded Moses to *speak* to the rock (Numbers 20:8). Here Moses *disobeyed* and instead struck the rock as he had previously (Numbers 20:11). It was because of this act of disobedience that God did not allow Moses to enter Canaan (Numbers 20:12, 27:12–14; Deuteronomy 32:49–51).

105. Who made the Ark of the Covenant? Deuteronomy 10:1–3 says Moses, but Exodus 37:1 says Bezalel.

Bifurcation fallacy. Bezalel, under the instruction of Moses, made the Ark of the Covenant (Deuteronomy 10:1–3; Exodus 37:1). So, it is proper to say either Moses or Bezalel or both made the ark.

106. Who wrote the (second set of) Ten Commandments? Exodus 34:1 says the Lord, but Exodus 34:27 says Moses.

Bifurcation fallacy. God wrote the Ten Commandments (for the second time) on stone tablets (Exodus 34:1). Before these stone tablets were placed in the Ark of the Covenant, Moses copied onto scrolls all that God had written (Exodus 34:27). If Moses had not done so, then how would we know what the Ten Commandments are? The original stone tablets have been lost.

107. Who was Zechariah's father? Jehoiada according to 2 Chronicles 24:20–21 but Berechiah according to Matthew 23:35.

Bifurcation fallacy, equivocation fallacy, and semantic range fallacy. Second Chronicles 24:20–21 lists the father of Zechariah as *Jehoiada*, whereas Matthew 23:35 lists him as *Berechiah*. Is this a contradiction? In order to conclude such, the critic must have made at least *three* errors in reasoning. First, we must ask, "Which Zechariah?" There are several men with this name mentioned in Scripture. To treat them as if they are all one person is to commit the fallacy of equivocation. Namely, Zechariah (Zecharias) the father of John the Baptist (Luke 1:59–60) is not the same person as Zechariah the prophet, grandson of Iddo (Zechariah 1:1), who is not the same person as Zechariah the priest (2 Chronicles 24:20), who is not the same as King Zechariah, son of Jeroboam (2 Kings 14:29). These are different people, so it would be no contradiction to point out that they have different fathers.

Second, the critic commits the semantic anachronism fallacy in forgetting that "father" in both Hebrew and Greek can refer to a grandfather or more distant descendent. There is no contradiction in saying that Jesus is a son of David (Matthew 1:1) and a son of Joseph (Luke 3:24). Christ was the legal descendant of both (see #58.)

Finally, the critic commits the bifurcation fallacy in failing to recognize that a person can have more than one name. If Christ in Matthew 23:35 is referring to the same Zechariah mentioned in 2 Chronicles 24:20–21, then the father may have had two names — both Jehoiada and Berechiah. This is common in Scripture: Saul/Paul, Jacob/Israel, Simon/Peter, etc.

108. How was Zedekiah related to Nebuchadnezzar? Through an uncle according to 2 Kings 24:17 but a brother according to 2 Chronicles 36:10.

Semantic range fallacy. Zedekiah was Nebuchadnezzar's uncle (2 Kings 24:17). Second Chronicles 36:10 describes Zedekiah as his 'ach (Hebrew) which is rendered "brother" in the KJV but is rendered as "kinsman" in the NAS. This word has a range of meanings, including a literal "brother," but its range also includes other close relatives — such as an uncle or nephew. The same word is used to describe Abraham's relationship to Lot in Genesis 13:8, 14:14, 16, yet Lot was Abraham's nephew. So, there is no inconsistency.

109. Who was Zerubbabel's father? Pedaiah (1 Chronicles 3:19) or Shealtiel (Ezra 3:2; Nehemiah 12:1; Haggai 1:1; Matthew 1:12; Luke 3:27)?

Semantic range fallacy and equivocation. The word "son" can refer to a grandson or more distant descendant, as in "the sons of Israel" (Exodus 6:11–13, 26–27). It can also refer to a biological son or a legally adopted son. So, there are several ways in which a person can have more than one father. Zerubbabel was the son of Shealtiel (Ezra 3:2; Nehemiah 12:1; Haggai 1:1; Matthew 1:12; Luke 3:27), and also the son of Pedaiah (1 Chronicles 3:19). As one likely possibility, Zerubbabel may have been the biological son of Pedaiah and the legal son of Shealtiel. This would occur if Shealtiel died before his wife, with no children; his brother Pedaiah would marry his widow and raise the first son as the legal descendent of Shealtiel, who is biologically his uncle. This was the normal Hebrew custom (Deuteronomy 25:5–6).

TIMING OF EVENTS

We here examine claims that the Bible contradicts itself concerning the timing of events. Suppose one verse claims that event A happened before event B, but another verse claims that event B happened first. That would be problematic. But in many cases, the reader has merely inferred the order of events whereas the text itself does not state which happened first. Many of the alleged contradictions listed in this section are alleviated simply by reading the text carefully without unwarranted assumptions.

110. When did Jesus ascend into heaven? Luke 24:1–51 and Mark 16:9–19 contradict John 20:26, which contradicts Acts 13:31, which contradicts Acts 1:2–3, 9.

Failure to read the text carefully. Luke 24 does not give the date or time of Christ's ascension — only that it was some time after the Resurrection, after He had led the disciples to Bethany (Luke 24:50). Mark 16:9–19 likewise does not give the date or time of Christ's ascension — only that it was sometime after the Resurrection (Mark 16:9, 14, 19). The Gospel of John does not mention the ascension at all, though we can deduce from it that Christ continued His earthly appearances for at least eight days after the Resurrection

(John 20:26), which is compatible with both Luke and Mark. Acts 13:31 states that Jesus was seen "for many days" after His Resurrection and before His ascension, which is consistent with all other accounts. Acts 1:2–3, 9 indicates that the time between Christ's Resurrection and ascension was at least 40 days. None of the other verses the critic lists contradict this.

111. When did Jacob rename Luz to Bethel? Genesis 28:18–19 contradicts Genesis 33:18, 35:6–7.

Bifurcation fallacy and failure to read the text carefully. Jacob first named Luz "Bethel" (which means "house of God" after departing from Beersheba and going toward Haran (Genesis 28:10–11, 18–19). Later, God commanded Jacob to return to Bethel (note that it was already called "Bethel" — Genesis 35:1) and to make an altar. Jacob did so and rechristened the place "El-bethel" (God of the house of God). Note that Jacob used a slightly different name in the rechristening. These events are separated in time, so where is any supposed contradiction?

112. On what day did the Temple burn? Second Kings 25:8–9 says on the seventh day, but Jeremiah 52:12–13 says on the tenth day.

Failure to read the text carefully, and specious reasoning. Actually, neither passage states the exact day that the Temple was burned. Rather, they speak of the day that Nebuzaradan "came to Jerusalem." Sometime after that, Nebuzaradan burned the Temple, perhaps on the same day or perhaps later. But English translations of 2 Kings 25:8 indicate that Nebuzaradan "came to Jerusalem" on the seventh day of the month, whereas Jeremiah 52:12 seems to indicate that Nebuzaradan "came to Jerusalem" on the tenth day of the month. Is this contradictory? In the original Hebrew, there are significant differences in wording that resolve any perceived problem, as shown in the following.

The Hebrew word translated "came" in both passages is "bow" and has a range of meanings, including "come" and also "go." So, it could refer to the time when Nebuzaradan *began* his journey from Riblah or when he arrived in Jerusalem. Thus, Nebuzaradan may have gone to Jerusalem (started his journey) on the seventh day and arrived in Jerusalem on the tenth day. Considering that Jerusalem is a three-day journey by horseback from Riblah, this seems extremely plausible. As even further support, in Jeremiah 52:12, the word "Jerusalem" is prefixed with a Hebrew preposition meaning "in." That is, Nebuzaradan entered into Jerusalem on the tenth day. But such a prefix is lacking in 2 Kings 25:8 because Nebuzaradan merely went to Jerusalem (i.e., began his journey) on the seventh day. In any case, there is no contradiction because the sense is different between the two passages.

113. Did the cock crow before or after Peter's denial? Matthew 26:70, 72, 74; Luke 22:57–60; and John 18:17, 25–27 all disagree with Mark 14:67–72.

Bifurcation fallacy. The correct answer is: neither. The rooster crowed (the second time) *simultaneously* with Peter's third denial. Luke's account makes this abundantly clear, that "Immediately, while he was still speaking, a rooster crowed." Matthew, Mark, and John also confirm that this occurred "immediately", e.g., at the same time as Peter's third denial. Where is any alleged inconsistency?

114. When did the Temple curtain rip? Luke 23:45–46 indicates that it happened before the death of Christ, which disagrees with Matthew 27:50–51 and Mark 15:37–38.

Failure to read the text carefully and specious reasoning. The Temple veil was torn from top to bottom at the time of Christ's death. Matthew, Mark, and Luke all confirm this. The critic seems to have erroneously assumed that the order in which something is *mentioned* in Scripture is the order in which it *happened*, but there is no rational basis for this assumption and there are many counter-examples. Luke 23:45–46 mentions the veil first, then the death of Christ, but it does not say that the veil was torn *before* Christ's death. Matthew

27:50–51 mentions the death first and then the tearing of the veil. But none of the accounts give the precise order, so how could there be any contradiction? They all agree that the veil was torn at the time of Christ's death.

115. When did the women (or woman) arrive at the sepulcher? John 20:1 says it was before sunrise, but Matthew 28:1 and Mark 16:1–2 say that it was very early, at sunrise.

Failure to read the text carefully. Any narrative naturally gives certain details and omits others. And it is human nature to "fill in" missing details with our own imagination, as is easily done with the various Gospel accounts of the women finding the empty tomb of Christ. The details *we imagine* between the various accounts may conflict with each other — but not the actual accounts. Notice that there is no actual contradiction whatsoever between the Gospels of Matthew, Mark, Luke, and John regarding when and how Jesus appeared to the women. All the Gospels report that this happened *after* the Sabbath, early in the morning on Resurrection Sunday (Matthew 28:1; Mark 16:1; Luke 24:1; and John 20:1).

Presumably, the critic is concerned about whether the women arrived before or after sunrise; but a careful reading of the text shows no controversy. No doubt, the women began their journey to the tomb while it was still relatively dark, but with it beginning to dawn (Matthew 28:1 and Luke 24:1). The paradox presumably consists of when they *arrived.* John 20:1 suggests that the arrival was before sunrise, the sky still being somewhat dark, whereas Mark 16:2 indicates that it was at or after sunrise. Matthew and Luke do not give the exact timing of arrival with respect to sunrise. But notice that Mark 16:2 indicates that *they* — that is Mary Magdalen *and* Mary the mother of James (and perhaps others: see Luke 24:10) — arrived at the tomb at or after sunrise. Whereas, John 20:1 states only that *Mary Magdalene* "came early to the tomb, while it was still dark." The women had been discussing who could roll away the stone (Mark 16:3) and perhaps this motivated Mary Magdalen to run ahead of the rest to get help with this matter, which is why she arrived earlier. So, there is no contradiction between one woman arriving before sunrise, while the rest of her group arrived at or *after* sunrise.

116. When did the earth dry after the Flood? Genesis 8:13 contradicts Genesis 8:14.

Semantic range fallacy. The land was dry by the 27th day of the second month (Genesis 8:14). The critic is apparently confused because Genesis 8:13 describes the ground as being "dried up" (NASB) on the first day of the first month. (Of course, even in English there is no *contradiction* in the ground being dry at one time, and then also being dry at another time.) But note that the Hebrew text uses a different word for "dried up" in verse 13 than the word for "dry" in verse 14. The word used in verse 13 has a variety of meanings (including "desolate" and "in ruins"), and its usage here suggests that the water was no longer upon the land, but that the land was still moist and muddy. Whereas, the word used in verse 14 suggests that the land was fully dry (and hard) at this later time. After all, there are degrees of dryness.

117. When was Eve created? Genesis 1:27 contradicts Genesis 2:20–22.

Failure to read the text carefully. Eve was made on the sixth day (Genesis 1:27, 31), after the creation of the animals and of Adam (Genesis 2:20–22). Where is there any inconsistency?

118. When did the cursed fig tree die? Matthew 21:19–20 indicates that it died instantly when Jesus cursed it, but Mark 11:13–14, 20–21 says it happened the next day.

Failure to read the text carefully. The fig tree immediately withered somewhat when Christ cursed it (Matthew 21:19), but it did *not* whither completely or die at that time. By the following morning, the tree had dried up completely from its roots (Mark 11:13–14, 19–21).

119. When did Jesus curse the fig tree? Before the temple visit (Mark 11:12–17) or after the temple visit (Matthew 21:12, 17–19)?

Failure to read the text carefully. By pulling selected verses out of context, the critic makes it sound as if there is an inconsistency: To read *only* Mark 11:12–17, we learn that Jesus cursed the fig tree *before* he came to the Temple. To read *only* Matthew 21:12, 17–19, we learn that Jesus cursed the fig tree the day *after* His visit to the Temple. Which account is correct? Both are true, of course, since Jesus visited the Temple *twice* in two days. And both Matthew and Mark teach this (see Matthew 21:12, 18, 23 and Mark 11:11, 15). Jesus cursed the fig tree on the morning of the day after His first Temple visit, and before His second Temple visit (Matthew 21:10–23; Mark 11:11–15). This type of silly error shows that the critic is not engaging in serious scholarship in trying to discern the truth of the matter, but is merely interested in distorting the text to justify his sin.

120. When was the Holy Ghost given? John 7:39, 20:22 and Acts 2:1–4 contradict Mark 12:36; Luke 1:15, 41, 67, 2:25; and Acts 1:16.

Equivocation fallacy. "Given" in what sense? The Holy Spirit has always been present in the world, from the very beginning (Genesis 1:1–2). And He has indwelt believers throughout time (Psalm 51:11; Isaiah 63:11; John 20:22; Mark 12:36; Luke 1:15, 41, 67, 2:25; Acts 1:16). However, the Holy Spirit was "given" *in a new way* to empower believers *at Pentecost* (Acts 1:8, 2:1–4; John 7:39, 14:16, 26, 15:26, 16:7), as evidenced by speaking in other languages.

121. When was heaven created? Matthew 25:34 contradicts John 14:2.

Failure to read the text carefully. John 14:2 discusses the place that Christ prepares for His followers. Matthew 25:34 discusses the *kingdom* that was prepared from the foundation of the world to be inherited by the saved. Neither verse addresses when heaven (either the physical universe or the realm of God) was created, so obviously they cannot contradict on an issue they do not address.

122. At what time of day was Jesus crucified? Mark 15:25 contradicts John 19:14–16.

Semantic anachronism and failure to read the text carefully. The crucifixion was not an instantaneous event. It took time. Furthermore, precise time-keeping was neither possible nor necessary at that point in history, so we should expect round numbers. Note that when the text is read carefully, only Mark's gospel gives the time of day that Christ was crucified — at the third hour (Mark 15:25). Inferring that Mark is using the Jewish reckoning of time, this would correspond to around 9:00 a.m.

The other Gospels do not state when Christ was crucified, but only indicate that there was darkness from the sixth to ninth hour (noon to 3:00 p.m.) while Jesus was still on the cross. This is fully consistent with Mark.

Had the critic read John 19:14–16 carefully, he would have realized that it does not mention the time of the crucifixion at all! Rather, John refers to the time at which Pilate questioned Jesus. John reports this as "about the sixth hour." The critic may have erroneously assumed that this was by Jewish reckoning, which would put it at noon. But that cannot be, because Mark indicates that the crucifixion had already started three hours before. It seems clear therefore that John is using the Roman reckoning of time — the same as ours, in which case the sixth hour is 6 a.m.

This reading is fully consistent with Mark 15:1, which states that Jesus was delivered to Pilate "early in the morning," i.e., around sunrise (~6:00 a.m.). After Pilate's judgment, there are roughly three hours before crucifixion, in which Jesus would have been brought to Golgotha to be mocked, spat upon, and finally nailed to the Cross. So, there is no apparent inconsistency when the texts are read carefully.

123. Were humans created before or after the other animals? *After* according to Genesis 1:25–27, but *before* according to Genesis 2:18–19.

Failure to read the text carefully. Genesis 1:25–27 indicates that animals were created before people. Genesis 2 does not give the order of creation, and thus there is no contradiction. In some English translations, Genesis 2:19 may seem to indicate that the animals were created after the events of verses 15–18, but *the text does not actually say this.* Hebrew verbs do not show tense in the same way as English, so tense must be supplied from context: "made" and "had [previously] made" would be written with the same verb form. The context here indicates that God brought the animals that He had *previously* made (before the creation of Adam) to Adam after the events of verses 15–18. This is seen in the Darby, Douay, and NIV translations of the passage. So, there is no inconsistency.

124. Which came first: the calling of Peter and Andrew or the imprisonment of John the Baptist? Mark 1:14–17 puts their calling *after* John's imprisonment, but John 1:40–42, 3:22–24 puts it *before*.

Bifurcation fallacy. Which calling? Peter and Andrew were called into the ministry of John the Baptist and met Jesus and spent time with Him before John the Baptist was imprisoned (John 1:35, 37, 40–42). At a later time, after John the Baptist had been imprisoned, Christ called Peter and Andrew to follow Him (Mark 1:14–17).

125. How old was Ishmael when he was abandoned by Abraham? Genesis 21:14–15, 18 indicates that he was a very young child, but Genesis 17:25, 21:5, 8 says that he was much older.

Bluff and failure to read the passages carefully. Ishmael was about 16 years old. Does any verse say otherwise? From Genesis 17:21–25, we learn that Ishmael was 13 one year before Isaac was born. Ishmael was sent away with Hagar when Isaac was weaned. Presumably, Isaac was around two years old at this time, which makes Ismael's age around 16 years. None of the verses listed by the critic contradict this. Perhaps the critic was confused by Genesis 21:15, where Hagar "left the boy under one of the bushes" and mistakenly thought that this implied that Ishmael was a baby. But context precludes this because

Ishmael was expelled for mocking Isaac (Genesis 21:9). (Parents of teenagers are familiar with the short-term energy of youth — which is known to fade when long-term endurance is the test.) The correct and rather obvious interpretation of verse 15 is that Ishmael was exhausted and dying from thirst, since the passage says, "When the water in the skin was used up. . . ."

126. When did Jehoash become king of Israel? Second Kings 13:1 contradicts 2 Kings 13:10.

Bluff and failure to read the text carefully. There is no apparent inconsistency here. Second Kings 13:10 states that Jehoash became king in the 37th year of Joash. He co-reigned for three years alongside his father and reigned alone for an additional 13 years after that. Second Kings 13:1 states that *Jehoahaz* (Jehoash's *father*) became king in the 23rd year of Joash. Perhaps the critic confused the names?

127. When was the man (or men) healed? Was it when Jesus departed from Jericho (Matthew 20:30; Mark 10:46) or before He came to Jericho (Luke 18:35)?

Failure to read the text carefully or to consult the original language. The blind men were healed as Jesus was departing from Jericho (Matthew 20:29–34; Mark 10:46–52). Luke informs us that one of these two blind men was begging when Jesus "was coming near Jericho" (Luke 18:35). Some readers might assume that this meant that Jesus was approaching Jericho, rather than leaving. But in fact, the Greek text of Luke 18:35 only indicates that Jesus was *near* Jericho at the time. Luke does not provide details of the timing. He only informs us of the outcome. The blind man cried to Jesus and was healed. Luke does *not* say that this happened *before* Jesus arrived at Jericho (we know it happened afterward), only that Jesus was near Jericho at the time. Luke merely *reports* of the healing before he reports of the events in Jericho. So, there is no genuine inconsistency.

128. Did Paul go to Jerusalem from Damascus immediately after his conversion? Acts 9:26 contradicts Galatians 1:16–17.

Bluff and failure to read the text carefully. No, Paul did not go to Jerusalem from Damascus immediately after his conversion (Acts 9:17–26; Galatians 1:16–17). No verse says otherwise. According to Acts 9:19, at least several days elapsed, and Acts 9:22 suggests that he spent considerable time in Damascus before going to Jerusalem. Galatians 1:16–18 agrees perfectly and states only that Paul went to Jerusalem three years later. In addition, this visit after three years may not have been the first visit, but rather the first time he went specifically to visit the Apostles (Galatians 1:17–18).

129. When was Jesus born? Matthew 2:1 and Luke 1:5 contradict Luke 2:1.

Bluff and specious reasoning. Jesus was born during the time when Caesar Augustus, the Emperor of Rome, ordered a census, during the time that Herod was king of Judea (Matthew 2:1; Luke 1:5, 2:1). There is no apparent inconsistency. I can only suppose that the critic is ignorant of history, in supposing that Augustus could not be emperor of Rome while Herod was king of Judea. But history shows that Rome permitted its nations to have their local kings and religions, so long as they submitted to Roman rule. This is not unlike the so-called "Holy Roman Empire" of Europe's Dark Ages, which featured many European "kings," who were administratively accountable to one European "emperor."

130. When did God kill Leviathan and the sea dragon? In the past (Psalm 74:13–14) or in the future (Isaiah 27:1)?

Bifurcation fallacy and genre fallacy. Both Psalm 74 and Isaiah 27 are written in Hebrew poetic style, where we expect to find non-literal figures of speech. In Isaiah 27:1, the Lord is said to "punish Leviathan" — a great sea creature, which in this passage represents an evil nation. God has punished evil nations *on many occasions* and will again (e.g., Genesis 19:24), in accordance with His own just and wise purposes. So, it is not a singular event. Similarly, Psalm 74:13–14 seems to refer to such an occasion, perhaps alluding to the destruction of the Egyptians at the Red Sea. In any case, God has done such things *many times*, so where is there any contradiction?

131. Did Elisha receive Elijah's mantle before or after Elijah was taken up into heaven? First Kings 19:19 says *before*, but 2 Kings 2:11–13 says *after*.

Bifurcation fallacy. The answer of course is both. The first time Elijah put his mantle on Elisha signified the latter's call into the prophetic office. When Elijah was taken up into heaven, Elisha again took up his mantle, signifying that Elisha was Elijah's successor. Why would the critic assume that a mantle can only be put on once?

132. When did Noah enter the Ark? Genesis 7:7–10 contradicts Genesis 7:11–13.

Bluff and failure to read the text carefully. Genesis 7:7–10 does not say when Noah entered the ark. It only teaches that the Flood came upon the earth "after the seven days" of grace that the Lord had granted in verse 4. But these verses do not directly say which day Noah entered the Ark, only that he *did* enter the Ark (Genesis 7:5–7). However, since God had told Noah in verses 1–4 that the Flood would happen after seven more days, there was no reason for Noah to enter the Ark before the seventh day. Moreover, verse 7 indicates that Noah and his family boarded the Ark "because of the water of the flood," which seems to imply that they boarded on the day when the rain began. And what do we read in Genesis 7:11–13? We learn that Noah and his family entered the Ark on the very day that the Flood began. The verses show perfect harmony, again revealing the lack of scholarship of the critic.

133. Was Jesus crucified the day before or the day after the Passover meal? John 19:14–16 contradicts Mark 14:12, 15:25.

Semantic anachronism fallacy and failure to read the text carefully. The answer is: neither. Jesus was crucified *on the day* of Passover — by Jewish reckoning. Recall that Jewish days began at sunset, and went until the following sunset. The Passover was celebrated on the 14th day of the month of Nisan (Numbers 9:3, 5). On the Passion Week, this day would begin at sunset on Thursday, and end at sunset on Friday. Jesus therefore celebrated the Passover meal on Thursday evening after sunset (Mark 14:12–18) and was crucified on Friday (Mark 15:25), which is still Passover by the Jewish calendar.

John 19:14–16 indicates that Christ was crucified at the time of "the preparation of the Passover." The critic perhaps assumes that this means that the Passover was to take place on the following day — *but the text does not say this.* So, there can be no contradiction since John 19:14–16 does not actually say when the Passover is. What are we to make of the phrase "the preparation of the Passover"? Since Friday before sunset was still the day of Passover, some people might have yet to perform it and might have been preparing for it.

Alternatively, the preparation was likely for the Sabbath day, since work was not permitted on the Sabbath. But this would be a special Sabbath day because it occurred on the week of Passover. Hence, it was the preparation (for the Sabbath) of the Passover week. The NIV even renders the passage this way, which the critic apparently did not bother to check. Thus, regardless of the precise meaning of this phrase, any alleged contradiction exists only in the critic's imagination — not in the text.

134. Were plants created before or after humans? Genesis 1:11–13, 27–31 says before, but Genesis 2:4–7 says after.

Failure to read the text carefully or to consult the original language. Plants, in general, were created before humans. Plants were made on day 3 (Genesis 1:11–13), humans on day 6 (Genesis 1:27–31).

Genesis 2:4–7 does not contradict this at all. Rather, it describes in greater detail the events of day 6. The Hebrew words rendered "shrub of the field" and "plant of the field" in Genesis 2:5 refer to *cultivated* plants. That is, no plants existed that were *the result of human agriculture*. The first plants had been supernaturally created by God. Genesis 2:8 confirms that plants predate humans because God put the man in the garden that He had previously planted.

135. When did Satan enter Judas? Before the Passover meal (Luke 22:3, 7) or during it (John 13:27)?

Bifurcation fallacy and specious reasoning. This can't happen more than once? Satan entered Judas when the Passover was approaching (Luke 22:1–3), and again when he had eaten the morsel (John 13:27). Where is there any contradiction?

136. When did David meet Saul? First Samuel 16:21–23 contradicts 1 Samuel 17:55–58.

Failure to read the text carefully. Neither text actually states when David first met Saul. David played the harp for Saul and became his armor-bearer (1 Samuel 16:14–23). After the battle with Goliath, King Saul asks, "Whose son is this young man?" (1 Samuel 17:55–58). It seems as if Saul had forgotten that David was the son of Jesse. Perhaps he had. But how is that in any way a *contradiction*?

Furthermore, it is very easy to forget a name or family connection when we see someone out of the usual context: perhaps at the supermarket we see a teacher or friend from school. The name might escape us for a moment because our mind functions by association. David had previously only appeared to Saul as a musician — a young boy playing the harp. Now suddenly Saul sees a young man who had slain a giant. Is this really the same boy who played the harp for Saul? Saul's reaction seems very realistic and understandable. In any case, there is no contradiction here.

137. When were the stars made? Genesis 1:16–19 says on the fourth day — after the earth, but Job 38:4–7 says that the stars already existed when the foundations of the earth were laid.

Genre fallacy and failure to read the text carefully. Genesis 1:16–19 indicates that stars were made on the fourth day of the creation week. Earth was made on the first day but was not finished until the sixth day. So, earth was unfinished and still being shaped by God when God made the stars. Job 38:4–7 shows full agreement with this. Though this section of Job is poetic, its meaning is that Job was not alive during the creation week, when the earth and stars were formed. Note that Job 38 does not give a specific order in which the events of Genesis transpired, but merely refers back to some of them.

138. When did Jesus' temple "tantrum" occur? John 2:11–16 contradicts Luke 19:36–45 and Matthew 21:1–13, which contradicts Mark 11:1–17.

Question-begging epithet fallacy and bifurcation fallacy. By the way the critic phrased this claim ("tantrum"), he suggests that Jesus behaved in a childish fashion, but no evidence for this is presented. So, his claim is merely a question-begging epithet fallacy. On the contrary, God's anger at the irreverent desecration of His holy Temple was very justified and appropriate. So, when did Jesus overturn the tables in righteous anger? One time was after the wedding in Cana, just before the Passover (John 2:11–16). He did this again at *another time* shortly after the triumphal entry (Luke 19:36–45; Matthew 21:1–13; Mark 11:1–17). Why did the critic arbitrarily assume that Jesus only did this once? Wouldn't God be angry *every* time people defame His temple?

CAUSE AND EFFECT

In this chapter we examine claims that the Bible contradicts itself concerning causation — who or what caused a particular event to happen. One verse lists one cause, but another verse lists a different cause. Which is correct? In most cases, causation is multi-faceted. Most events have *multiple* causes, so two different verses may correctly give two different causes with no contradiction. For example, what causes rain? Is it moisture in the air, the air temperature dropping below the dew point, a cold front, gravity pulling on the water droplets, natural forces, or God? All of these are causes. There is no contradiction between these causes, only compatible differences. It is the bifurcation fallacy to assume that a given effect must have only one cause. Furthermore, just because two events happen at about the same time does not necessarily imply the one caused the other. This is the false-cause fallacy. These errors in reasoning account for many of the critic's blunders in this section.

139. Was Abraham justified by faith or by works? Romans 4:2 says by *faith*, but James 2:21 says by *works*.

Bifurcation fallacy. Abraham was justified both by faith and by works (James 2:24, 26). To "justify" means either to be in right moral standing or to show that one is (morally) in right standing. Abraham was justified by faith *before God* since God knows all things — including Abraham's faith (James 2:23). God sees our hearts (1 Samuel 16:7), so we are justified before God by our faith alone, which God can see. But men cannot see another man's faith. They only see the outward works that follow from inward faith. Therefore, Abraham was justified *before men* by the works that followed from his faith, since men cannot see faith but can see works. James *explicitly* teaches this (James 2:18–26).

140. Who makes people deaf and blind? Exodus 4:11 and John 9:1–3 say God, but Mark 9:17, 25 indicate that an unclean spirit is responsible.

Bifurcation fallacy. God makes all things happen according to the counsel of His will (Isaiah 46:10; Daniel 4:35; Exodus 4:11; John 9:1–3). And God often uses *means* to accomplish His will (Isaiah 46:10–11; Proverbs 16:9, 20:24, 21:1; Mark 9:17, 25). Even the demons are used by God to accomplish His will (1 Kings 22:21; 2 Corinthians 12:7). The Bible teaches that God ordains both the ends and the means. So, where is the contradiction in God causing something to happen by using His creations?

141. Does the blood of animal sacrifices take away sin? Leviticus 4:20, 26, 31, 35, 5:10, 16, 18, 6:7, 17:11 and Numbers 15:27–28, 29:5 all say *yes*, but Hebrews 10:4, 11 say *no*.

Failure to read the text carefully. The Bible categorically states that animal sacrifice cannot take away sin (Hebrews 10:4, 11), and no verse contradicts this. None of the Old Testament verses the critic lists say that animal sacrifice can take away sin. Rather, animal sacrifice was used to "cover" or "atone for" sin in a symbolic act that foreshadowed the Messiah, who would actually take away sin. That's why animal sacrifices had to be repeated (Hebrews 10:1–2). Note that God was willing to forgive sins long before the sins were actually paid for by Christ. But only Christ could actually *take away* sin, as Hebrews 10:1–14 abundantly states.

142. Who destroyed Sodom and Gomorrah? Genesis 19:13 says angels, but Genesis 19:24 says God.

Bifurcation fallacy. God destroyed Sodom and Gomorrah using His angels (Genesis 19:13, 24). So, it is accurate to say "God's angels destroyed Sodom and Gomorrah," or "God destroyed Sodom and Gomorrah." There is no contradiction, since God's action was accomplished by His spiritual ministers. God often works through means, and so the Bible teaches dual causality (Isaiah 46:9–11).

143. Is Salvation by faith alone? *Yes* according to Mark 16:16; John 3:18, 36; Acts 16:30–31; Romans 1:16–17, 3:20, 28, 4:2, 13, 5:1, 10:9; Galatians 2:16, 3:11–12; Ephesians 2:8–9; Titus 3:5. *No,* salvation is by works according to Psalm 62:12; Proverbs 10:16; Jeremiah 17:10; Ezekiel 18:27; Matthew 5:20, 12:37, 16:27, 19:17, 25:41–46; Luke 10:26–28; John 5:29; Romans 2:6, 13; 2 Corinthians 5:10, 11:15; Philippians 2:12; James 2:14, 17, 21–25; 1 Peter 1:17; Revelation 2:23, 20:12–13, 22:14.

False-cause fallacy, sweeping generalization fallacy, and failure to read the text carefully. Salvation is by God's grace, received by faith and not by works (Ephesians 2:8–9; Mark 16:16; John 3:18, 36; Acts 16:30–31; Romans 1:16–17, 3:20, 28, 4:2, 13, 5:1, 10:9–10; Galatians 2:16, 3:11–12; Titus 3:5). The Scriptures unilaterally teach this, and no Scripture contradicts it. So, what of the Scriptures that the critic lists are supposedly incompatible? The critic makes three errors in thinking that these passages are somehow contradictory.

First, it is clear by the verses the critic chose that he has committed the false-cause fallacy. This is the error of assuming a false cause-and-effect relationship between two things that are correlated. For example, smoke and fire are correlated — they often go together. A child might conclude, "Therefore, smoke *causes* fire." But this conclusion is erroneous. It is the fire that causes the smoke. Fast-moving clouds do not cause wind, and palm trees do not cause sunshine. Correlation does not prove causation.

Likewise, the Bible teaches that good works and salvation are correlated, as we will see below. That is, those who practice good works tend to also be those who are eternally saved. The critic falsely concludes then that the good works have *caused* the salvation. But the Bible nowhere teaches this, and in fact teaches the *opposite*. Good works are the *effect* of salvation, not the cause. When a person is truly saved by God's grace received through faith, that person desires to please God and to do good works. Almost all the verses the critic lists as supposedly contrary to salvation by grace, merely show that salvation and works are *correlated*, which is perfectly compatible with good works following salvation by grace.

For example, in Matthew 25:41–46 Jesus tells of the fate of those who did not do good works — that they go into eternal punishment, but the righteous to eternal life. But does this passage teach that good works are the *cause* of righteousness or of eternal life? No. They are the *effect*. Those who have repented and have been made righteous by Christ's atonement desire to please God and obey His commandments (1 John 2:29, 3–5). Those who are unrepentant generally act wickedly and do not obey the commandments with right goals and motives (1 John 2:11, 3:3–10). Likewise, John 5:29; Romans 2:13; Philippians 2:12; and Revelation 22:14 teach that good works *go with* salvation, just as wicked deeds go with damnation. But *none* of these teach that good works are the cause of salvation. No Scripture does. Good works are but the lifestyle of those who have been saved by God's grace.

Likewise, James 2:14 and 17 teach that the kind of faith that is needed for salvation is one that produces good works. "Faith" that does not result in works is not a genuine saving faith but a "dead" one. Note that James does *not* teach that good works are the *cause* of salvation (or saving faith) — rather, good works follow saving faith and are associated with it. James 2:21–25 does not address the cause of salvation, but rather addresses the topic of *justification* before men, as indicated in verse 18. Justification before men is the outward, visible evidence (good works) of inward righteousness (salvation by grace through faith).

The critic also makes a second error — the sweeping generalization fallacy. This is when a person assumes that a general trend has no exceptions, when there is evidence to the contrary. Generally, God gives people exactly what they deserve. But salvation is an exception, because it is *better* than what anyone deserves. So, when we read passages like Psalm 62:12; Romans 2:6; Jeremiah 17:10; 2 Corinthians 5:10; 1 Peter 1:17; and Revelation 2:23 that teach that God rewards every man according to his work, we need to ask if the Bible allows any exceptions to this generalization. Of course it does — salvation is not something we have earned (Titus 3:5).

Of the remaining passages, the critic has simply not read the text carefully. For example, Proverbs 10:16 states that the "wages of the righteous is life" — but this verse does not mention what the cause of eternal salvation is. Nor does it mention "works." The righteous — those who have received Christ's imputed righteousness — will inherit eternal life, but not because of works. Ezekiel 18:27 discusses the man who turns away from his sin and repents and begins practicing righteousness — his life will be saved. However, the text does *not* say that his eternal salvation can be earned or is a result of good works. The fact that the man repents shows that he has received *by faith* the salvation that comes from God's grace.

In Matthew 5:20, Jesus warns that unless a person's righteousness exceeds that of the scribes and Pharisees, the person will not enter the kingdom of heaven. The scribes and Pharisees were the religious leaders of the day, *yet their good works were not sufficient to warrant salvation.* Far from contradicting salvation by grace through faith, this passage confirms it. If the top religious leaders cannot be saved by their good works, how much less those of us who are common sinners? Only by receiving Christ's imputed righteousness by faith can a person be counted as righteous (Romans 4:22–24).

Matthew 12:37 is no exception — it points out that our own words (not "works") will be used as evidence in the court of God. That is, our words will either give evidence of our salvation by God's grace or our lack thereof. Matthew 16:27 indicates again that God will "reward each according to his works" — indicating God's fairness and justice. But this does not negate God's grace and mercy, in God also giving us above and beyond what we have earned — things that cannot be earned, such as salvation.

In Matthew 19:17, Jesus tells the rich young man, "But if you want to enter into life, keep the commandments." Notice first that Jesus does *not* say that keeping the commandments will necessarily result in salvation, as if the former could ever be the cause of the latter. So, there is no contradiction. Moreover, one of God's commandments is to repent and believe on His name (Matthew 4:17; Acts 2:38, 3:19, 8:22, 17:30). But the salvation that God gives to the repentant person is His *gift* and cannot be earned from obedience. Likewise, Luke 10:26–28 does not teach that salvation is earned by obedience, only that they go together. By analogy, if there's smoke, there's fire, yet smoke is not the cause of the fire. The saved will desire to walk in obedience (1 John 3:7–9).

In 2 Corinthians 11:15, we read that Satan's servants, in the end, are judged according to their deeds. Well, yes, since they have not received God's grace through faith, they are condemned by their evil works. All those who are unsaved will be judged by their works, and no one will be saved by their works (Romans 3:20; Galatians 2:16). Revelation 20:12–13 teaches this explicitly, as the critic might have realized if he had read on to verse 15. Those who have their name written in God's book of life, the saved, are not judged on their (insufficient) works.

144. Who forces non-believers to disbelieve? John 12:40 and 2 Thessalonians 2:11–12 indicate that God does, but 2 Corinthians 4:3–4 indicates that it is Satan.

Bifurcation fallacy and question-begging epithet. Of course, no one "forces" non-believers to disbelieve contrary to their wishes. Such loaded language obscures a legitimate question: What is the *cause* of the unbeliever's disbelief? But in supposing that there is only one cause, the critic commits the bifurcation fallacy.

Does God "blind the eyes" of the wicked so that they do not understand the Gospel and repent (John 12:40; 2 Thessalonians 2:11–12)? Or does Satan do this (2 Corinthians 4:3–4)? Or do the people themselves close their own eyes and refuse to see (Matthew

13:15)? The answer of course is: all of the above. God is sovereign, and therefore uses both people and Satan to accomplish His sovereign purpose (Isaiah 46:9–11). God blinds the eyes of those who do not wish to see, and He uses Satan to do this, and He uses the desires of the wicked to do this. The Bible therefore endorses dual-causality. Where is there any contradiction whatsoever in supposing that both God and Satan are causal agents in the blinding of the spiritual eyes of the wicked?

145. Who hardened Pharaoh's heart? God hardened Pharaoh's heart according to Exodus 4:21, 7:3, 13, 9:12, 10:1, 20, 27, 11:10, 14:4, 8, 17, but Pharaoh hardened his own heart according to Exodus 8:32, 9:34; and 1 Samuel 6:6.

Bifurcation fallacy. Both God and Pharaoh hardened Pharaoh's heart (Exodus 4:12, 7:3, 13, 8:32, 9:12, 34, 10:1, 20, 27, 11:10, 14:4, 8, 17; 1 Samuel 6:6). There is no rational reason why it would have to be just one or the other. People sometimes work together to produce an outcome. Likewise, God can use men to accomplish aspects of His plan (Isaiah 46:10–11).

146. Who sent the Holy Ghost? Jesus did so according to John 15:26, but God the Father did so according to John 14:26.

Bifurcation fallacy. God (both God the Son and God the Father) sent the Holy Spirit (John 14:26, 15:26). Even John 15:26 indicates that Jesus sent the Holy Spirit "*from* the Father," so clearly both persons were doing the sending.

147. Who brought evil on Job? Was it Satan (Job 2:7) or God (Job 42:11)?

Bifurcation fallacy. God uses means to accomplish His will (Isaiah 46:10–11), even Satan. God used Satan to test Job. So, it is fair to say that Satan brought adversities on Job, and God brought adversities on Job (Job 2:7, 42:11). Dual causality is perfectly logical and is at the heart of Christianity. After all, God used men to write *His* Word (2 Peter 1:21; 2 Timothy 3:16). Those who study logic are well aware that most effects have a proximate cause and one or more distal causes. This same analysis is well developed in Anglo-American tort law, under the phrase "proximate causation."

148. Who cast Jonah into the sea? Men (Jonah 1:15) or God (Jonah 2:3)?

Bifurcation fallacy. (Same as #140, #142, #144). God often uses people to accomplish His plan. Men, enabled by God, cast Jonah into the sea (Jonah 1:15, 2:3). So, Jonah was right to poetically say that "You [God] had cast me into the deep."

149. How did King Josiah die? Second Kings 22:20 contradicts 2 Kings 23:29–30 and 2 Chronicles 35:23–24.

Failure to read the text carefully. Josiah was mortally wounded in combat at Megiddo by Pharaoh Neco, specifically by Neco's archers on his orders (2 Kings 23:20–30; 2 Chronicles 35:23–24). Second Kings 22:20 does not contradict this; rather, it confirms that Josiah would not live to see the calamity that God would bring upon Judea but that he would die while Judea is at peace — which he did.

150. Was Rahab saved by faith or works? Hebrews 11:31 says by faith, but James 2:25 says by works.

Semantic range fallacy and failure to read the text carefully and in context. Rahab was *saved* by faith (Hebrews 11:31). She was *justified* by works (James 2:25). These are two different things. In the context of James, to "justify" means to *show or demonstrate* that one is in right standing, which is not the same thing as *being* in the right standing (salvation). The context of James 2 (see James 2:17–20) is *showing* to others that we are in right standing with God; this is accomplished through works, since people cannot observe faith apart from works. Salvation is by faith alone; justification before men is by works resulting from faith. James 2:17–26 makes this abundantly clear.

151. Who raised Jesus from the dead? Jesus said that He would do this Himself in John 2:19–21, but Acts 2:24, 32, 4:10, 13:30; Galatians 1:1; Colossians 2:12; and 1 Thessalonians 1:10 say that God did.

Bifurcation fallacy. *God* raised Jesus from the dead (Acts 2:24, 32, 3:15, 4:10, 5:30, 10:40, 13:30; Colossians 2:12): God the Father (Galatians 1:1; Acts 3:26; Romans 6:4; 1 Thessalonians 1:10), God the Son (John 2:19–21, 10:17–18), and God the Holy Spirit (1 Peter 3:18; Romans 8:11). All members of the Trinity were involved in the Resurrection of Christ, and no verse contradicts this.

152. How did Saul die? First Samuel 31:4–6 and 1 Chronicles 10:4 contradict 1 Samuel 1:8–10, which contradicts 2 Samuel 21:12, which contradicts 1 Chronicles 10:14.

Bluff. Only the first two passages describe in detail (the proximate cause of) how Saul died, and 1 Chronicles 10:14 gives the distal cause. The rest of the verses only state what happened afterward, with full consistency.

Saul died in a losing battle by falling on his own sword (1 Samuel 31:1–6; 1 Chronicles 10:4). When the Philistines arrived and found Saul's dead body, they cut off his head and hung his body on the wall of Beth-shan (1 Samuel 31:8–10). The men of Jabesh-gildead then went by night and removed Saul's body, burned it, and buried the bones in Jabesh (1 Samuel 21:11–13). David then took the bones from there and buried them in the country of Benjamin in Zela (2 Samuel 21:12–14). First Chronicles 10:13–14 indicate that Saul's demise was part of God's plan and was ultimately a result of Saul's sin against God. So, where is the alleged contradiction?

153. What must you do to be saved? Matthew 5:20, 6:1, 7:1, 7–8, 10:22, 12:37, 16.27, 19:30, 25:34–36; Mark 10:31, 13:13; Luke 6:24, 37, 19:23–24; John 5:29; Romans 2:6, 13; Psalm 62:12; Jeremiah 17:10; 2 Corinthians 5:10, 11:15; James 2:14, 5:1; 1 Peter 1:17; Ezekiel 18:27; 2 Thessalonians 2:10, 24:13; 1 John 4:7; and Revelation 2:23, 20:12–13 contradict Mathew 7:21, 10:42, 16:25, 18:3, 19:17–19, 29, 22:14; Mark 8:35, 38, 9:41, 10:29–30, 16:16; Luke 9:24, 10:26, 13:23–24, 18:18–22, 29–30; John 3:3, 5, 16, 5:24, 6:37, 44, 50, 9:11, 12:25, 17:33; Acts 2:21, 16:31; Romans 3:28, 5:1, 8:29–30, 10:9, 13, 11:26; 1 Corinthians 1:21, 5:1–5, 7:14, 16, 15:29; Galatians 2:16; Ephesians 2:8; James 2:17, 3:36, 6:40, 47; Titus 3:5; 1 Timothy 2:14–15; 2 Timothy 2:11; Ephesians 1:4–5, 6:53–54; and Revelation 14:4, 12, 22:14.

Bluff, failure to read the text carefully or in context, false-cause fallacy, and elephant hurling. Most of the passages listed by the critic do not discuss eternal salvation and merely reveal his shallow thinking and ignorance of Scripture. Perhaps he thinks by listing many verses that we will be intimidated and just take his word for it (the fallacy of elephant hurling). But that would not be scholarly. The critic has not reasoned logically from these passages. Even the question "what must you *do* to be saved" begs the question — the Bible teaches that there is no work you can do to earn salvation. It is entirely by God's grace, and the believer receives salvation by faith which itself is a gift from God (Ephesians 2:8–9).

Many of the passages chosen indicate that the critic has committed the false-cause fallacy. This is the error in assuming that when there is a link between A and B, that A must be the cause of B. In reality, B might be the cause of A, or C might be the cause of both A and B. Obesity is often correlated with poor diet and lack of exercise. But obesity is not the cause of poor diet and exercise. Rather, in many cases, poor diet and lack of exercise cause obesity. Likewise, good works and salvation go together. But this doesn't mean that good works cause salvation. The Bible teaches the reverse: that salvation is the cause of good works. Had the critic known this obvious biblical truth, he would not have listed most of the verses above.

The Bible unilaterally teaches that eternal salvation is (a) God's gift (Ephesians 2:8), (b) always undeserved (Titus 3:5), (c) received through faith in Christ (Ephesians 2:8), (d) accomplished by Christ's substitutionary atonement on the Cross (2 Corinthians 5:21; 1 John 2:2; Hebrews 2:9, 14–15), (e) professed with the mouth (Romans 10:9–10). Eternal salvation (f) cannot be achieved or supplemented by good works (Ephesians 2:8–9; Titus 3:5), (g) but always results in good works (James 2:14–26; 1 John 2:4), and (h) results in the repentant believer being considered righteous by receiving Christ's righteousness (2 Corinthians 4:21; Romans 4:3). All the verses listed by the critic are fully consistent with the above principles and with each other. Let's look at each one specifically.

Matthew 5:20 — Only the righteousness received by faith in Christ results in salvation; good works are insufficient (b, c). The Pharisees lacked such faith and therefore lacked righteousness.

Matthew 6:1 — does not discuss eternal salvation, but rather the rewards that follow from good works, which salvation does not (f).

Matthew 7:1; Luke 6:37 — does not relate to eternal salvation, but rather regards making judgments.

Matthew 7:7–8 — not specifically relating to salvation; though God is pleased to give salvation to the repentant who genuinely ask for it (e).

Matthew 10:22; Mark 13:13 — is not speaking specifically of eternal salvation, but enduring tribulation. Nonetheless, those who are genuinely saved will endure (Hebrews 10:38–39).

Matthew 12:37 — genuine salvation is exhibited by a profession of faith (e).

Matthew 16:27 — good deeds follow from salvation (g) but are not the cause (f). The critic has committed the false-cause fallacy in thinking that good works are the *cause* of salvation simply on the basis that they are *correlated*. Salvation is the cause of good works.

Matthew 19:30 — does not discuss eternal salvation.

Matthew 25:34–36; Mark 10:31 — good works follow from salvation (g). They are not the cause (f). The critic again has committed the false-cause fallacy.

Luke 6:24 — does not discuss the cause of salvation, but only points out that it cannot be bought with money.

Luke 19:23–24 — a parable about obedience, not salvation *per se*. Nonetheless, the saved desire to obey God (g).

John 5:29 — good works follow from salvation (g), they are not the cause (f). Thus, those who do good works out of gratitude for salvation will inherit eternal life — but not because of works. Again, the critic has committed the false-cause fallacy.

Romans 2:6 — deals with the justice of God, not salvation. Christ's righteousness is imputed to the believer, so God treats them as if they had upheld God's law perfectly, as Christ did (h). Those who are saved receive God's mercy while Christ pays the penalty for their sin, resulting in justice.

Romans 2:13 — those who are saved will want to obey God's law, and will be justified (g).

Psalm 62:12; Jeremiah 17:10; 2 Corinthians 5:10; Revelation 2:23 — deals with the justice of God, not salvation *per se*. Christ's righteousness is imputed to believers, so God treats them as if they had upheld God's law perfectly, as Christ did (h). Moreover, salvation always results in good deeds (g).

2 Corinthians 11:15 — Those who reject Christ will be judged by their works, which never result in salvation (b).

James 2:14 — saving faith results in good works (g). Good works are the effect, not the cause, of faith (f). The critic has again committed the false-cause fallacy.

James 5:1 — salvation is God's gift and cannot be bought with money (a).

1 Peter 1:17 — again, this speaks of God's justice, not His mercy in extending salvation to undeserving, repentant sinners. But those who are saved are imputed Christ's righteousness, as if they obeyed God's law perfectly and never sinned (h).

Ezekiel 18:27 — this refers to a wicked man who repents of his sin and receives God's gift of salvation. Such a person will then practice justice and righteousness (g). But such good deeds are not the cause of his salvation (f), rather, God's grace is (a). Again, the critic commits the false-cause fallacy.

2 Thessalonians 2:10 — those who do not receive God's gracious gift of salvation through faith in Christ will not be saved (a, b, c).

2 Thessalonians 24:13 — no such verse exists.

1 John 4:17 — in context (1 John 4:15–16), those who have genuine faith in Christ, who profess His name, can have confidence in the day of judgment because they are saved (c, e, h).

Revelation 20:12–13 — in context, (see Revelation 20:15), those whose names are not recorded in the book of life, that is those who have not received Christ as Savior, will be judged according to the deeds, and none of them will be saved (b, c, f).

Matthew 7:21 — not everyone who claims to be saved really is.

Matthew 10:42; Mark 9:41 — this has nothing to do with eternal salvation, but rather deals with the rewards of good works.

Matthew 18:3 — only those who have childlike faith in Christ can be saved (c, f).

Matthew 16:25; Mark 8:35; Luke 9:24; John 12:25 — those who "lose their life" for Christ's sake are saved, because only someone who has received Christ as Lord would be willing to give up his or her life for Christ. Salvation is the cause, willing obedience is the effect.

Matthew 19:17–19; Luke 18:18 — Jesus does *not* say that keeping the commandments would cause a person to be saved; rather He says to keep the commandments, one of which is to repent of sin and have faith in God (Isaiah 55:7). It's a pity the critic didn't read the verses that follow. The rich young man claimed to have followed all the commandments, yet Jesus said that he was still *lacking* (Matthew 19:20–23; Luke 18:22–24). The man was unwilling to give up his possessions for the sake of following Christ. Yet, salvation is by God's grace received only through faith in Christ (a, b, c).

Matthew 19:29; Mark 10:29–30; Luke 18:29–30 — those who make such sacrifices for Christ's sake will inherit eternal life, but the former is not the cause of the latter. Rather, salvation is the cause of obedience. Again, the critic has committed the false-cause fallacy.

Matthew 22:14 — Many hear the Gospel and are called out by it, but only those who repent and receive Christ as Savior are saved.

Mark 8:38 — Those who are ashamed of Christ and His words are not saved.

Mark 16:16 — Salvation is received only by genuine faith in Christ (c); obedience by baptism follows (g). Those who don't believe in Christ cannot be saved (b).

Luke 10:26 — Jesus asks a question. The person who loves the Lord with all his heart will repent of sin and receive Christ as Savior.

Luke 13:23–24 — The path of righteousness can be difficult, and many people are unwilling to give up sin and receive Christ as Lord.

John 3:3, 5, 16, 5:24 — Salvation is only by God's grace, by faith in Christ, which is being "born again."

John 6:27 — Does not speak to the cause of salvation; rather this passage addresses those who are already saved, working for heavenly treasure that endures forever in the eternal state. Such blessings are in addition to the salvation that cannot be merited.

John 6:44 — Salvation is God's unmerited gift (a).

John 6:50 — The bread from heaven is Christ (John 6:51). Salvation is only through Him (c).

John 9:11 — Christ gives sight to the blind. The passage does not address eternal salvation.

John 17:33 — No such verse exists.

Acts 2:21 — Those who call upon the name of the Lord, an indication of their repentance and willingness to receive Christ (Romans 10:9–10, 13), will be saved (a, c, e).

Acts 16:31 — Salvation is received through faith in Christ (c).

Romans 3:28; 5:1 — Salvation, justification before God, is through faith in Christ, not by works (c, f).

Romans 8:29–30; Ephesians 1:4–5 — Salvation is God's gift and is by His choice (a).

Romans 10:9, 13 — Salvation is by faith in Christ and is confessed by the mouth (c, e).

Romans 11:26 — Salvation comes from God; Christ takes away sin (a, d).

1 Corinthians 1:21 — Salvation is God's gift, received through faith.

1 Corinthians 5:1–5 — Does not address the cause of salvation; rather it deals with church discipline.

1 Corinthians 7:14, 16 — Does not address the cause of salvation; rather it shows how godly people can have a positive influence on others, perhaps leading the unbeliever to Christ.

1 Corinthians 15:29 — An argument for the physical resurrection, not eternal salvation.

Galatians 2:16 — Salvation, justification before God, is by faith in Christ, not works (a, b, c, f).

Ephesians 2:8 — Salvation is God's gift, received through faith in Christ (a, c).

James 2:17 — Genuine saving faith in Christ is always accompanied by good works. Faith that does not result in good works is a "dead" faith that does not save (g). See James 2:26.

James 3:36, 4:40, 47 do not exist.

Titus 3:5 — Salvation is given by God's mercy, not by works (a, b, f).

1 Timothy 2:14–15 — Salvation is received by faith in Christ (c, d). Christ was brought into the world as a descendant of Eve.

2 Timothy 2:11 — Salvation is received by faith in Christ — His dying on the Cross represents us and our sin (c, d, h).

Ephesians 6:53–54 — Does not exist.

Revelation 14:12 — Addresses persevering the faith, not the cause of salvation.

Revelation 14:4 — Those who follow the lamb are those who have been purchased by God, a reference to His salvation. This again shows that genuine salvation results in obedience.

Revelation 22:14 — Those whose robes are washed (in the blood of the Lamb, a reference to salvation by faith in Christ found in Revelation 7:14) are those who are saved.

154. Who tempted David to number Israel? Second Samuel 24:1 says it was the Lord, but 1 Chronicles 21:1 says it was Satan.

Bifurcation fallacy, and failure to read the text carefully. God normally uses means to accomplish His plan, just as He used men to write His Word. So, was Scripture written by men or God? The correct answer is both. Who provoked David against Israel? When God permits something to happen, it can be said that He did it, even though He is not the proximate cause. Thus, both God and an adversary (likely *the* adversary Satan) can be said to have provoked David. The adversary is the proximate cause, while God is a distal cause. This is even clearer in the original language of 1 Samuel 24:1, which indicates that God's anger burned against Israel and "*one* incited David." The referent to the word "one" is left ambiguous, but from 2 Chronicles 21:1, we know it to be an adversary ("Satan" means *adversary*).

However, David still had a choice in how to respond to such provocation. David chose to sin, as God knew he would, and God appropriately punished David and Israel for their sins. Though God did not directly tempt David (no Scripture teaches such), the Lord in His wrath did not prevent David from being tempted by Satan and from acting sinfully. Presumably, the critic thinks that this is somehow contradictory. But why? God can use Satan to accomplish His plan, as He did at the crucifixion.

DIFFERENCES IN DETAILS

Some passages of Scripture provide details that seem to be incompatible with details listed in other sections. Critics often point to differences in how the authors of the four Gospels report events. Undeniably, there are differences. But are these genuinely contradictory or are they *compatible differences*? There is nothing erroneous about one person reporting that an event takes place after sunrise, while another person says it happened in the morning. The wording may differ, but there is no conflict of facts. Human nature is to let the imagination fill in the details not provided in the text — details like where people were standing, how many people were present beyond those specifically mentioned, or exactly when an event happened when the time is not recorded. Often the contradictions are in the reader's imagination, not in the text.

155. There are two creation accounts — Genesis 1:25–27 contradicts Genesis 2:18–22.

Failure to read the text carefully and specious reasoning. Genesis 1:25–27 describes the creation of the animals and human beings. Genesis 2:18–22 refers back to the creation of these animals, and goes on to describe Adam naming them and then the subsequent creation of Eve. It does not say when the animals were created — we read that only in Genesis 1:25–31. So, where is the alleged inconsistency?

156. Was Ahaz buried with his fathers? Second Kings 16:20 contradicts 2 Chronicles 16:20.

Failure to read the text carefully. First, there is no 2 Chronicles 16:20. Perhaps the critic meant 2 Chronicles 28:27. However, both 2 Kings 16:20 and 2 Chronicles 28:27 affirm that indeed Ahaz was buried with his fathers, e.g., in the city of Jerusalem. Perhaps the critic is confused because Ahaz was not buried *in the same tomb* as the kings of Israel. But he was buried in the same city, and both 2 Kings 16:20 and 2 Chronicles 28:27 refer to this in saying that "So, Ahaz slept [was buried] with his fathers."

157. Did the city of Ai exist after Joshua destroyed it? Joshua 8:28 indicates that it was destroyed, but Nehemiah 7:32 mentions people coming from Ai, implying that it still existed.

Specious reasoning and failure to distinguish different times. The city of Ai was utterly destroyed by Joshua and remained unoccupied *at the time the Book of Joshua was written* (Joshua 8:28). The city was later rebuilt (or perhaps a different city with the same name) and was occupied by the Israelites after the Babylonian captivity (Nehemiah 7:32). Perhaps the critic is unaware that the events of Nehemiah transpired about one thousand years later than Joshua. A contradiction is "A and not-A *at the same time* and in the same sense." But where is the supposed contradiction between a city being unoccupied at one time, and then occupied a thousand years later?

158. Does God want some to go to hell? First Timothy 2:3–4 and 2 Peter 3:9 contradict Proverbs 16:4; John 12:40; Romans 9:18; and 2 Thessalonians 2:11–12.

Equivocation fallacy on the word "want." Does a righteous judge *want* to sentence a serial murderer to death? In one sense, no; it would be upsetting to condemn any person to death. He may not enjoy it, nor does he approve of the murderer's actions that require the death penalty. Yet, in another sense, the judge does *want* this because it is the right penalty, accomplishes justice (especially for the families of the victims), and protects the innocent from any further violence. The judge does not approve of the murderer's actions, and he may not enjoy the sentencing, but he does plan to sentence the guilty man because it is the right thing to do.

Likewise, God does not approve of sin, and God would be pleased to save anyone who genuinely repents and trusts in Him. He will readily pay their penalty and save them from hell. God has no pleasure in the death of the wicked; rather He is pleased to save *anyone* who repents (Ezekiel 18:23, 32, 33:11). God approves of repentance and He commands everyone everywhere to repent — not just some (Acts 17:30). But, for those who stubbornly refuse God's offers of grace and mercy, God will honor their perverse choice, and allow them to experience the consequences of their depravity: hell. God *plans* this and justice demands it (Luke 13:1–9; Proverbs 16:4; John 12:40; Romans 9:18, 21–22; 2 Thessalonians 2:10–12). However, God does not *approve* of their sin, and would be pleased to save them from hell if only they would repent (Isaiah 55:7; 1 Timothy 2:3–4; 2 Peter 3:8; Romans 10:13).

All of the above passages agree with this, and therefore with each other. None of them teach that God both wants and does not want something at the same time *and in the same sense*, and thus there is no contradiction.

159. Was David alone when asking for the holy bread at Nob? First Samuel 21:1 contradicts Matthew 12:3–4.

Equivocation fallacy, and failure to read the text carefully. David came to Ahimelech without any attendants, and his companions may have waited in another place. So, David was alone in his meeting with Ahimelech (1 Samuel 21:1). But David did share the bread with his companions as both 1 Samuel 21:4–5 implies and Matthew 12:3–4 states.

160. How should the Ammonites be treated? Deuteronomy 2:19, 37 state that Ammonites should be treated in peace, but in Judges 11:32 and Jeremiah 49:2, the Lord authorizes war against Ammon.

Failure to distinguish different times and circumstances. Originally, Ammon was to be allowed to peacefully co-exist with Israel, and not to be conquered by it (Deuteronomy 2:19, 37). However, in the course of time, Ammon made war against Israel (Judges 11:4–5). Therefore, God allowed Israel to conquer Ammon (Judges 11:30–32). There is no apparent contradiction between making peace with a peaceful nation at one time, and then going to war *at a later time* when the nation becomes violent and attacks its neighbors.

161. How long does God's anger last? Psalms 30:5; Jeremiah 3:12; and Micah 7:18 all indicate that God's anger is very brief, whereas Numbers 32:13; Jeremiah 17:4; Malachi 1:4; and Matthew 25:41, 46 all indicate that God's anger is long or even eternal.

Bifurcation fallacy and failure to consult the original language. First, there are several different types of anger, wrath, indignation, and displeasure. These are often indicated by the specific Hebrew or Greek word used in the context, and can denote very significant distinctions. The critic rolls all these together as if they were one.

Second, the Bible teaches that God's anger toward the unrepentant is quite different from His anger toward believers. *For the redeemed,* God's anger is brief (Psalm 30:5 ['aph]; Jeremiah 3:12 [panim]; Micah 7:18 ['aph]). For the *unrepentant,* God's anger lasts long (Numbers 32:13 ['aph]; Hebrews 3:10 [prosochthizo] 3:11 [orgê]); even forever (Jeremiah 17:4 ['aph]; Malachi 1:4 [za'am]; Matthew 25:41, 46 [refers to punishment, without explicit mention of "anger" or "wrath"]). The last of these verses (Mathew 25:46 [referring to "punishment"]) very explicitly teaches that the difference depends on whether the person is positionally righteous or wicked, so the critic's error here really is inexcusable.

162. From what were the animals created? Genesis 1:20 contradicts Genesis 2:19.

Failure to read the text carefully and argument from silence. Genesis 1:20 does not say from what source the swimming and flying creatures were made. Genesis 2:19 indicates that land creatures and birds were made from the ground.

163. Where did Jesus first appear to the 11 disciples after the Resurrection? Matthew 28:16 indicates a mountain in Galilee, but this contradicts Mark 16:14; Luke 24:33–37; John 20:19.

Failure to read the text carefully. Jesus met with His disciples at several *different* times after the Resurrection and at several different locations. None of the texts listed by the critic contradict this by listing two different locations as both being the *first* appearance of Christ. Matthew 28:16–17 tells of Christ meeting with His disciples in Galilee, though it does not say or even imply that this was their *first* meeting. Mark 16:14 tells of Christ meeting with His disciples, though the location and date are not specified. But this was not the *first* appearance for all, since Mark 16:12 indicates that Christ appeared to two of His disciples when they were walking to the country, probably to Emmaus. Luke 24:33–37 reports of a meeting of the disciples in Jerusalem, but even this text indicates that Simon had seen Him previously (verse 34). And two disciples had previously seen Jesus on the road to Emmaus, which is about seven miles from Jerusalem (Luke 24:15). The Jerusalem meeting would seem to be the first time that the majority of disciples, all except Thomas (John 20:24), saw the resurrected Christ, since this happened on the same day as the Resurrection (Luke 24:1, 21, 33, 36). John 20:19–24 also confirms this meeting, though it does not give the location. All these accounts are compatible, so where is the alleged contradiction?

164. What was in the Ark of the Covenant? First Kings 8:9 and 2 Chronicles 5:10 say that the Ark contained *only* the stone tablets of the ten commandments, but Hebrews 9:4 says that the Ark also contained a jar of manna and Aaron's rod.

Failure to distinguish different times. At one time, the Ark of the Covenant held the stone tablets of the Ten Commandments, a golden jar of manna, and Aaron's rod (Hebrews 9:4; Exodus 16:33; Numbers 17:10). At a *later* time, *after* the Ark had been recovered from the Philistines, it contained only the stone tablets of the Ten Commandments (1 Kings 8:9; 2 Chronicles 5:10). The jar of manna and Aaron's rod had apparently been removed by that time. Furthermore, the Hebrew text of Exodus 16:33, 34 and Numbers 16:25 can be translated to indicate that the objects had been placed *in front* of the Ark, not within it.

165. Was Asa perfect? First Kings 15:14 and 2 Chronicles 15:17 say *yes*, but 2 Chronicles 16:7, 10, 12 indicate that he sinned.

Equivocation fallacy. Among other things, "perfect" can mean (1) positionally righteous, e.g., forgiven, or (2) sinless in practice. Only Jesus is sinless in practice, but the redeemed are positionally righteous. Asa was positionally righteous and perfect in that sense (1 Kings 15:14; 2 Chronicles 15:17; Romans 4:5). But Asa was not perfectly sinless in practice (2 Chronicles 16:7, 10, 12; Romans 3:23).

166. On what did Jesus ride into Jerusalem? Matthew 21:5–7 disagrees with Mark 11:7 and Luke 19:35, which contradict John 12:14.

Bluff and failure to read the text. Jesus rode on a young donkey (a colt) as Matthew 21:5–7; Mark 11:7; Luke 19:35; and John 12:14–15 all confirm. The account in Matthew also mentions that an (adult) donkey was brought along as well; the other Gospels do not mention this, but neither to they deny it. So, there is no inconsistency at all. Perhaps the critic did not realize that a "colt" is the Old English word for a young donkey?

167. Is the day of the Lord at hand? First Thessalonians 4:15–17, 5:23 contradict 2 Thessalonians 2:2–3.

Bifurcation fallacy and failure to read the text carefully. The 1 Thessalonian passages cited by the critic do not even mention "the day of the Lord," so it's hard to take the critic seriously here. While 2 Thessalonians 2:2 does mention the day of the Lord, the verse is not addressing whether the day is near or far. Rather, it is addressing the error of those who believed that it had already happened, when in fact it had not. In fact, the premise of the critic's claim is flawed because the "day of the Lord" does not refer *just* to the second coming. It may (depending on the immediate context of a given passage) refer to that. But it is also used of any time when God powerfully acts in history, especially in judgment (Isaiah 13:6, 9; Ezekiel 13:5, 30:3; Joel 1:15, 2:1, 11, 31, 3:14; Amos 5:18, 20; Obadiah 1:15; Zephaniah 1:7–8; 1 Thessalonians 5:2; 2 Peter 3:10). So, the day of the Lord is near whenever God is about to come either spiritually or physically.

168. How many languages were there before the Tower of Babel was built? Genesis 11:1, 6–9 indicate that there was only one, but Genesis 10:5, 20, 31 speak of multiple languages.

Failure to read the text carefully. There was one language before Babel (Genesis 11:1). Genesis 10:5, 20, 31 all refer to people who lived *after* God confused the languages at Babel. This is obvious because Genesis 10:6–10 indicate that Nimrod was the third generation from Noah, and his kingdom began at Babel. Yet Genesis 10:5, 20, and 31 all describe the splitting by languages that happened *after* the third generation from Noah. The critic erroneously assumed that all the events described in Genesis 10 preceded all the events of Genesis 11. But the text indicates otherwise.

169. In whose name is baptism to be performed? Matthew 28:19 contradicts Acts 2:38, 8:16, 10:48, 19:5.

Subset fallacy and incidental fallacy. Baptism is to be performed in the name of God. God has many names and is Triune. So, baptism may be done in the name of the Father, Son, and Holy Spirit (Matthew 28:19), or in the name of (the Son) Jesus (Acts 2:38, 8:16, 10:48, 19:5). Where is the supposed contradiction? Furthermore, only one of these passages is a command — Matthew 28:19. The other passages merely report what people did. So, even if people were not following the command properly, it is not a contradiction in the Bible to report this. The critic has fallaciously supposed that the Bible necessarily endorses that which it merely records; this is the incidental fallacy.

170. Who was to blame for original sin? First Timothy 2:14 says Eve, but Romans 5:12 says man (Adam).

Equivocation fallacy on the word "sin." Adam alone is to blame for original sin (Romans 5:12) because he deliberately broke God's law. This is the meaning of the Greek word translated "sin" in Romans 5:12 [*hamartia*]. Notice that 1 Timothy does *not* state that Eve sinned; it does not use the word *hamartia*. Eve did transgress God's law before Adam did. But unlike Adam, Eve was deceived (1 Timothy 2:14). The Bible uses a different word for transgression committed in ignorance [*parabasis*].

171. How old was Benjamin when his clan migrated to Egypt? Genesis 44:20, 22 say he was little, but Genesis 46:8, 21 indicate he was old enough to have sons.

Failure to read the text carefully. Genesis 44:20–22 does not give the age of Benjamin at all. Verse 20 indicates that Benjamin was "little" from the Hebrew word *qaton*, which can mean young, or physically small, or insignificant, or "least" in the sense that Benjamin was the youngest brother. But the age isn't given. Neither does Genesis 46:8–21 give Benjamin's age. Verse 21 lists his sons. But the text doesn't say which if any of these had yet been born when Jacob's family moved to Egypt, though they may well have been. So, how can these two chapters possibly contradict on the age of Benjamin, when neither chapter gives the age of Benjamin?

172. Should every man bear his own burden? Galatians 6:5 contradicts Galatians 6:2.

Equivocation fallacy. The critic has fallaciously assumed that "burden" is being used in the same sense in verse 2 as it is in verse 5. Not only does context preclude this, but the original Greek word is not the same between these two verses. Verse 2 uses the Greek word *baros* for "burden" and has the meaning of a weight or trouble. In context with verse one, Paul is teaching that Christians ought to volunteer to help one another with their spiritual difficulties, gently restoring those who have sinned. Verse five uses the word *phortion* for "burden" which has the meaning of a "load." In context with verse 4, Paul is teaching that each person should be concerned with the work that has been assigned to him, and not presumptuously judge others of their assignments. There is no contradiction in instructing people to help each other, but reminding them that they will answer to God for their own assignments, and not another's.

173. Who buried Jesus? Matthew 27:57–60; Mark 15:43–46; and Luke 23:50–53 contradict John 19:38–42, which contradicts Acts 13:27–29.

Subset fallacy and failure to read the text carefully. Joseph of Arimathea buried Jesus (Matthew 27:57–60; Mark 15:43–46; Luke 23:50–53; John 19:38–42). The Gospel of John adds that Joseph was helped by Nicodemus. But this is not contrary to the other Gospels in any way. They all affirm that Joseph buried Jesus. Does Acts 13:27–29 contradict this? Not at all. Acts 13:27–29 does not even mention the specific names of those who buried Jesus.

174. Did God command the Israelites to make Him burnt offerings? Exodus 8:27, 10:25, 20:24, 29:16–18 all say *yes*, but Jeremiah 7:22 says *no*.

Failure to read the text carefully, and to consider context. The Lord did command the Israelites to offer burnt offerings for their sin as a foreshadow of Christ. Jeremiah 7:22 does not contradict this, because it states that God did not command burnt offerings *in the day that He brought them out of Egypt* — that is, at that time. Indeed, at the time of the Exodus from Egypt, after the Passover and before the giving of the Law at Sinai, we do not find any instance of the Lord commanding the Israelites to offer sacrifices. Instead, God commanded them to listen to His voice and walk in His ways (Jeremiah 7:23; Exodus 15:26, 19:5–6) — which is far more important to God than sacrifice.

The context of Jeremiah 7:22 indicates that God prefers obedience to sacrifice, which is a common theme in Scripture (1 Samuel 15:22; Proverbs 21:3; Hosea 6:6; Ecclesiastes 5:1). Indeed, if people would obey God perfectly — as He desires — there would be no need for sacrifice. Animal sacrifice is never something that God desires for Himself, but rather was given to people because of their sins to point to the Messiah (Hebrews 10:5–9; Psalm 51:16; Isaiah 1:11, 16–17).

175. Who appeared to Moses in the burning bush? Exodus 3:4 and Mark 12:26 say God, but Exodus 3:2 and Acts 7:35 say it was the *Angel* of the Lord.

Bifurcation fallacy. God the Son spoke to Moses in the burning bush. The critic appears to be ignorant of the fact that one of the names of Christ is the "Angel of the Lord" (Genesis 22:11–12, 15–17). So, God the Son, the Angel of the Lord, is the person who spoke to Moses in the burning bush (Exodus 3:2, 4; Mark 12:26; Acts 7:35).

176. What became of Cain? Genesis 4:11–12 contradicts Genesis 4:16–17.

Failure to read the text carefully. Both Genesis 4:11–12 and Genesis 4:16–17 affirm that Cain left the area and wandered in the land of Nod east of Eden. "Nod" means "wandering." So, apparently Cain remained a fugitive and wanderer in that part of the world.

177. Was Jesus taken to Caiaphas or Annas first? Matthew 26:57; Mark 14:53; and Luke 22:54 say Caiaphas, but John 18:13 says Annas.

Failure to read the text carefully. Jesus was taken to Annas first, and then to Caiaphas (John 18:13–24). None of the above verses contradict this. Caiaphas was the high priest at the time, and Annas, as Caiaphas's father-in-law, was also called the high priest, because he had held the office previously. Note that Matthew, Mark, and Luke do not mention the first meeting with Annas. But neither do they deny it, so there is no contradiction at all.

178. Will those who call on the Lord be delivered? Joel 2:32; Acts 2:21; and Romans 10:13 say *yes*, but Matthew 7:21; Jeremiah 14:12; Ezekiel 8:18; and Micah 3:4 contradict that.

Equivocation fallacy. To "call upon the Lord" does not simply mean to ask the Lord for something. Rather it means to have a repentant attitude of faithful submission to God, trusting Him for salvation. All those who genuinely repent and trust in the Lord and call upon His name will be saved (Joel 2:32; Acts 2:21; Romans 10:13). Matthew 7:21; Jeremiah 14:12; Ezekiel 8:18; and Micah 3:4 all describe those who have *failed* to repent, who have *not* trusted in the Lord, and who have *not* called upon God *for salvation*. There is no inconsistency in God saving those who repent, and choosing not to save those who do not repent (John 3:18).

179. Did God kill all the Egyptian cattle in the sixth plague? Exodus 9:3–6, says *yes*; however, cattle still exist in Exodus 9:19, 12:29, implying that not all of them died.

Failure to read the text carefully. In the sixth plague all the livestock of Egypt that were *in the field* died (Exodus 9:3). This is what the "all" refers to in verse 6 — *all that were in the field* in the land of Egypt. Those that were not in the field presumably survived, and are seen again in the seventh plague, along with any new livestock that may have been acquired in the intervening time (Exodus 9:19–20, 25). Of those cattle that survived both the six and seventh plagues, along with any new cattle that were acquired, the firstborn of them died in the tenth plague (Exodus 12:29). Where is any inconsistency?

180. Is it okay to have a census? Second Chronicles 2:17 contradicts 2 Samuel 24:1 and 1 Chronicles 21:2.

Sweeping generalization fallacy. Like many things, there is nothing wrong with having a census — providing it is done in the right way and with the right motive (Exodus 30:12; Numbers 1:2; 2 Chronicles 2:17). Therefore, we must conclude that David's sin in taking a census of Israel and Judea was either that he did it in the wrong way, or with the wrong motive (or both) since it was displeasing to God and to David's conscience (1 Chronicles 21:7–8; 2 Samuel 24:10). How might David have erred?

As one possibility, when a census was taken, biblical law required a small ransom to be collected from each person for the Lord (Exodus 30:12). David may have failed to do so. Moreover, the Bible teaches that intentions matter, and that a person can sin in his heart even if there is no outward sinful action (Matthew 5:28; Exodus 20:17). David may have had an unrighteous motive, perhaps an arrogant pride in the size of his army, rather than rightly attributing Israel's success ultimately to God. Indeed, Joab asked why David would "delight" in this thing (2 Samuel 24:3), and pointed out that it would be a "cause of guilt to Israel." Since 1 Chronicles 21:1–2 indicates that Satan provoked David to conduct the census, it is clear that David's motives were improper. Of course, God was ultimately behind this and used this sin to humble David so that he might renew his faith in God. There was clearly something wrong with *the way* in which David conducted this census, even though a census in general is not inherently wrong.

181. Did the centurion ask Jesus directly to help his slave? Matthew 8:5–8 says *yes*, but Luke 7:1–7 says that the centurion sent messengers instead.

Failure to read the text carefully and argument from silence. Neither Matthew 8:5–8 nor Luke 7:1–7 teach that the centurion asked Jesus directly, that is, in person. Luke 7:1–7 specifically denies this, saying that the centurion spoke to Christ by sending messengers. The account in Matthew does not mention the messengers, but neither does it deny that the centurion spoke through messengers. So, there is no contradiction or inconsistency.

182. What did the centurion call Jesus when He died? Mark 15:39 and Matthew 27:54 contradict Luke 23:47.

Bifurcation fallacy. The centurion declared both that Christ was innocent (Luke 23:47), and that Christ was the Son of God (Matthew 27:54; Mark 15:39). There is simply no logical reason why the centurion could not have said both of these things.

183. Is childbearing sinful? Leviticus 12:6–7 indicates that it is, because it requires a sin offering, but Genesis 1:28 and 1 Timothy 2:15 indicate that it is not.

Failure to read the text and specious reasoning. Of course, it is not sinful to marry and bear children, and the Bible nowhere teaches any such thing. Leviticus 12:6–7 was a purification ritual associated with the Old Testament ceremonial laws, which stressed holiness and pointed forward to Christ's coming and the New Covenant. Nowhere does Leviticus 12:6–7 even remotely suggest that childbearing is sinful. Rather, it reminds us that we are all born sinful (Psalm 51:5) because Adam sinned (Romans 5:12).

184. How did Jesus respond when questioned by the high priest? Matthew 26:63–64 and Luke 22:70 contradict Mark 14:62.

Bifurcation fallacy. It's hard to take the critic seriously when there is not even any apparent inconsistency between these three accounts.

All agree that Jesus affirmed that He is the Son of God. Each Gospel is a summary only of Christ's life and ministry; as such, each Gospel leaves out some events and statements of Christ that others include. But they do not contradict each other. Christ's statement went something like this: "You have said it; nevertheless I tell you, yes, I am; and hereafter you shall see the Son of man sitting at the right hand of the power of God, and coming with the clouds of heaven." Matthew 26:64, Luke 22:69–70, and Mark 14:62 all record various portions of Christ's answer, with no inconsistency whatsoever.

185. Is circumcision required? Genesis 17:7, 10, 13, 19, and Leviticus 12:3 teach that it is, but Galatians 5:2 and Colossians 2:10–11 say otherwise.

Failure to distinguish different times. First, we must ask "required for *what?*" The critic's question is ambiguous. Circumcision of the flesh was required for *full obedience* to God *for Abraham and his male descendants under the Old Covenant administration* (Genesis 17:7–11; Leviticus 12:3). It is not now, nor has it ever been, a requirement for salvation (Romans 4:3, 9–10), but was an outward sign of inward faith for the Old Testament administration (Romans 4:11). Since it pointed forward to Christ's first coming, circumcision was set aside in the New Testament (Galatians 5:1–12). All the Scriptures consistently teach this, without any discrepancy.

186. To whom were the cities of Exhtaol and Zoreah given? Joshua 15:20, 33 contradicts Joshua 19:40–41.

Failure to distinguish different times. Eshtaol and Zorah were originally allocated to Judah (Joshua 15:20, 33), but later were given to Dan (Joshua 19:40–41). After the captivity in Babylon, they were inhabited by the children of Judah (Nehemiah 11:29). Is the critic really unaware that national boundaries can change with time?

187. What color was Jesus' robe? Matthew 27:28 says *"scarlet,"* but Mark 15:17 and John 19:2 say it was *"purple."*

Bifurcation fallacy and failure to read the text carefully. John indicates (and Mark confirms) that Jesus was dressed in a purple *garment* (*himation* in Greek). Matthew teaches that Jesus was dressed with a scarlet *robe* (*chlamus* in Greek). Why would it be impossible to wear a purple garment with a scarlet robe? (Even one garment, if its exact color were something in between red and purple, might be accurately described by either color.)

188. Did Jesus forewarn the Apostles of His death and Resurrection? Matthew 20:18–19, 26:31–32; Mark 8:31,10:33–34, 14:28; and Luke 18:31–33 all say He did, but John 20:9 indicates that He did not.

Failure to read the text carefully. Yes. Jesus told His disciples many times of His upcoming death and Resurrection (Matthew 20:18–19, 26:31–32; Mark 8:31, 10:33–34; Luke 18:31–33). But they failed to understand (John 20:9). This is a failure on their part certainly, but where is there any inconsistency or contradiction in the text? The inexcusable nature of the critic's error here is made obvious by his failure to read just one more verse than what he listed: Luke 18:31–33 *and 34.*

189. Did Jesus ask God to save Him from crucifixion? Matthew 26:36, 42; Mark 14:35–36; and Luke 22:41–42 all contradict John 12:27.

Failure to read the text carefully. Jesus was willing to die to do His Father's will (Matthew 26:42). He asked, "if it were possible," that is, *if there were any other way to accomplish salvation, if the Father were willing* that He might be spared the crucifixion (Mark 14:35–36; Luke 22:41). But since there isn't, He was fully willing to go to the Cross. John 12:27 confirms this. Hebrews 5:7 teaches that Christ's prayer was answered — so obviously Christ was not asking for an unconditional release from the crucifixion since He was in fact crucified.

The critic's mistake here, in failing to read the text carefully, is to confuse a conditional request with a categorical one. A conditional statement has the form "if p then q" where a categorical one is simply "q." In the conditional statement, if the antecedent "p" is not true, then the consequent "q" does not necessarily follow. In the case of Christ's prayer, "p" is "salvation were possible apart from the crucifixion of Christ and God were willing" and "q" is "may I escape crucifixion." Christ had a purpose in asking this prayer in this form. Since the Father would certainly honor the prayer of His Son, and since He did (Hebrews 5:7), Christ's prayer proves that salvation would not be possible apart from the crucifixion — a key element in biblical theology.

190. Will God curse the earth? Malachi 4:6 contradicts Genesis 8:21.

Failure to read the text carefully in context. In Genesis 8:21–22, God promises never again to curse the ground *in the sense of* destroying every living thing on its surface by water, as long as the earth remains. No Scripture contradicts this. Malachi 4:6 indicates that God will send Elijah the prophet to bring restoration, so that God will *not* "smite the land with a curse." There is no mention of a world-destroying flood in Malachi 4:6. So, there is not even an *apparent* contradiction between these two passages.

191. Are those who obey the law cursed? Galatians 3:10 contradicts Deuteronomy 27:26.

Failure to read the text carefully. No, it is *disobedience* that brings a curse (Deuteronomy 27:26). God promises to *bless* those who obey His law (Deuteronomy 28:1–14). Galatians 3:10 *confirms* this in saying that "cursed is everyone who does *not* abide by all things written in the book of the law, to perform them." Indeed, Galatians 3:10 quotes from Deuteronomy 27:26. Where is the alleged contradiction?

192. Who carried Jesus' Cross? John 19:17 says that Jesus carried His own Cross, but Matthew 27:32; Mark 15:21; and Luke 23:26 say that Simon did.

Subset fallacy. Jesus and Simon together carried the Cross. Jesus was weak from His scourging, and so the Roman soldiers ordered Simon to assist in carrying His Cross. John 19:17 does not mention Simon's assistance, but neither does it deny it. Matthew 27:32 and Mark 15:21 do mention Simon carrying the Cross, but do not specifically mention that this was in assistance to Christ. Luke 23:26 indicates that the Cross was placed on Simon "to carry behind Jesus" suggesting that Jesus led carrying the front whereas Simon followed carrying the rear. Where is there any inconsistency?

193. David never sinned (he was clean and righteous). Second Samuel 22:21, 25 and 1 Kings 3:14, 9:4, 14:8 indicate that David was clean and righteous, but 1 Kings 15:5 says that he was clean except for his actions against Uriah, and 2 Samuel 24:10 indicates that David acted wickedly.

Straw-man fallacy and equivocation. Other than Christ, all men have sinned (Romans 3:23; Hebrews 4:15; 1 John 1:8). Those who continue in sin are unrighteous and "unclean" in God's sight. However, those who repent of sin and trust in Christ for salvation, God forgives, cleanses (1 John 1:7,9), and treats as if they had not sinned (Romans 4:3, 5, 10:10; Titus 3:5). Our sin is imputed to Christ, while His righteousness is imputed to us (2 Corinthians 5:21; Phillipians 3:9). The forgiven are therefore righteous in principle, even though they continue to struggle with sin at times in practice (1 John 1:8, 2:1–3). So, "righteous" can mean either (1) never having sinned, or (2) having one's sins forgiven. And there is a third meaning too; the Bible uses the word "righteous" for outward, every-day practical obedience to God's Word, even if that obedience is not absolute (Job 1:8; Genesis 6:9; Proverbs 12:10; Ecclesiastes 7:15).

So, was David "righteous?" It depends on which definition is being used *in context*. Was David righteous in the sense that he had never sinned? Of course not (Psalm 4:1, 4, 51:3; 2 Samuel 24:10), for no one is (Romans 3:23; 1 John 1:8). Was David righteous in the sense of pursuing God and generally living by God's commands daily? Yes — except for his sins regarding Uriah (1 Kings 15:5; 2 Samuel 22:21, 25; 1 Kings 3:14, 9:4, 14:8). Was David righteous in principle — in the sense of forgiven? Yes (2 Samuel 12:13; Psalm 51:1–2). So, once we go beyond the critic's superficial and careless reading of the text, we find that the Scriptures are rigorously consistent on this issue.

194. To whom did Peter deny knowing Jesus? Matthew 26:69–73 disagrees with Mark 14:66–71, which disagrees with Luke 22:54–60, which contradicts John 18:15–17, 25–27.

Bifurcation fallacy and failure to read the text carefully. Peter denied knowing Jesus to a number of people. The first to accuse Peter of knowing Christ was a servant girl of the high priest (Matthew 26:69; Mark 14:66–67; Luke 22:56; John 18:17). Then a servant girl began saying *to others* in the crowd (not to Peter) that Peter was with Christ (Matthew 26:71; Mark 14:69). The members of this crowd then accused him, some saying "You are not also one of His disciples are you?" (John 18:25) and one in particular saying, "You are one of them too!" (Luke 22:58), which Peter denied (Luke 22:58; John 18:25). After about an hour, the bystanders again began to accuse Peter (Mark 14:70; Luke 22:59). They had noticed that Peter was Galilean, and talked like one of Christ's disciples (Matthew 26:73; Mark 14:70; Luke 22:59). And one of the bystanders that accused Peter had seen him in the garden with Christ (John 18:26). Peter, for the third time, denied these accusations, and the rooster crowed (Matthew 26:74; Mark 14:71–72; Luke 22:60; John 18:27). Though each account provides some details that another account may omit, there does not appear to be any inconsistency at all.

195. Who can cast out devils in the name of Jesus? Mark 16:17 says believers. However, Matthew 7:21–23; Mark 9:38; and Luke 9:49 say unbelievers.

Fallacy of denying the antecedent. Mark 16:17 teaches that one of the signs that will accompany New Testament believers is that they will cast out demons in Christ's name. It does *not* say that *all* believers will do this or at all times. Nor does it say that *only* believers will do this. The critic's error seems to be the fallacy of denying the antecedent, which has this form:

If p then q	[example: If it is snowing, then it must be cold outside]
Not p	[It is not snowing]
Therefore not q	[Therefore it is not cold outside]

The example provided shows why this kind of reasoning is fallacious — for it is possible to be cold outside and still not snowing. In the case of Mark 16:17, p is "one is a believer," and q is "he or she may cast out demons in Christ's name." The critic then considers the case of non-believers ("not p") and erroneously concludes that they cannot cast out demons in Christ's name. But this is fallacious. No Scripture states that unbelievers cannot cast out demons in Christ's name. So, Mark 16:17; Matthew 7:21–23; Mark 9:38; and Luke 9:49 all confirm that casting out demons in Christ's name is a characteristic typically but not exclusively associated with a Christian, and thus is not proof that one is a Christian.

196. Where did the devils ask not to go? Mark 5:9–10 says out of the country, whereas Luke 8:30–31 says into the abyss.

Bifurcation fallacy. They asked Christ not to send them out of the country (Mark 5:9) nor into the abyss (Luke 8:31). There is no reason to suppose that they did not request both. And these are perfectly compatible requests since the abyss is certainly out of the country.

197. Is divorce ever permissible? Matthew 19:6 says *no*, but Matthew 5:32, 19:9 says that it is acceptable in cases of adultery, 1 Corinthians 7:15 says it is acceptable if the unbeliever initiates it, whereas Deuteronomy 24:1–2 indicates that divorce is okay.

Failure to read the context and sweeping generalization fallacy. Yes, divorce is permissible, but *only* for sexual impurity such as adultery — otherwise it is sinful. Matthew 19:6 gives the general principle, that we should not separate what God has joined (the husband and wife) and Matthew 19:9 further clarifies that all divorce is considered the sin of adultery, with the exception of divorce for cases of fornication (sexual sin). Matthew 5:32 confirms this *exactly* — that divorce is the sin of adultery except for divorce on the basis of fornication. Deuteronomy 24:1 also confirms this principle — that a man may only divorce his wife if he "has found some indecency in her" — a reference to sexual impurity. All these verses are perfectly consistent. First Corinthians 7:15 deals with how a Christian should respond if her unbelieving husband decides to divorce her. This would be sinful on his part of course, but the Bible teaches that *she* has not sinned in allowing him to proceed with the divorce. Where is there any contradiction, or even any *apparent* inconsistency?

198. Who put the robe on Jesus? Luke 23:11 says Herod and his soldiers, but Matthew 27:27–28 says the soldiers of the governor, and Mark 15:15–17 and John 19:1–2 just say the soldiers.

Failure to read the text carefully. All the texts affirm that the soldiers put the robe on Jesus. Luke 23:11 mentions that these were Herod's soldiers, acting under his authority. And so the text rightly says, "Herod with his soldiers" dressed Christ in a robe. Matthew 27:27–28 further confirms that these "soldiers of the governor" (Herod) put the robe on Christ. Mark 15:16–17 and John 19:2 also both confirm that the soldiers dressed Him. Where is any inconsistency?

199. Does God dwell in darkness or in light? First Kings 8:12; 2 Chronicles 6:1; and Psalm 18:11, 97:2 contradict 1 Timothy 6:15–16.

Bifurcation fallacy and equivocation fallacy. God is a spirit (John 4:24), not a material being with a location in space (1 Kings 8:27). Yet, He sees all and His power is immediately available everywhere, so we speak of God as being "omnipresent" (Psalm 139:7–8). In that sense, He dwells everywhere (Jeremiah 23:24), and darkness and light are alike to Him (Psalm 139:12). As all-powerful, He can also manifest physically in a specific location as He pleases. And so we can make sense of passages like 1 Kings 8:12; 2 Chronicles 6:1; Psalm 18:11, 97:2. The Bible also speaks of "light" metaphorically as a symbol of God's holiness, purity, and knowledge (John 3:19, 9:5, 12:46). It is in *this* sense that God dwells in "unapproachable light" (1 Timothy 6:15–16), even though He is fully present in the darkest corner. The critic is clearly not interested in reading the text as the authors intended, but in distorting it to his own purpose.

200. What kind of animals may we eat? *None* according to Genesis 1:29; Proverbs 23:20; Daniel 1:8; and Romans 14:21. Only *"clean" animals* according to Deuteronomy 14:7–8 and Leviticus 11:2–4. *All animals* according to Genesis 9:3; Mark 7:18–20; Luke 10:8; Acts 10:9–13; 1 Corinthians 10:25; Romans 14:2; and 1 Timothy 4:1–3.

Failure to distinguish different times and circumstances and failure to read the text carefully. God originally designed humans and animals to be vegetarian (Genesis 1:29–30). At a *later time*, after the Flood, God permitted people to eat the meat of any animal (Genesis 9:3). Sometime *after that*, God placed additional restrictions on the kinds of meat that the *Israelites* were permitted to eat; this symbolically showed their separation as God's chosen people under the Old Testament administration before the coming of Christ (Leviticus 20:24–26; Daniel 1:8; Deuteronomy 14:7–20; Leviticus 11:2–23). At a *later time*, when Christ came, God removed the dietary restrictions on the Israelites because the Old Testament administration had expired (Mark 7:18–20; Luke 10:8; Acts 10:9–15; 1 Corinthians 10:25–27; 1 Timothy 4:1–5).

Note that Proverbs 23:20 does not restrict the type of food that people may consume, but rather the *quantity* thereof; it instructs people not to be gluttons, and so it is irrelevant to the question the critic has posed. Likewise, Romans 14:2, 21 does not place any restrictions on the Christian's diet. It merely warns against doing things in front of others that might make them stumble in their faith (1 Corinthians 10:28–32).

201. How should the Edomites be treated? Deuteronomy 23:7 says as brothers, but 2 Kings 14:3, 7; Ezekiel 25:13; and Obadiah 1, 8–9 say as enemies.

Failure to read the text in context, hasty generalization fallacy, and incidental fallacy. Deuteronomy 23 deals with the Old Testament purity laws, in listing what manner of people may be permitted in the assembly of the Temple ceremonies. Verse 7 indicates that Edomites were permitted in the assembly, providing that they were a third generation follower of God (Deuteronomy 23:8). The passage says nothing about how *all* Edomites should be treated in general. And none of the other passages contradict Deuteronomy 23:7, by, for example, forbidding a third generation proselyte from Edom from being part of the Temple assembly.

Nor does 2 Kings 14:3,7 prescribe how Edomites, in general, should be treated. Rather, it describes what Amaziah did — he killed many Edomites. The Bible does not necessarily endorse the actions it records. So, it is fallacious to conclude that something is right simply on the basis that the Bible records that it happened — the incidental fallacy. Likewise, Ezekiel 25:13 says nothing about how Edomites should be treated in general. Rather, it describes God's wrath against the people of Edom (at that time), and God's destruction of Edom. Obadiah 1:8–9 likewise describes God's bringing of vengeance upon Edom. But none of the passages listed address the critic's question of how Edomites should be treated.

202. Did Jesus, Mary, and Joseph go to Egypt or Nazareth? Matthew 2:14 says Egypt, but Luke 2:39 says Nazareth.

Bifurcation fallacy and failure to distinguish different times. They went first to Egypt (Matthew 2:14–15), and then later to Nazareth after Herod died (Matthew 2:20–23; Luke 2:39).

203. When will the end of the world come? Matthew 10:23 contradicts Matthew 24:14.

Failure to read the text carefully. Matthew 10:23 does not even touch on the issue of the end of the world. Therefore, it cannot contradict any passage on that particular issue. Rather, Matthew 10:23 tells of a time when the "Son of Man comes." This does not speak of the final day, but rather of a near-term, coming of Christ, much like the many times God came in judgment, even though He did not appear visibly or physically (e.g., Isaiah 19:1; Micah 1:3). That this coming was to take place soon (and thus does not refer to the final coming at the end of history) is clear because Christ said it would happen before they finished going through the cities.

Matthew 24:14 does not contradict Matthew 10:23, but rather speaks of a time when the Gospel would be preached to the entire world (Greek: *oikoumene* — a reference to the inhabited, civilized world), and says that the end would follow. Whether this is the end of the world, or some other end, only context will tell. But either way, this does not contradict Matthew 10:23 which says nothing about the end of the world.

204. How should we treat our enemies? Exodus 23:4; Proverbs 25:21; Matthew 5:44; and Luke 6:35 all indicate that enemies should be treated with loving compassion. But the following passages suggest the opposite: Psalm 35:6, 8, 55:15, 58:6–7, 69:22–28, 83:9–10, 83:15–17, 109:6–14; Lamentations 1:21–22, 3:64–66; 1 Corinthians 16:22.

Bifurcation and failure to read the text carefully (in context). Answer: Biblically. Oh, does the critic want more details? Then he must ask more specifically: how should we treat our enemies *in which context?* Obviously, the details of how we treat enemies in battle may be different from how we treat them in peacetime. How we treat an enemy who poses no immediate threat to us may differ from the way we treat someone who is actively trying to kill us. The Bible teaches that the specific response to our enemy depends greatly on the circumstances, as opposed to the critic's naïve and simplistic thinking.

When there is no immediate threat, when at peace, we should treat our enemies fairly, peaceably, and with compassion (Exodus 23:4; Proverbs 25:21; Matthew 5:44; Luke 6:35). On the other hand, enemies in battle during a just war are to be slain (Deuteronomy 20:16). And it is therefore appropriate to pray for victory, and thus the destruction of one's enemies under such circumstances (Psalm 35:6–9, 55:15, 69:22–28, 83:9–10, 15–17). Moreover, people are permitted to defend themselves with lethal force against an enemy who is potentially going to kill them (Exodus 22:2–3). Certain crimes are to be punished by death, though this right and responsibility belongs only to those authorized as representatives of civil government (Exodus 20:12; Romans 13:4). And it is right to pray for justice in such cases (Psalms 58:6–7, 109:6–14; Lamentations 1:21–22, 3:64–66). However, none of these verses contradict each other by giving two contrary instructions for the *same* circumstance.

Note that 1 Corinthians 16:22 says nothing about how to treat an enemy. Rather it refers to the excommunication of a person who continually shows that he does not love the Lord. This is for the person's good (1 Corinthians 5:5), and is therefore an act of love just as a father disciplining a child (Hebrews 12:5–11; 1 Corinthians 11:32).

205. Has anyone ever ascended into heaven? John 3:13 says no one but Christ, yet, Genesis 5:24; 2 Kings 2:11; and Hebrews 11:5 give several other examples.

Failure to read the text in context. In verse 12, Jesus asks Nicodemus, "If I told you earthly things and you do not believe, how shall you believe if I tell you heavenly things?" In other words, if Nicodemus was unwilling to believe Jesus about earthly matters which he could verify with his own senses, then how could he possibly trust him on heavenly matters which he could *not* possibly verify with his own senses? And why is it that people on earth are unable to verify heavenly matters with their own senses? Verse 13 explains, because no one living on earth has ever ascended to heaven so as to see heavenly things *and return to report them* — except Jesus who originated there (John 3:13). So, no one *currently living* on earth has ever ascended to heaven and returned so as to report what he or she has seen. But there have been people taken directly to heaven that *remain there* (Genesis 5:24; 2 Kings 2:11; Hebrews 11:5) and are thus not able to report to us what they have seen. So, there is no inconsistency when the passages are read *in context*.

206. Were the men with Paul knocked to the ground? Acts 26:14 says *yes*, but Acts 9:7 says they stood.

Failure to distinguish different times and semantic range fallacy. The men with Saul/Paul did indeed fall to the ground (Acts 26:14) when the light flashed, and no passage says otherwise. But of course, they did not remain on the ground for the rest of their lives; at some point they stood up, though Paul apparently remained prostrate until Jesus had finished speaking. The rest "stood speechless" (Acts 9:7) while Christ was speaking. Of course, the phrase "stood speechless" is not necessarily referring to their posture anyway, just as one can "stand firm" while in a seated position. So, the critic has made two errors in thinking that these passages contradict each other.

207. Who bought the potter's field? Matthew 27:6–7 says the chief priests did, but Acts 1:18 says that Judas did.

Failure to read the text carefully. The chief priests bought the potter's field *on behalf of Judas and using his money* (Matthew 27:3–7). The field rightly can be said to be acquired by Judas "with the price of his wickedness" since he furnished the means for doing it (Acts 1:18), though the action was carried out by the chief priests.

208. To whom did Jesus make His first post-Resurrection appearance? Matthew 28:1, 9 says to two people both named "Mary." However, Mark 16:9 and John 20:11–14 indicate just one Mary, whereas Luke 24:13–31 says He appeared to the two disciples on the road to Emmaus. However, 1 Corinthians 15:4–5 teaches that He first appeared to Cephas (Peter).

Failure to read the text carefully. (See also #18.) Most of these texts (Matthew 28:1; John 20:11–14; Luke 24:13–31; 1 Corinthians 15:4) do not say anything about a *first* appearance, and thus they cannot contradict on something that they do not mention. Mark 16:9 suggests that Mary Magdalene was apparently the first to see the resurrected Christ. Recall that she arrived at the tomb ahead of the other Mary, and saw Jesus before the rest of the women. This is fully consistent with all the other passages the critic lists; none of them state that someone other than Mary Magdalene was *first*.

209. Did everyone (except for Noah and his family) die in the Flood? Genesis 7:21–23 says *yes*, but Genesis 6:4 and Numbers 13:33 indicate that some other people (the nephilim) survived.

Specious reasoning. Yes, everyone except Noah and his family died during the Flood (Genesis 7:21–23) and no Scripture contradicts this. The nephilim (the "giants" or "fallen ones") mentioned in Genesis 6:4 are obviously not the same nephilim mentioned in Numbers 13:33 — the latter were born over one thousand years after the Flood, so there is no excuse for the critic in making such an obvious blunder.

210. Which flying creeping things may we eat? Deuteronomy 14:19 says none, but Leviticus 11:21–23 lists several that may be eaten.

Sweeping generalization fallacy. The Bible gives a generalization in Deuteronomy 14:19 and again in Leviticus 11:20 that winged creeping things (presumably a reference to insects) are to be considered unclean. But does the Bible go on to give any exceptions to this generalization? Yes. In Leviticus 11:20 the general trend is given, and in the following verses (Leviticus 11:21–23) the exceptions are listed — including grasshoppers and crickets. The critic should have realized this by reading Leviticus 11:21–23 in context, starting just one verse earlier, Leviticus 11:20, which is nearly identical to Deuteronomy 14:19, and thus not contradictory at all. Deuteronomy was written *after* Leviticus, and so there was no need to re-list the exceptions in chapter 14.

211. From what were the fowls created? Genesis 1:20–21 contradicts Genesis 2:19.

Failure to read the text carefully. (Same error as #155.) Genesis 2:19 seems to suggest that birds were made from the ground. Note that Genesis 1:20–21 does not say *from what* the birds were created, so it cannot contradict since it says nothing about the source material.

212. Were the disciples frightened or gladdened when they saw Jesus? They were frightened according to Luke 24:37, but gladdened according to John 20:20.

Failure to distinguish different times. They were initially startled and frightened (Luke 24:37), but as Jesus talked with them, they were overcome with joy and amazement (Luke 24:38–41; John 20:20).

213. Who gave the law to Moses? God (Exodus 19:20, 20:22) or angels (Galatians 3:19)?

Bifurcation fallacy and failure to read the text carefully. God gave the law to Moses using angels (Acts 7:53; Exodus 19:20, 20:22; Galatians 3:19; Hebrews 2:2). "Angel" means messenger. Note that Christ, who is Himself God, is often called "the Angel of the Lord" (Genesis 16:9, 13, 22:15–16).

214. Who was greater: Jesus, Solomon, or John the Baptist? *Solomon,* according to 1 Kings 3:12; *Jesus,* according to Matthew 12:42; Luke 11:31; and Colossians 2:2–3; *John the Baptist,* according to Matthew 11:11.

Failure to distinguish different senses, and failure to read the text carefully. First we must ask, who was "greater" *in what sense of the word?* Do we mean "greater" in wisdom, "greater" in power, "greater" in moral character, or "greater" in prophetic word? After all, Tim can be better than John at tennis, while John is better than Tim at chess. There would be no contradiction in this.

God gave Solomon a wise and discerning heart superior to any man before him or anyone to arise after him (1 Kings 3:11). This obviously excludes God Himself, who is not a man and did not arise after Solomon; thus, Jesus as God is infinitely wise and therefore wiser than Solomon (Colossians 2:2–3; Matthew 12:42). But, it is reasonable to conclude that Solomon was greater *in wisdom* than John the Baptist.

John the Baptist was the greatest *prophet* to be born naturally (Matthew 11:11). The phrase "born of women" is a figure of speech indicating one who is born into the world in the natural way (e.g., Job 14:1). This would exclude Christ who was miraculously conceived (Luke 1:34–35). But John the Baptist was greater than any prophet before him — that this greatness refers to the prophetic office is indicated in verse 9 (which the critic failed to include) and even more clearly in the parallel account in Luke 7:28 "among those born of women there is not a greater *prophet* than John the Baptist." So, *in terms of the prophetic office*, John the Baptist was greater than Solomon. But Jesus is superior in wisdom, character, power, and prophetic office to both (Mark 1:6–7; Luke 3:16, 11:31; Matthew 12:42).

215. Was Mary Magdalene happy or sad when she saw the risen Jesus? Matthew 28:8–12 contradicts John 20:11–15.

Failure to distinguish different times and failure to read the text carefully. *Before* Mary realized that Jesus was risen, *before* she recognized Jesus, she was understandably sad (John 20:11–15). But *after* she recognized that Jesus was alive, she was exceedingly joyful (Matthew 28:8; John 20:16–18).

216. Did Herod think Jesus was John the Baptist? Matthew 14:1–2 and Mark 6:16 contradict Luke 9:9.

Failure to read the text carefully. Apparently, Herod did think that it was possible that Jesus was a resurrected John the Baptist (Matthew 14:1–2; Mark 6:16). But, perhaps after trying to persuade himself that this just couldn't be so, he wanted to see for sure (Luke 9:9). None of the above verses contradict each other.

217. Where did Joseph's brothers find the hidden money? Genesis 42:29–35 contradicts Genesis 42:27, 43:21.

Bluff and failure to read the text carefully. All accounts agree that the money was found in the sacks (Genesis 42:27, 35, 43:21). Genesis 42:27 and 43:21 further specify that it was in the "mouth" (opening) of the sack, that is, inside near the top and resting on top of the remaining contents. There is no inconsistency, apparent or real.

218. Is only God holy? Revelation 15:4 says *yes*, but Exodus 22:31; Leviticus 11:44–45, 19:2, 20:7; Deuteronomy 7:6; Isaiah 4:3; Psalm 16:10, 86:2; Luke 2:23; and 1 Corinthians 7:14 all indicate that certain people are holy as well.

Failure to distinguish different senses. In Scripture, the word "holy" can mean perfectly righteous and without sin — having never sinned (Isaiah 5:16; Hebrews 4:15; 1 Peter 1:15–16). Or it can refer to the imputed righteousness that sinners inherent when God saves them (Philippians 3:9; Romans 3:22; Titus 3:5) — they are "washed clean" and counted as righteous even though they have sinned (1 John 1:9; Romans 4:3, 9). Only God is holy in the first sense (Revelation 15:4; Isaiah 45:21). He alone is perfect and without sin (Hebrews 4:15; Isaiah 40:25; Psalm 16:10). He commands us to be this way too (Exodus 22:31; Leviticus 11:44–45, 19:2, 20:7; Luke 2:23), though we all fall short and none of us are righteous by our own merit (Romans 3:23; Job 15:14–16; Psalm 130:3; Isaiah 53:6, 64:4; 1 John 1:8). But all those who have repented of sin and trusted in God for salvation are holy in the second sense — by Christ's imputed righteousness

(Hebrews 3:1; Deuteronomy 7:6; Isaiah 4:3; Psalm 86:2; 1 Corinthians 7:14). So, there is no inconsistency.

219. How should homosexuals be treated? Should they be executed according to Leviticus 20:13? Or should they be removed from the land according to 1 Kings 15:11–12?

Failure to read the text carefully and incidental fallacy. The obligation of the state is to punish those caught in homosexual behavior (by two or more witnesses) with the death penalty (Leviticus 20:13). No Scripture teaches otherwise. First Kings 15:11–12 does not prescribe how homosexual sins should be treated, rather it describes how one particular king did treat them. What people do and what they *should* do are often different things. The text indicates that Asa "put away" the (male) cult prostitutes. He may have done this by executing them in obedience to biblical law. Regardless, there is no contradiction in the text.

220. If a husband believes, is his wife saved also? *Yes,* **according to 1 Corinthians 7:14 and Acts 16:31, but not necessarily according to 1 Corinthians 7:16.**

False-cause fallacy. Answer: not necessarily. People are saved by God's grace through faith in Christ — not by being married to someone who is saved (Ephesians 2:8–9; Romans 10:9–10). However, if a man becomes a Christian, and decides not to divorce his unbelieving wife, he will have a positive influence on her, and she will become a better person (sanctified) for it (1 Corinthians 7:14). His influence may even lead her to salvation in Christ (1 Corinthians 7:16; Acts 16:31, 34). But Christ is the actual cause of salvation, not marriage. These passages all agree on this.

221. Were the men or angels inside or outside the tomb when the women arrived? Matthew 28:2 contradicts Mark 16:5; Luke 24:3–4; and John 20:11–12.

Failure to read the text carefully. Matthew 28:2 does not say where the angel (that had rolled the stone away) was *when the women arrived.*

Though, Matthew 28:5–8 strongly implies that he was within the tomb — see verse 8. This agrees with Mark 16:5; Luke 24:3–4; and John 20:11–12. Where is the supposed contradiction?

222. Can God stop iron chariots? Judges 4:13–16 says *yes*, but Judges 1:19 says *no*.

Failure to read the text carefully. God can do whatsoever He pleases. He can easily stop chariots and has done so (Judges 4:13–16). The tribe of Judah, however, couldn't always drive out chariots due to their lack of faith (Judges 1:19; Matthew 17:19–20).

223. Did Jeconiah have any sons? Jeremiah 22:28–30 indicates that he would not, but 1 Chronicles 3:17–18 and Matthew 1:12 say that he did.

Failure to read the text carefully. Yes, Jeconiah had sons (1 Chronicles 3:17–18; Matthew 1:12). Jeremiah 22:28–30 does not say otherwise. Rather it says that Jeconiah (Coniah) is despised, and should be written down (considered as if) childless, not in an absolute sense, but rather that none of his physical descendants would ever sit on the throne. His royal line was thus ended. That Jeremiah 22:28–30 does not refer to lack of offspring, but rather lack of *royal* offspring is made evident in verse 30, which mentions his descendants: "For none of his descendants shall prosper sitting on the throne of David, and ruling anymore in Judah." History confirms that they never did.

224. What will happen to Jews when they die? Matthew 8:12 contradicts Romans 11:26.

Bifurcation fallacy and failure to read the text in context. Those Jews who reject Christ will be cast into outer darkness (Matthew 8:12), along with the Gentiles who reject Christ. Those Jews who repent and trust in Christ will be saved (Romans 11:26), along with the Gentiles who trust in Christ (Romans 10:12; Galatians 3:28). In terms of salvation, there is no difference between Jews and Gentiles (Galatians 3:28).

225. Will there be many Jews? Genesis 26:4 says *yes*, which contradicts Genesis 4:27.

Failure to read the text in context, and to distinguish different times. Yes, Abraham's descendants would be many (Genesis 26:4), as history confirms. There is no Genesis 4:27. Perhaps the critic refers to Deuteronomy 4:27? But in context, this passage is giving a *conditional* promise. Beginning in verse 23, Moses promises that *if* the Israelites should act wickedly, then God would destroy many of them and disperse the rest so that there would be relatively few left. But this does not contradict God's promise that Abraham would have a humanly uncountable number of descendants, even if those descendants (at a later time) became wicked and were scattered and reduced. Even if God had chosen to destroy them completely, His promise would still be true since Abraham did indeed have many descendants. Furthermore, the critic's fallacious worldview may be slipping in here. The Bible indicates that people continue to have conscious existence after death, either in heaven or in hell. Thus, all of Abraham's innumerable descendants still exist, either in life or in death.

226. Did God commend or condemn Jehu for the killings at Jezreel? Second Kings 10:30 and 2 Chronicles 22:2 indicate that God approved, but Hosea 1:4 indicates that God did *not* approve.

Failure to distinguish different times and failure to read the text in context. Jehu was authorized by God to execute the wicked house of Ahab in Jezreel — including the Baal worshipers (2 Kings 9:6–7, 10:18–30). This he did and was commended and blessed for his obedience (2 Kings 10:30). But (as the critic would have noticed if he had read just one more verse), Jehu then began committing the same sins as those he slaughtered, including idolatry (2 Kings 10:29–31). By biblical law, when passing judgment on a criminal, the judge must himself be innocent of that crime, otherwise, his judgment is considered unjust (Romans 2:1). Thus, when Jehu committed the same sins as those he had deposed, his actions in previously deposing them can no longer be considered right, because he was acting *hypocritically*. All the good that he might have accomplished in overthrowing the wicked persons that came before him was undone, and so their blood was spilled in vain. And for *this* reason, God punished him (Hosea 1:4).

227. Where was Joash buried? Second Kings 12:20–21 contradicts 2 Chronicles 24:24–25.

Bifurcation fallacy. Joash was buried "with his fathers" — in the same city as they were buried — the city of David (Jerusalem), but not in the tombs of the kings (2 Kings 12:20–21; 2 Chronicles 24:24–25). Where is there any inconsistency?

228. How did Judas die? By hanging himself (Matthew 27:5) or by falling (Acts 1:18)?

Bifurcation fallacy. Judas committed suicide by hanging himself (Matthew 27:5). Acts 1:18 does not contradict this, but does give additional details; it indicates (after hanging himself) Judas fell and burst open. Far from contradicting, these verses spectacularly confirm biblical prophecy as documented in Appendix 8 of Dr. Arnold Fruchtenbaum's book *Messianic Christology*.[1]

229. Did Judas identify Jesus with a kiss? Matthew 26:47–49; Mark 14:43–45; and Luke 22:47–48 contradict John 18:3–5.

Fallacy of argument from silence. Yes, Judas identified Jesus with a kiss (Matthew 26:47–49; Mark 14:43–45; Luke 22:47–48). John 18:3–5 does not mention the kiss, but it does not deny or contradict it. Each author chose which details to record, and which to omit, with no contradictions.

---

1. Dr. Arnold Fruchtenbaum, *Messianic Christology* (Tustin, CA: Ariel Ministries, 1998).

230. Was Keturah Abraham's wife or concubine? Genesis 25:1 says wife, but 1 Chronicles 1:32 says concubine.

Bifurcation fallacy. A concubine *is* a wife, though generally considered a secondary one. So, if Keturah was a concubine, which she was (1 Chronicles 1:32), then she was a wife. It is possible that Abraham "promoted" Keturah to be his primary wife after the death of Sarah. Note that the original Hebrew text uses the same word (*ishshah*) for both "wife" and "woman." Context alone determines which is meant. Thus, the Bible indicates that "Abraham took a 'woman' and her name was Keturah" (Genesis 25:1).

231. To kill or not to kill. God allows and even commands men to kill other men in Exodus 32:27; Numbers 15:35; and 1 Samuel 15:2–3. But God forbids men to kill other men in Exodus 20:13, 23:7; Deuteronomy 5:17; Mark 10:19; Luke 18:20;and Matthew 19:18.

Failure to read the text carefully and distinguish sense. The Bible forbids *murder* — the *unlawful* taking of a human life (Exodus 20:13; Deuteronomy 5:17; Mark 10:19; Luke 18:20; Matthew 19:18). As such, killing someone during peacetime who is not guilty of a capital offence is unlawful (Exodus 23:7). But the law allows the taking of life during a just war (1 Samuel 15:2–3), for self-defense or the necessary defense of others whose lives are endangered (Luke 22:35–38; Esther 8:11–12; Exodus 22:2–3), or for a capital crime (Numbers 15:30–35; Exodus 32:27). The Scriptures consistently follow these principles.

232. What were the last words of Jesus? Matthew 27:46 contradicts Luke 23:46, which contradicts John 19:30.

Failure to read the text carefully. The critic cites Matthew 27:46, where Christ quotes Psalm 22. But if the critic had bothered to read just four more verses, he would have realized that even Matthew indicates that this was *not* the last thing Christ said on the Cross (Matthew 27:46–50). In fact, Matthew does not record Christ's last words — only that whatever He said, He did so in a loud voice (Matthew 27:50). John records Christ saying, "It is finished" and then reports that Christ died, but the text does not say that the death happened instantly after Christ said these words, or that no other words were said. Luke, however, does seem to indicate that "Father, into your hands I commit my spirit" were Christ's last words before His death, since "having said this, He breathed His last" (Luke 23:46). None of the other verses contradict this. Incidentally, Christ's last recorded words are "Surely I come quickly" (Revelation 22:20).

233. Should we obey human or divine law? Acts 5:29 contradicts 1 Peter 2:13, which contradicts Romans 13:1–2.

Bifurcation fallacy. When possible, we should obey *both* God's law and the civil law of the land, because civil authority is authorized by God (Romans 13:1–7; 1 Peter 2:13–14). However, if it is not possible to obey the civil law without violating God's law, then it is right to disobey the civil law of the land for the sake of obeying God (Acts 5:29, 4:19; Daniel 3:1–30).

234. Has the sun ever stood still in the sky for 24 hours? Joshua 10:12–13 contradicts Genesis 10:22.

Bluff and specious reasoning. Yes, the sun (and moon) were visibly stopped by God for about a day during a battle between Israel and the Amorites (Joshua 10:12–13), a supernatural event that was not to be repeated (Joshua 10:14). No verse contradicts this. The critic lists Genesis 10:22, which doesn't even touch the issue. Perhaps he meant Genesis 8:22; but this merely teaches that the cycles of nature will continue in the future. It does *not* say that all days will be of equal length.

235. Who is the Lord of this world? *God* according to Joshua 2:11, 3:13; 2 Kings 19:15; 1 Chronicles 16:14, 16:31; Ezra 5:11; Job 34:13; Psalm 47:2, 7, 59:13, 83:18, 96:10, 97:1, 5, 99:1; Isaiah 37:16, 54:5; Micah 4:13; Zechariah 4:14, 6:5; Matthew 11:25; Luke 10:21; and Acts 17:24. The *devil* according to Matthew 4:8–9; Luke 4:5–7; John 12:31, 14:30, 16:11; and 2 Corinthians 4:4.

Bifurcation fallacy and specious reasoning. We might just as well ask, "Who owns the cattle on a particular hill: the farmer or God?" The farmer might indeed own them. But also, and in a greater sense, God owns them because God owns all the cattle on all the hills (Psalm 50:10). This is an example of co-ownership, just as the prophetic writing of Scripture as accomplished by co-authorship (2 Peter 1:18–21; 2 Timothy 3:16). Likewise, there are many "lords" in this world who have authority (1 Corinthians 8:5); even Satan is sometimes called the "god of this world" (2 Corinthians 4:4) and "ruler of this world" (John 12:31, 14:30, 16:11) since, temporarily and by God's permission, he has such influence.

But God has authority over all earthly kings and even over Satan (John 19:10–11; Psalm 2:6–7, 10–12) and is therefore the ultimate Lord (Joshua 2:11, 3:13; 2 Kings 19:15; 1 Chronicles 16:14, 31; Ezra 5:11, 34:13; Psalm 47:2, 7, 59:13, 83:18, 96:10, 97:1, 5; 99:1; Isaiah 37:16, 54:5; Micah 4:13; Zechariah 4:14, 6:5; Matthew 11:25; Luke 10:21; Acts 17:24). God indeed is the King of kings, and Lord of lords (Revelation 19:16, 17:14; 1 Timothy 6:15).

The critic is not thinking clearly in citing Matthew 4:8–9; Luke 4:5–7 where Satan promises to give Jesus all the kingdoms of the world if only Christ would bow down to him. Satan is a liar (John 8:44) and these are not ultimately his nations to give. The nations ultimately belong to Christ (Psalm 2:8; Daniel 7:13–14; Matthew 28:18).

236. Should we love or hate our brother? We should love our brother according to Leviticus 19:17–18 and John 3:15, 4:20–21. However, we should hate our brother according to Luke 14:26.

Failure to read the text in context. Of course we should love our brother and not hate him (Leviticus 19:17–18; 1 John 3:15, 4:20–21). Jesus does not contradict this, but rather affirms it (Matthew 5:22–24), and so it should be obvious that Jesus is not teaching us to hate others in Luke 14:26. Rather, as was His common teaching style (e.g., Matthew 7:4), Christ was using *hyperbole* to make a point. This is the technique of exaggerating something for emphasis. In this case, Jesus was teaching that we ought to love Him *so much more* than even our biological family and that the latter is like "hate" *by comparison*. Obviously, he is not teaching that we should literally hate others, since He taught that we ought to love even our enemies (Matthew 5:44).

237. Is marriage a good thing? *Yes,* **according to Genesis 2:18; Proverbs 18:22; Ecclesiastes 9:9; Matthew 19:5; 1 Timothy 4:1–3; and Hebrews 13:4.** *No* **according to 1 Corinthians 7:1, 7–8.**

Failure to read the text carefully and to distinguish sense. Like many things in life, marriage has pros and cons. But how would that be a *contradiction* since the pros and cons are different? The positive aspects of marriage are that it provides a helper and uniquely suitable companion for man (Genesis 2:18; Proverbs 18:22) with whom to enjoy life (Ecclesiastes 9:9), was instituted by God (Genesis 2:18, 21–24; Matthew 19:5–6; 1 Timothy 4:1–3; Hebrews 13:4) to produce godly children (Malachi 2:15), can produce sanctification (1 Corinthians 7:14), and helps reduce the temptation for fornication (1 Corinthians 7:2,9). On the other hand, if unchecked, marriage can divert our attention away from God (1 Corinthians 7:1, 7–8). The Bible also warns of the negative consequences of entering into marriage with a contentious woman (Proverbs 21:9, 25:24). Really, there is no verse that says that marriage is *bad* — only that there are drawbacks. There is no inconsistency, either real or apparent.

238. Was Moses meek? Numbers 12:3 says *yes,* **which contradicts Numbers 31:14–18.**

Failure to read the text carefully and specious reasoning. Yes, Moses was very meek/humble (Numbers 12:3). *No verse says otherwise.*

Certainly. Numbers 31:14–18 does not deny this. Rather, the latter passage shows that Moses was rightly angered when the people of Israel sinned. A person who is meek or humble is one who does not have an attitude of arrogance or pride; but a meek/humble person may become angry for good reasons. Jesus was also very meek, and yet exhibited righteous anger at sin (Matthew 11:29; Mark 11:15). There is no contradiction because meekness and anger are not contrary.

239. Is God merciful? *Yes* according to Exodus 34:6; Deuteronomy 4:31; 2 Samuel 24:14; 1 Chronicles 16:34; Psalm 25:8, 86:5, 100:5, 103:8, 106:1, 107:1, 118:1, 136:1, 145:9; Jeremiah 3:12, 33:11; Lamentations 3:33; Joel 2:13; Micah 7:18; 2 Corinthians 1:3; James 5:11; and 1 John 4:16. *No* according to Exodus 34:6–7; Numbers 25:4; Deuteronomy 7:16; 1 Samuel 6:19, 15:2–3; Lamentations 2:2, 2:17, 3:43, 13:14, 16:3–7; Ezekiel 7:4, 9, 9:5–6; and Micah 1:12.

Specious reasoning. God is merciful and full of compassion, *and no verse says that He isn't*. After all, God promises to save and have compassion on anyone who repents and calls upon Him (Isaiah 55:7). That's pretty merciful! He is certainly merciful and compassionate (Exodus 34:6; Deuteronomy 4:31; 2 Samuel 24:14; 1 Chronicles 16:34; Psalm 25:8, 86:5, 100:5, 103:8, 106:1, 107:1, 118:1, 136:1, 145:9; Jeremiah 3:12, 33:11; Lamentations 3:32–33; Joel 2:13; Micah 7:18; 2 Corinthians 1:3; James 5:11; 1 John 4:16).

But God is *also* just, and therefore does not extend mercy to those who are *unrepentant*, but gives them justice (Exodus 34:7; Numbers 25:4; Deuteronomy 7:16; 1 Samuel 6:19, 15:2–3; Lamentations 2:2, 17, 3:43; *Jeremiah* 13:14, 16:3–7; Ezekiel 7:4, 9, 9:5–6; Micah 1:12). There is no inconsistency in the merciful God showing His mercy to the repentant, and His justice to the unrepentant. After all, just because God is full of mercy doesn't mean that He is required to extend that mercy to everyone. (A man can be *generous*, and yet still not give away everything he has to *everyone*).

240. How did God say the Moabites should be treated? Deuteronomy 2:9 says peaceably — that the Israelites should not attack them. However, in Judges 3:28–30 and Jeremiah 48:2, God encourages the Israelites to attack Moab.

Failure to distinguish different times/circumstances and to read the text carefully. None of the above passages say how "the Moabites should be treated." So, obviously they cannot contradict on an issue that they do not address. In Deuteronomy 2:9, God forbids Israel from provoking Moab to war and from taking their land; for God did not give that land to Israel. In Judges 3:12–14, we read that God permitted Moab to attack Israel and possessed some of its land for 18 years, due to Israel's disobedience. When Israel repented and cried to God (verse 15), God allowed Israel to take back *their own land* that Moab was possessing (Judges 3:28–30). Where is there any inconsistency? Moreover, Jeremiah 48:2 prophesies of what will happen with Moab, saying nothing about how the Moabites "should be treated" by Israel. So, again we see that the critic just isn't reading the text accurately or thinking carefully.

241. Did any Moabite enter the congregation of the Lord? Deuteronomy 23:3 and Nehemiah 13:1 contradict Ruth 1:4, 4:13, 17.

Bluff and failure to read the text carefully. Moabites were certainly allowed (and encouraged) to repent of their sins and become part of God's people. Ruth did so (Ruth 1:4, 4:13, 17). However, Moabites were not permitted to enter the "assembly of the Lord" (the ruling body of either the church or state of Israel) until the tenth generation (Deuteronomy 23:3; Nehemiah 13:1). Ruth did not. So, where is there any contradiction?

242. Is money good or bad? Ecclesiastes 10:19 contradicts 1 Timothy 6:10.

Bifurcation fallacy and failure to read the text carefully. Neither. Money is not inherently good or bad; it can be used for good purposes or for bad purposes. Money can be used for enjoyment (Ecclesiastes

10:19), which is fine. Note that the critic has repeated the common error of thinking that 1 Timothy 6:10 says something negative about money — it does not. It states that the *love of* money is the root of all sorts of evil — not money itself.

243. Did Jesus preach His first sermon on a mountain or a plain? Matthew 5:1–3 says mountain, but Luke 6:17, 20 says plain.

Failure to read the text carefully. Jesus preached the beatitudes on the mountain (Matthew 5:1–3). Around that time, it was on a section of *level ground* (a "plain"), perhaps a level part of the mountain or at its base, where Christ *healed* many (Luke 6:17). Luke confirms that Christ had descended some ways on the mountain to heal the sick (Luke 6:12, 17) in the level spot. Whether this was at the base of the mountain, which Christ then re-ascended to begin speaking, or whether Christ was already at some elevation on the mountain in the level area, neither Gospel says. So, obviously, they cannot contradict each other.

244. What is God's name? Exodus 6:2–3 contradicts Exodus 34:14, which contradicts Exodus 3:14.

Bifurcation fallacy and specious reasoning. God has *many* names — many more than the critic listed. But how is that in any way even slightly *contradictory?* Judge Joseph Smith might be called, "Joseph," "Joe," "Mr. Smith," "Judge Smith," "Your Honor," and so on. God is the LORD (YHWH), God Almighty (Exodus 6:2–3), He is called "Jealous" (Exodus 34:14), and the "I AM" (Exodus 3:14), to name just a few.

245. What's new? Ecclesiastes 1:9 says nothing is new. But new things are mentioned in Isaiah 43:19, 65:17; Jeremiah 31:22; 2 Corinthians 5:17; 2 Peter 3:13; and Revelation 21:1.

Failure to read the text in context and to consider the time and sense. Ecclesiastes 1:9 poetically expresses the truth that, in the present world, nature has uniformity such that there are no new natural creations. After all, God finished His work of creating this universe by the seventh day (Genesis 2:2–3); and although new animals or people may be born, they are the same kinds as originally created and are made from old material that has been recycled since creation. Thus, *today, in the present* (or precisely King Solomon's present — our past), nothing is genuinely new *"under the sun"* — a reference to the natural/physical universe.

None of the other verses listed by the critic deal with the *present, physical* universe. They either deal with a *future* physical universe, or the *spiritual* world. It should be obvious that Isaiah 43:19 speaks of something that will happen in Isaiah's *future:* "Behold, I *will* do something new." So, that can't contradict what Solomon was saying about the present. Likewise, Isaiah 65:17 speaks of Isaiah's future, not the present. Had the critic read Jeremiah 31:22 *in context* (see verse 6 and verse 31) he would have seen that this too is referring to a *future* act of God.

Second Peter 3:13 specifically says "we are looking for" (expecting in the future) new heavens and a new earth. The new heaven and earth is also mentioned in Revelation 21:1. Second Corinthians 5:17 speaks of the present, but it is a *spiritual* creation and thus not a natural one ("under the sun"). This passage speaks of the new nature a Christian becomes when he is saved; but obviously the physical body does not become new at this present time. So, there is no apparent inconstancy because the sense is different. There is nothing new in the *natural* world in the *present*, but there are new *spiritual* creations in the present and new natural creations in the *future*.

246. What is the correct new moon sacrifice? Numbers 28:11 gives a different procedure from Ezekiel 46:6.

Failure to distinguish different times. At which time period? How would it be contradictory for God to specify different ceremonial procedures for *different times*? The events of Ezekiel take place over eight hundred years after the events of Numbers. The ceremonial laws prescribed for Moses during the Exodus and the early days of Israel before the construction of the temple were binding for that time period (Numbers 28:11). If God prescribed different ceremonial laws for the times of the kings after the Temple was constructed, that is His prerogative (Ezekiel 46:6). Under the New Testament, animal sacrifice is not required at all (Hebrews 10:11–12; Galatians 4:9–11).

247. How should nonbelievers be treated? *Kill them,* **according to Deuteronomy 13:6–10.** *Do not be bound to them,* **according to 2 Corinthians 6:14–17;** *love them,* **according to Leviticus 19:18; Matthew 4:44, 22:39; Mark 12:31; Luke 6:27, 6:31, 10:27; Romans 13:9–10; Galatians 5:14; and James 2:8, 7:12.**

Hasty generalization fallacy and sweeping generalization fallacy. Obviously, the details of how a person is to be treated will depend on the circumstances. An unbeliever who is a violent murderer should be treated differently from one who lives peaceably and obeys the law. It would be ridiculous to argue that since some unbelievers (murderers, rapists) ought to be punished by execution, that therefore *all* unbelievers ought to be punished by execution. And yet, this is precisely the sort of ridiculous reasoning employed by the critic in alleging any inconsistency in the above passages. But there is no genuine inconsistency at all. Consider the following.

Deuteronomy 13:6–10 describes a wicked person who has enjoyed the blessings of living in a land of God-fearing people, a person who then rebels against God and attempts to entice others to join in his high treason. Obviously, that wicked traitor is to be punished. But an unbeliever who abides by civil law should not be punished by civil authority (Romans 13:3–4). No Scripture contradicts this principle.

Second Corinthians 6:14–17 specifies that a believer should not marry an unbeliever. No Scripture contradicts this principle.

Leviticus 19:18 indicates that we should not take personal vengeance, for justice is the responsibility of God and civil magistrates that act as His representatives (Romans 13:1–4). And the verse teaches that we ought to love our neighbor as ourselves — in context this refers to the people of God (verses 16–17). No verse contradicts this. The passage is confirmed in Matthew 22:39; Mark 12:31; Romans 13:9–10; Galatians 5:14; James 2:8; and Luke 10:27, each showing that we ought to show great love to those who treat us well (Luke 10:29–37).

James 7:12 does not exist. Matthew 4:44 does not exist. But perhaps the critic meant Matthew 5:44 where we are taught to love even our enemies — those who persecute us.

Luke 6:27 teaches that we are to love our enemies (consistent with Old Testament Law: Exodus 23:4–5) — those people who mistreat us (Luke 6:28) but not so far as to attempt to murder us, for which self-defense would be an appropriate response (Exodus 22:2–3). Luke 6:31 teaches that we ought to treat others as we would want to be treated. So, where is there any inconsistency?

248. Was the tomb opened or closed when the women arrived? Luke 24:2; Mark 16:3–4; and John 20:1 contradict Matthew 28:2.

Bluff and failure to read the text carefully. All these texts agree that the stone had been rolled away by the time the women reached the tomb. Matthew 28:2 records the rolling away of the stone, but it does not teach that the women had already arrived. They arrived later.

249. Who owns the earth? *The Lord* does, according to Genesis 14:19, 22; Exodus 9:29, 19:5; Deuteronomy 10:14; 1 Chronicles 29:11; Psalm 24:1, 50:12, 89:11; 1 Corinthians 10:26. *The devil* does, according to Matthew 4:8–9 and Luke 4:5–6. *Men* do, according to Psalm 115:16.

Bifurcation fallacy and specious reasoning. God owns everything, including the earth (Genesis 14:19, 22; Exodus 9:29, 19:5; Deuteronomy 10:14; 1 Chronicles 29:11; Psalm 24:1, 50:12, 89:11; 1 Corinthians 10:26). God graciously delegates aspects of His rule over earth to mankind (Psalm 115:16; Genesis 1:26–28). Thus, people can own possessions as a steward (e.g., Job 1:3; Matthew 21:33), but God owns everything as a King. (See #147.)

The critic's reasoning is absurd in listing Matthew 4:8–9 and Luke 4:5–6. In these two passages, Satan attempts to swindle Christ by offering Him the kingdoms of the world, which of course Christ already owns as God. These passages do not contradict the rest of Scriptures; on the contrary, they confirm that Satan is a liar. Christ wasn't fooled. But, apparently, the critic was.

250. How should parents be treated? Exodus 20:12; Deuteronomy 5:16; Ephesians 6:2; Proverbs 1:8, 23:22; and Malachi 4:6 indicate that parents should be treated with respect and honor in contradiction to Matthew 12:47–48, 23:9, 3:32–33 and Luke 9:59–60, 14:26.

Bluff and failure to read the text carefully. Parents should be treated with respect and honor (Exodus 20:12; Deuteronomy 5:16; Ephesians 6:2; Proverbs 1:8, 23:22; Malachi 4:6). No verse contradicts this. Jesus is being perfectly respectful to His mother in Matthew 12:47–50 and Mark 3:32–35 when He includes all those who trust in Him as His family. The critic might have realized this if he had read just two more verses. Likewise, what is disrespectful about Christ denying that no one can be father over our conscience except God in Matthew 23:9? In Luke 9:59–62, Jesus explains that our allegiance to our Creator rightly comes before even family (as the critic might have realized if he had read just two more verses). Obviously, showing more respect to God doesn't remotely imply that we should be disrespectful to family! The verses he selected again show that the critic is not interested in serious scholarship.

And what of Luke 14:26? Does Jesus here mean that we should literally hate our family? As the context of verses 27–33 makes clear, and as was His standard teaching style, Jesus uses *hyperbole* to illustrate the principle of putting God first. Namely, we ought to love God to such an extent that our love for family is like hate by comparison. He does *not* teach that we should literally hate family; he teaches that we ought to love family (Matthew 15:4), and yet love God so much more (Matthew 22:36–40).

251. Did Paul see Jesus on the road to Damascus? First Corinthians 9:1 contradicts Acts 9:8 and 1 Corinthians 15:8.

Bluff and failure to read the text carefully. *None* of the verses listed by the critic actually state whether Paul saw Jesus on the road to Damascus! First Corinthians 9:1 and 15:8 both teach that Paul saw Jesus, but neither state whether this happened on the road to Damascus or at some other time. Nor does Acts 9:1–8 (nor Acts 22:6–11, nor Acts 26:13–18) state whether Paul saw Jesus — only that Paul *heard* Jesus and saw a *light*. Now how could these verses possibly contradict on an issue that none of them even address? Again we see that the critic is not engaged in scholarly analysis; any contradictions exist only in his imagination — not in the text.

252. Did Paul visit all of the disciples when he went to Jerusalem after his conversion? *Yes*, according to Acts 9:26–28, but no according to Galatians 1:18–19.

Failure to read the text carefully. No, Paul did not visit all of the disciples or Apostles when he went to Jerusalem. Of the Apostles, Paul only saw Peter and James (Galatians 1:18–19). Acts 9:26–28 does *not* state that Paul saw *all* the Apostles/disciples; it only says that Barnabas brought Paul to see the Apostles (Peter and James). Any contradiction exists only in the critic's imagination — not in the text.

253. Is God warlike or peaceful? Warlike according to Exodus 15:3 and Psalm 18:34, 144:1. Peaceful according to Romans 15:33; 1 Corinthians 14:33; 2 Thessalonians 3:16; and Hebrews 13:20.

Bifurcation fallacy and failure to recognize different times. The critic's objection is absurd, a bit like asking "Was George Washington warlike or peaceful?" Obviously, in times of peace, Washington was peaceful; but in times of war, he knew how to do battle. Likewise, God grants peace when appropriate — in fact, there would be only peace if everyone loved and obeyed God. And God brings war and calamity when appropriate, especially to those who are in rebellion against Him. Passages such as Isaiah 45:7; Ecclesiastes 7:14; and Jeremiah 18:7–9, explicitly teach this.

Notice that God *never* grants peace and war *at the same time and in the same sense*, which is what would be required for a contradiction. So, God is rightly called a warrior (Exodus 15:3), and helps the righteous in battle (Psalm 18:34, 144:1) so as to remove the wicked. And when people live according to God's instructions, He is happy to grant them peace (Romans 15:33; 1 Corinthians 14:33; 2 Thessalonians 3:16; Hebrews 13:20). Any good king would do the same.

254. Who wrote the Pentateuch? Deuteronomy 1:1, 31:9 says that Moses did, which contradicts Numbers 12:3 and Deuteronomy 34:5–6, 34:10.

Sweeping generalization fallacy. Moses wrote the bulk of the Pentateuch, and is therefore rightly called its author (Deuteronomy 1:1, 31:9). God is also the author, since He inspired all of what was written in Scripture (2 Timothy 3:16). Of course, Numbers 12:3 is fully consistent with this; Moses is allowed to write in the third person point of view, even about himself. What about Deuteronomy 34:5–6, 10 which records Moses's death and seems to be written afterward? Most likely Joshua wrote this final chapter of Deuteronomy. If the author of a book dies before its completion and someone else writes the last chapter, the author is still the author of the book. Where is there any contradiction? (Furthermore, since Moses wrote by inspiration of God, we cannot discount the possibility that he prophetically reported his own future death.)

255. Were the Pharisees baptized by John? Matthew 3:7–11 contradicts Luke 7:29–30.

Sweeping generalization fallacy and failure to read the text carefully. Matthew 3:7–11 does not directly say whether the Pharisees were baptized by John; rather it states only that many of the Pharisees were coming for baptism when John saw them and called them a "brood of vipers." Presumably, John did not baptize them since that would have indicated their repentance and symbolized their participation in the family of God. This agrees completely with Luke 7:29–30 where the Pharisees who rejected God's purpose had not been baptized by John. Of course, it would be a sweeping generalization fallacy to conclude that since the Pharisees *in general* had rejected God and were not baptized by John, that there were no exceptions. Presumably, if an individual Pharisee had repented of his sin and trusted in Christ as Lord, John would have been willing to baptize him.

256. Should we try to please others? Romans 15:2 and 1 Corinthians 10:33 contradict Galatians 1:10.

Sweeping generalization fallacy and failure to read the text in context. The Christian should seek peace with others when it is possible (Hebrews 12:14) as long as it does not require us to sin (Acts 5:29). Thus, pleasing others is a secondary consideration to pleasing God. And when we are faced with a dilemma in which it is only possible to please either God or men, we are morally obligated to obey God (Acts 4:19; Genesis 3:17; 1 Samuel 15:24; Matthew 7:8). Jesus confirms that the first and greatest commandment is to love the Lord, and the second is to love our neighbor as ourselves (Matthew 22:38). Note also that loving a neighbor is not the same as trying to "please" him.

All the verses listed by the critic agree with this principle. Note that he has taken Romans 15:2 out of context; in context with verse 1, the passage teaches that we should not be solely concerned about *ourselves*, but about others too; the passage does not teach that pleasing others is more important than pleasing God. Likewise, 1 Corinthians 10:31–33 teaches that we should do all things for the glory of *God*, and avoid giving offense to people when this does not conflict with our duty to God.In Galatians 1:10, Paul confirms that his primary goal is to please God rather than men.

257. What did Jesus do after His baptism? Mark 1:12–13 says He went into the wilderness, but John 1:35, 43, 2:1 says that He and His disciples went to Galilee.

Bluff. Jesus did many things after His baptism, including living the rest of His life on earth. Perhaps the critic wants to know what happened *immediately* afterward. But the Gospel of John does not mention the baptism of Jesus, nor what happened immediately afterward. So, obviously it cannot contradict on something that it does not mention. John 1:32 implies that the events of John 1:35–2:1 happened sometime after Jesus was baptized (compare with Mark 1:9–10). Mark 1:12–13 indicates that Jesus went into the wilderness for 40 days after His baptism, and no verse contradicts this.

258. How much power did Jesus have? Matthew 20:23 and Mark 6:5 indicate that His power was *limited*, but Matthew 28:18 indicates that His power was *unlimited*.

Semantic range fallacy, failure to check the original language, and to read the text in context. In Hebrew custom, when it is not fitting or appropriate to do something it is customary to say "I *cannot* do it" (Genesis 19:22, 37:4). We use this way of speaking in English too. Consider a lactose-intolerant person being offered an ice cream cone. He might say, "No thank you. I can't eat dairy products." Does this mean the person lacks the ability to put the ice cream in his mouth and swallow? Of course not. Rather, it means that it would not be appropriate for him to do so, because it would have deleterious consequences on his health.

So, when Jesus "could not" work many miracles in His hometown (Mark 6:5), this was not for lack of *ability*; rather, it would have been *inappropriate* for Him to bless those who had such a stubborn lack of faith (Mark 6:6). Likewise, it was completely inappropriate for the sons of Zebedee to have their mother ask Jesus for them to sit beside His throne (Matthew 20:21–23). Jesus "could not" grant that request because it was sinful, *not* because He lacked any ability. Jesus has all power in heaven and on earth (Matthew 28:18). But, as God,

He cannot deny Himself (2 Timothy 2:13). Thus, Jesus cannot act wickedly. This is not due to lack of power, but rather because Jesus is fully good.

259. Do Christians know how to pray? In Matthew 6:9–13 Jesus tells them how, but in Romans 8:26, Paul says they don't know how.

Specious reasoning. We know the appropriate *outline* for prayer; but we do not always know for what *specifically* to pray. Jesus gives a basic outline for prayer in Matthew 6:9–13. But we often need help to know what details we should insert into that outline. The Holy Spirit helps us in this area (Romans 8:26). Where is there any inconsistency?

260. Is every word of God pure? *Yes* according to Psalm 2:6, 119:140 and Proverbs 30:5. But this contradicts 2 Kings 18:27; Ezekiel 23:20; Habakkuk 2:16; and Malachi 2:3.

Equivocation fallacy. The critic never defines what he means by "pure," or he might have realized his error. Every Word of God is pure in the sense that everything God affirms is perfectly true and infallible (Psalm 119:140, 160; Proverbs 30:5; 2 Timothy 3:16). Thus, even when the Bible records the wicked actions of wicked men, it does so with perfect accuracy. The Word is pure, since it perfectly records the actions of individuals, though such actions may be detestable, and the punishment of the wicked may be unpleasant.

The Hebrew word translated "pure" in Psalm 119:140 is the word that would be used to describe gold that has been refined so that it is uncontaminated. In similar fashion, God's Word is pure, tested, perfectly true from beginning to end, and uncontaminated by anything false. No Scripture contradicts this. The passages listed by the critic (2 Kings 18:27; Ezekiel 23:20; Habakkuk 2:16; Malachi 2:3) are no exception; they may displease the critic's emotions, but they all truthfully report what was said. Psalm 2:6 does not address the issue.

261. Can God be found through reason alone? Romans 1:20 says *yes*, but Job 11:7 says *no*.

Failure to read the text in context. No, God cannot be found by *unaided* reasoning apart from revelation (because humans could know *nothing* apart from divine revelation — Proverbs 1:7; Colossians 2:3). Romans 1:20 is perfectly consistent with this when read *in context with the previous two verses.* Romans 1:18–19 teach that God has *revealed* Himself to all people. That is why we inescapably recognize the handiwork of the Creator when we look at the creation (Romans 1:20). Job 11:7 inerrantly records the words of Zophar who rhetorically asks if God's limits can be discovered by man. But this question is not relevant to the issue of whether God can be "found through reason alone." In any case, it does not contradict Romans 1:20.

262. Did Mary Magdalene recognize Jesus when He first appeared to her? Matthew 28:9 contradicts John 20:14, which contradicts Luke 24:23.

Failure to read the text carefully, failure to distinguish different times, and a bluff. When Mary first saw Jesus she did not recognize Him (John 20:14–15). But as soon as He spoke her name, she did recognize Him (John 20:16). The other Gospels do not record Mary's initial and momentary inability to recognize Christ, but Matthew 28:9 affirms that Mary and the other women did worship Jesus — perfectly consistent with Matthew 28:9. Notice that Luke 24:23 says nothing about the issue, demonstrating again that the critic is not careful and honest in his claims.

263. Did both thieves revile Jesus? Mark 15:32 and Matthew 27:44 say *yes*, but Luke 23:39–42 says only one did.

Failure to distinguish different times and failure to read the text carefully. Luke 23:39–42 indicates that one thief insulted Jesus, while the other was repentant. However, Mark 15:32 and Matthew 27:44 simply say that those [plural] who were crucified with Christ were insulting Him. Do we have a contradiction? Hardly. It is entirely reasonable that both thieves initially mocked Christ, and *at a later time* one repented. (Consider how Saul of Tarsus changed his attitude and behavior toward Christ.) The critic has failed to consider that the above passages may both be truthfully reporting what happened at two different times.

Furthermore, as is customary of Hebrew style (Luke was a Gentile, but Matthew and Mark were Hebrews), Matthew and Mark may have been using synecdoche — representing an individual by the group. The phrase, "the people shouted for joy" doesn't necessarily imply that every person in the group shouted, only a representative sample. Thus, the one thief on the cross may represent both. Yet, the critic has arbitrarily dismissed this possibility as well.

264. Is wealth a sign of righteousness or of wickedness? Righteousness, according to Psalm 37:25, 12:1, 3, and Proverbs 15:6. Wickedness, according to Matthew 19:23–24; Luke 6:24; and James 5:1.

Bifurcation fallacy. Wealth is *neither* a sign of righteousness nor of wickedness. A righteous man may be either wealthy (2 Chronicles 1:11–12) or poor (Matthew 3:4, 11:11; Luke 16:20–22). A wicked man may be either wealthy (Luke 6:24–26; James 5:1–6) or poor (Matthew 18:23–34). As a general rule, God does provide for His people so that they are not without the necessities of life for extended time, which is the sense of Psalm 37:25. But God never promises that all who obey Him will be wealthy in this world. (The critic also seems to misunderstand that "wealth and riches" in poetic contexts like Psalm 112:1–3 and Proverbs 15:6 often refer to the spiritual blessings that God does promise to those who trust in Him.) Note that Jesus does not say that a rich man cannot enter heaven in Matthew 19:23 — only that it is hard for him.

265. How should Sabbath-breakers be punished? By being "cut off" according to Exodus 31:14, but by being executed, according to Exodus 31:14–15, 35:2 and Numbers 15:32–36.

Bifurcation fallacy. How Sabbath-breakers should be punished depends on the way in which they break the Sabbath, as the critic would have realized if he had read the context. If a person violates the Sabbath day *unintentionally*, then under the Old Testament administration he must offer a sin-offering and will be forgiven (Numbers 15:27–29). But, at that time, if a person broke the Sabbath day law *intentionally*, in open defiance and high treason against the Lord, then that person was to be cut off from God's people (Numbers 15:30–31).

The punishment was to fit the crime; thus, the severity of the punishment was to match the severity of the defiance. It may be that lesser displays of defiance against God simply require being "cut off" from God's people by exclusion from religious ceremonies, while greater displays of defiance (witnessed by two or more people — Deuteronomy 17:6) require being "cut off" completely by execution (Numbers 15:32–36; Exodus 31:14–15, 35:2). In any case, there is no apparent contradiction in the listed verses.

266. Who may offer sacrifices to God? Leviticus 17:1–5 and Numbers 18:6–8 contradict 1 Samuel 1:1–2, 20, 7:7–9.

Bluff. Anyone may bring a sacrifice to the Lord, as long as it is done in the right way. Once the Tabernacle was established, God appointed the Levites to perform the sacrifices. Under the Mosaic administration, people would bring their sacrifices to the Tabernacle/Temple, and only the priests were permitted to enter and perform the sacrifice (Leviticus 17:1–9; Numbers 18:6–8). There were exceptions and provisions for those who lived too far to readily travel to the Temple (Deuteronomy 12:21). First Samuel 1:1–3, 20 is perfectly consistent with this; Elkanah sacrificed through the priests (1 Samuel 1:3) as required by law. Samuel was himself a priest of God, and sacrificed appropriately (1 Samuel 7:7–9).

267. Did Saul's family die with him? *Yes*, according to 1 Chronicles 10:6, but *no*, according to 2 Samuel 2:7–9.

Bifurcation fallacy. Some members of his family did die on the same day as Saul, and others did not. Saul had at least six sons. They were Armoni, Mephibosheth (2 Samuel 21:8), Jonathan, Malchi-shua,

Abinadab, and Esh-baal (1 Chronicles 9:39). Three of Saul's sons died with him in battle — Jonathan, Abinadab, and Malchi-shua (1 Chronicles 10:2,6). Thus, all of Saul's house who followed him into battle perished with him, which is the contextual meaning of 1 Chronicles 10:6. Mephibosheth, Ishbosheth (Esh-Baal) and Armoni apparently did not participate in battle, and thus lived for a time afterward (2 Samuel 2:7–9), though they were later killed (2 Samuel 4:5–8, 21:8).

268. Was Sisera asleep when he was murdered? *Yes,* **according to Judges 4:21, but** *no,* **according to Judges 5:26–27.**

Bluff. Failure to read the text in context. Sisera was asleep when he was killed (Judges 4:21) and no verse says otherwise. Beginning in Judges 5:1 we read of the song that Deborah and Barak sang. In verses 26–27 they sing about the killing of Sisera. Though poetic, their song is consistent with the historical account, and does not contradict by suggesting that Sisera was not asleep. So, where is there any inconsistency?

269. Is all Scripture inspired by God? **Second Timothy 3:16 says** *yes,* **but 1 Corinthians 7:12, 25 says** *no.*

Specious reasoning. Of course all Scripture is inspired by God (2 Timothy 3:16), and no verse contradicts this. But not all Scripture is in the form of *commands* from God. Some Scripture gives general principles of wisdom; also, some Scripture reports historical events in a historical narrative format. In 1 Corinthians 7:25, Paul explains that he is not giving a command, but he gives an opinion on the matter — an opinion that he writes under divine inspiration. But just because it's not a command doesn't mean it's not a divinely inspired principle.

270. Should you serve God alone? *Yes,* **according to Matthew 4:10, 23:10. But the following passages direct us to serve others in addition to God: Ephesians 6:5; Colossians 3:18, 20, 22; 1 Timothy 6:1; Titus 2:9; and 1 Peter 2:18.**

Failure to read the text carefully or in context and equivocation. In Matthew 4:10, Jesus quotes Deuteronomy 6:13 — which in context (see Deuteronomy 6:14) indicates that God alone is to be worshiped and served *as God*; it is the *worshiping of other gods* that is forbidden — not service to others in general. We have only one ultimate allegiance/authority (Matthew 23:30) who is to be served and worshiped in the religious sense.

But this does not deny the possibility of secondary human authority figures that can and should be obeyed and served in a less-than-ultimate sense. Indeed, all earthly authority comes from God anyway (Romans 13:1). We therefore should submit to our leaders (Hebrews 13:17) and indeed all those God has instituted to have authority over us (Ephesians 6:5; Colossians 3:18–23; 1 Timothy 6:1; Titus 2:9; 1 Peter 2:18), since they act as representatives of God (Romans 13:1). But they are not to be worshiped or served *in an idolatrous way*, as if they literally were another god. The Bible therefore forbids idolatry, but permits and encourages reverent submission and service.

271. What is the earth set upon? The earth rests on nothing according to Job 26:7, but the earth rests on pillars according to 1 Samuel 2:8 and Job 9:6.

Genre fallacy and failure to read the text in context. All the passages cited by the critic exhibit synonymous parallelism: the defining characteristic of Hebrew poetry. This demonstrates that these passages are poetic in nature, and should be interpreted as such. The earth physically hangs upon nothing, being suspended in space, as poetically described in Job 26:7. There is no difficulty in that passage.

Do 1 Samuel 2:8 and Job 9:6 contradict this? Presumably, the critic thinks that the biblical authors meant for the "pillars of the earth" to be taken in a physical sense. If so, then he has violated the genre principle because in biblical literature, "pillars" are used as a word-picture to denote *stability*. Consider Proverbs 9:1 where "Wisdom" is said to rest on seven pillars — but this *can't mean physical pillars since wisdom is non-physical*. In Revelation 3:12 and Galatians 2:9, people who are steadfast are referred to as pillars. In 1 Timothy 3:15, the Church is referred to as the pillar of truth. Thus, in context, 1 Samuel 2:8 and Job

9:6 teach that the earth is *stable*. This does not in any way contradict that the earth poetically hangs upon nothing — since it does so in a way that is stable.

272. How should a man who has sex with a menstruating woman be punished? He is counted as unclean for seven days according to Leviticus 15:24. However Leviticus 20:18 says he is to be cut off from the people.

Bifurcation fallacy and failure to read the text carefully and in context. The punishment depends on the circumstances. If the man lies with his wife, and he does *not* know that her menstruation has begun, then he is ceremonially unclean for seven days under the Old Testament administration (Leviticus 15:24). However, if he knows ahead of time that she is menstruating, and lies with her anyway in open rebellion to God's law, then under the Old Testament administration he was to be cut off from Israel (Leviticus 20:18). The two passages are fully consistent when the full context is considered.

273. What did the sign over Jesus' head say? "This is Jesus the King of the Jews" (Matthew 27:37), "The King of the Jews" (Mark 15:26), "This is the King of the Jews" (Luke 23:38), or "Jesus the Nazarene, the King of the Jews" (John 19:19)?

Bifurcation fallacy, and subset fallacy. The Gospels all agree that the inscription indicated that Jesus is "the King of the Jews." But the Gospels record three different variations of the inscription. Which one is correct? They all are, of course! That's because there were three different inscriptions, as the critic would have known if he had read *only one more verse in John* (John 19:20).

John 19:20 reports that the inscription was written in three different languages (Greek, Hebrew, and Latin). Thus, there were three inscriptions, worded slightly differently. Matthew, Luke, and John each correctly record one of the inscriptions in one of the three languages. So, there is no contradiction. And Mark gives only part of the title — the part that is the same between all three languages — with full consistency.

274. What did Judas do with the silver? Acts 1:18 says he bought a field with it. However, Matthew 27:5 says he threw it back into the sanctuary.

Bifurcation fallacy. Judas threw the money back into the temple, and a field was bought with it on his behalf (Matthew 27:5; Acts 1:18). So, rightly can we say that Judas bought a field with his money, though he did not make the transaction himself (Matthew 27:6–8). (See Fruchtenbaum's book *Messianic Christology*, appendix 8.[2])

275. Were the men or angels inside the tomb sitting or standing? They were sitting according to Mark 16:5 and John 20:11–12. However, they were standing according to Luke 24:3–4.

Failure to distinguish different times. John 20:11–12 happened at a different time from the events recorded in Mark 16:5 and Luke 24:3–4. Mary Magdalene arrived ahead of the rest of the women, and initially saw only that the stone had been rolled away (John 20:1). When she returned later and looked into the tomb, she saw two angels sitting (John 20:11–12). When the rest of the women arrived they saw at least one of the angels sitting at the right (Mark 16:5). The posture of the other angel is not stated in Mark's Gospel. The sitting angel may have then stood in greeting as is perhaps implied in Luke 24:3–4. However, the Greek words translated "stood" in Luke 24:3–4 do not necessarily refer to posture, but may be translated "suddenly appeared" as is translated in the New Living Translation. So, there is no inconsistency between the three passages when they are read in context.

276. What was Jesus' sixth commandment? Matthew 19:17–19 contradicts Mark 10:19, which contradicts Luke 18:20.

The fallacy of the argument from silence. The critic seems to think that if something isn't listed in the Bible, then it didn't occur. But the Bible itself explicitly refutes this (John 21:25). Thus, the Gospels each record *some* of the things Jesus did, and *some* of the things

---

2. Dr. Arnold Fruchtenbaum, *Messianic Christology* (Tustin, CA : Ariel Ministries, 1998).

He said. And the different authors made different choices regarding what to record and what to omit. But how is this in any way at all *contradictory*?

Some of the commandments Jesus quoted are recorded in Matthew 19:17–19; *some* are recorded in Mark 10:19; and *some* are recorded in Luke 18:20. None of these passages are contradictory; none affirm what another denies. But since they are partial lists, we have no way of knowing which commandment was the "sixth" that Jesus quoted at that particular time. And the writers are under no particular obligation to record the quotations in the same order in which they occurred chronologically. So, the critic's objection here is really quite silly.

277. Who brought Joseph into Egypt? Midianites (Genesis 37:36) or Ishmaelites (Genesis 37:28, 39:1)?

Bifurcation fallacy. Joseph was sold to a group of people that included both Ishmaelites and Midianites. The critic has not read the surrounding context or he would have known this (Genesis 37:25, 27–28). The Midianites appear to be the traders of the group that actually purchased Joseph (Genesis 37:28, 36). But since they traveled with the Ishmaelites, it is accurate to say that Joseph was brought to Egypt by both Ishmaelites and Midianites (Genesis 37:36, 39:1).

278. How many sons did God have? *Only one* (Jesus), according to John 3:18 and 1 John 4:9. *Adam* in addition to Jesus, per Luke 3:38. *Many*, according to Genesis 6:2–4; Job 1:6, 2:1, 38:6–7; and John 1:12.

Equivocation fallacy and genre fallacy. God has one *"only begotten"* Son (John 3:16, 18; 1 John 4:9), where the Greek phrase translated "only begotten" denotes "unique" or "one of a kind." There is only one Son who is of the same nature as God the Father, and therefore a person of the Trinity who is rightly called "God" (Hebrews 1:8). However, all who call upon God's name for salvation are adopted into God's family as children (John 1:12). And thus, God has many *adopted* sons —

believers (Luke 3:38; Genesis 6:2–4; Job 1:6; 2:1). That Christians are sons by the spirit of adoption is explicitly taught in Romans 8:15. So, there really is no excuse for the critic's blunder here.

The critic has also committed the genre fallacy in taking poetic sections of the Bible out of context as if they were literal narrative. The astute Bible scholar recognizes figures of speech when they occur in wisdom literature such as the Book of Job. By verbal imagery, even stars may be called "sons of God" (Job 38:7) since God is the "Father of lights" (James 1:17). But no one other than Jesus is ever called the "*only begotten* Son of God."

279. How did Jesus cure the blind man? Mark 8:22–25 contradicts John 9:1–6.

Equivocation fallacy: *which* blind man? Jesus healed *many* of the blind, and not always by the same method (Matthew 11:5). The blind man in Mark 8:22 is obviously a different person from the one in John 9:1–6, because the two men were healed in different ways.

280. How should strangers be treated? Exodus 22:21, 23:9; Leviticus 19:33–34; Deuteronomy 10:19; Jeremiah 22:3; Zechariah 7:10; and Matthew 25:35 indicate that strangers should be treated with fairness and love. However, this contradicts Numbers 1:51, 3:10, 38, 18:7 and Deuteronomy 7:2.

Sweeping generalization fallacy. All people should be treated rightly — meaning they should be rewarded for right behavior, and punished for wrong behavior. Since the majority of people don't commit capital crimes — rape, murder, etc., there are some general principles that apply to most people most of the time. This is true for the native or the "stranger." For example, in general, people should not be wronged, mistreated, or oppressed (Exodus 22:21, 23:9; Leviticus 19:33; Jeremiah 22:3; Zechariah 7:10); they should be loved (Leviticus 19:34; Deuteronomy 10:19; Matthew 25:35). The stranger who is innocent of a capital crime should not be put to death (Jeremiah 22:3).

However, God has authorized the use of force against those people (whether native or stranger — it makes no difference) who egregiously violate His laws. Thus, just as the innocent (of a capital crime) are protected under God's law, so the guilty are to be appropriately punished. Anything else would be unjust. Thus, public blasphemy is punishable by death. One example would be a non-priest who enters the tabernacle or desecrates the priesthood in disobedience to God's command (Numbers 1:51, 3:10, 38, 18:7). Wicked nations that are characterized by murder, rape, blasphemy, kidnapping, and so on, God will appropriately judge and He often used Israel to do it (Deuteronomy 7:1–2; Leviticus 18:24–25). Where is there any alleged contradiction in these passages?

281. Why did God turn the sundial back ten degrees? Second Kings 20:7–11 contradicts Isaiah 38:4.

Bluff and failure to read the text. God caused the shadow on the sundial to go back ten degrees as a sign to Hezekiah that God would indeed heal him, add 15 years to his life, and deliver him and the city out of the hand of the king of Assyria. Both 2 Kings 20:5–11 and Isaiah 38:4–8 explicitly state that this is the reason. There is not even a hint of inconsistency. Did the critic think that we wouldn't check?

282. Is Jesus peaceful? *Yes,* according to Luke 2:14; John 14:27, 16:33; and Acts 10:36. *No,* according to Matthew 10:34; Luke 12:51, 22:36; and Revelation 19:11.

Bifurcation fallacy. The critic's implication is that Jesus is either (A) always peaceful or (B) always non-peaceful. But such thinking is simplistic. Jesus brings peace ultimately to those who are repentant and have faith in Him; thus He is the Prince of Peace (Isaiah 9:6). However, to those who continue to rebel against Him, He destroys (Psalm 2:11–12). There is no contradiction or inconsistency in Jesus showing peace to some and destruction to others. In fact, God must eventually destroy the violently wicked from the earth in order for the righteous to experience peace!

Thus we see Christ's peace manifested to those with whom He is pleased (Luke 2:14), to His disciples (John 14:27), those who are in Him (John 16:33), those who are believers (Acts 10:36). And yet, to those who rebel in this world, even if they have family who are believers, Christ brings a "sword" (Matthew 10:34–36; Luke 12:51–53). So, that the righteous can have peace, God will destroy the unrighteous who prevent peace (Revelation 19:11). We also note that swords can be used defensively — to defend against attackers and as a deterrent to discourage them even from the attempt to disrupt the peace of the righteous (Luke 22:36). Where is the supposed contradiction?

283. Where did Jesus tell His disciples to go after His Resurrection? To Galilee, according to Matthew 28:10 and Mark 16:7, but Jerusalem, according to Luke 24:49 and Acts 1:4.

Bifurcation fallacy and failure to distinguish different times. Shortly after His Resurrection, Jesus told them to go to Galilee and He met with them there (Matthew 28:10; Mark 16:7). After this, He told them to wait in Jerusalem until the outpouring of the Holy Spirit at Pentecost (Luke 24:49; Acts 1:4). These happened at different times, obviously, as the critic would have realized if he had read the passages in context.

284. Did Jesus say, "Destroy this temple, and in three days I will raise it up"? John 2:19–21 contradicts Matthew 26:59–61 and Mark 14:57–58.

Failure to read the text carefully or in context. Yes, Jesus did say, "Destroy this temple, and in three days I will raise it up" — by which He meant His body (John 2:19–21). Matthew 26:59–61 and Mark 14:57–58 correctly report what *Christ's accusers claimed* He had said. They claimed that Christ had said that *He* would destroy the temple made with hands (a reference to the humanly constructed building) and rebuild it in three days. They were misquoting Him of course, and the Bible correctly records their statements — though their statements were inaccurate. The error belongs to the accusers, not the text of Scripture. The critic must not have read these passages carefully at all.

285. How did God address Jesus at His baptism? Mark 1:11 and Luke 3:22 contradict Matthew 3:17.

Bifurcation fallacy. "You are My beloved Son, in You I am well-pleased" seems to be the best English equivalent to the actual words spoken by God the Father to Christ at His baptism. The critic is perhaps bothered by the fact that Matthew puts the reference to Christ in third person rather than second person; "This is my beloved Son in whom I am well-pleased." But recall that quotation marks were not present in the original. Matthew's rendering is therefore likely what John or others reported to Matthew — not a quote of what God said, but rather the content or meaning appropriately rendered in third person by someone who is not Christ.

By analogy, consider two witnesses reporting an event to the police. The first witness named Mark says, "Then Betty said, 'This is my truck!' " The second witness named Matthew says, "Then Betty said that it was her truck." Now, a person would have to be rather dim to claim that the two versions are *contradictory*. Both are perfectly accurate. One is an exact quote, the other reports what was said from his perspective. Likewise, the Gospels of Mark and Luke appear to record the exact quote, whereas Matthew reports what happened from the point of view of a third person. In any case, there appears to be no inconsistency of fact: God stated that Christ was His Son and that He was well-pleased in Him.

286. What did the soldiers give Jesus to drink? Matthew 27:34 says "gall," but Mark 15:23 says "wine mixed with myrrh." Moreover, Luke 23:36 and John 19:29 say "sour wine" or "vinegar."

Bifurcation fallacy. Just before the crucifixion, they gave him wine mixed with myrrh, which Christ tasted, but refused to drink (Matthew 27:34; Mark 15:23). In Matthew, the text says "gall" rather than "myrrh," but "gall" is a general term for anything bitter, which includes myrrh. Later, during the crucifixion, they gave him sour wine, which Jesus did receive (Luke 23:36; John 19:29). It is unclear why the critic thought that there was any inconsistency here.

287. Did the men with Paul hear the voice? *Yes,* according to Acts 9:7, but *no,* according to Acts 22:9.

Equivocation fallacy. To "hear" can either mean to perceive sound or to understand words. The men with Paul may well have heard the voice of Christ, but they did not understand the voice. This is clear in modern translations of Acts 9:7 and Acts 22:9, such as the NASB, NIV, or NLT.

288. How did God tell Moses to get water from a rock? Moses was to strike the rock according to Exodus 17:5, but Moses was to speak to the rock according to Numbers 20:7–8.

Bifurcation fallacy and failure to distinguish two different events at different times (see #104). At *Rephidim,* God instructed Moses to *strike* the rock (Exodus 17:1, 6). At *Kadesh,* God commanded Moses to *speak* to the rock (Numbers 20:1, 7–8). The fact that the critic did notice that the command of God was different at these two different locations makes the critic's previous mistake (#104) absolutely inexcusable. This shows that he is not at all interested in the truth.

289. Was Jonah swallowed by a fish or a whale? Jonah 1:17 says fish, but Matthew 12:40 says whale.

Semantic anachronism fallacy. The Linnaean classification system by which whales are classified as "mammals" and not as "fish" was not invented until the 1700s. So, obviously the Bible isn't going to use that system.

The Greek word translated as "whale" in Matthew 12:40 in the KJV, is *ketos,* which includes both whales and large fish. Likewise, the Hebrew word for "fish" in Jonah 1:17 is *dag* and is not exactly the same as our modern Linnaean category. So, there is no inconsistency in the original Hebrew and Greek languages.

290. Who created heaven and earth? Genesis 1:1 and Isaiah 44:24 contradict John 1:6–10 and 1 Corinthians 8:6.

Bifurcation fallacy and specious reasoning. God created the heavens and the earth, specifically, God the Son — our Redeemer, the Lord Jesus (Genesis 1:1; Isaiah 44:24; John 1:6–10; 1 Corinthians 8:6; John 1:1–3; Hebrews 1:2) — though all the members of the Trinity seem to have been involved (e.g., Genesis 1:26). Does the critic honestly not realize that the Bible teaches that Jesus is God?

291. Who is for or against Jesus? Matthew 12:30 and Luke 11:23 contradict Mark 9:40 and Luke 9:50.

Specious reasoning. There is no inconsistency at all, not even an apparent one, between any of these passages. Collectively, they indicate that a person is either for Christ or against Christ, but that neutrality is not an option. In logic, this is called a biconditional: a person is for Christ if and only if he or she is not against Christ. Where is there even any hint of inconsistency?

292. Where did the women watching the crucifixion stand? At a distance from the Cross (Matthew 27:55; Mark 15:40; Luke 23:49) or by the Cross (John 19:25)?

Equivocation fallacy and failure to distinguish different times. None of the above verses give the specific location where the women stood. Matthew 27:55; Mark 15:40; and Luke 23:49, all indicate that the women were standing "at a distance" from the Cross. John 19:25 states that they were standing "by the Cross." But is that really a discrepancy? Note that none of these verses state that it was a *long* distance — merely "at *a* distance." Both "by" and "at a distance" are relative and subjective qualifiers. Both imply that there was some distance between the Cross and the women, and neither specifies exactly what that distance is. If the women were standing about 30 feet away from the Cross, it would be accurate to say they are standing "at a distance" from the Cross, and also accurate to say that they were "by the Cross."

We should also remember that the crucifixion lasted for hours, yet the critic seems to assume that no one moved for that entire time. Is that really reasonable? Couldn't the women have initially watched from a larger distance, and then moved closer to the Cross at a later time, perhaps to comfort Mary? In any case, there is no apparent inconsistency.

293. How are people judged by God? Matthew 12:37; Luke 10:26–28; and John 5:29 contradict Mark 16:16 and John 3:3, 18, 36.

Bifurcation fallacy and false-cause fallacy. Implicit in the critic's question is the claim that either all people are judged on the basis of their own works, or all people are saved by their faith in Christ. But this is a bifurcation fallacy because the truth is neither of these options. Rather, those who have not trusted in Christ are judged on the basis of their own works — which always results in condemnation (Romans 3:20; Revelation 20:13–15). And those who have trusted in Christ are redeemed on this basis and are "born again" and saved by faith (Mark 16:16; John 3:3, 18, 36).

Furthermore, the Bible teaches that salvation results in a person wanting to obey God (1 John 2:3–6), and therefore doing good works (Matthew 5:16). These good works are not an effort to merit salvation, but are out of gratitude for the salvation we have freely received (Hebrews 12:28). All the above Scriptures agree with this.

Namely, those who trust in Christ will confess Him as Lord, and thus are justified by their words (Romans 10:9–10; Matthew 12:37). Those who are saved will want to obey God's commandments (1 John 2:3–6), and will therefore love God and will love others (Luke 10:26). The critic commits the false-cause fallacy in thinking that John 5:29 teaches that good works result in salvation. John 5:29 does not teach that good works are the cause of salvation — only that there is a *correlation* between good works and salvation. But correlation does not imply causation. And from 1 John 2:3–6 we understand that salvation is the cause, and good works are the *effect* — the exact opposite of the critic's assumption.

Furthermore, the type of "judgment" involved in a particular Scripture passage's context may be different from the meaning of "judgment" elsewhere, due to the specific meaning of the biblical words that are translated (into English) as "judge" or "judgment." To illustrate, the English words "judge" or judgment" appear as translations of different Hebrew words (*dîn, dûn palal, pelilah, shaphat, ta'am, yakach*) and also of different Greek words (*anakrinô, diakrinô, dikastês, dikaiôma, hêgeomai, krinô, kritês*). Thus, in addition to recognizing context, it is also important — before jumping to hasty conclusions about "consistency" in what the Bible teaches about "judgment" — to learn which of the various meanings (of "judgment") is involved in any given Scripture passage.

294. Did Zedekiah see the king of Babylon? *Yes,* according to Jeremiah 34:3, but 2 Kings 25:7 says he was blind.

Failure to read the text carefully or in context. Yes, Zedekiah was captured, brought to Babylon, and saw the king of Babylon face to face, as prophesied in Jeremiah 34:3, and fulfilled in 2 Kings 25:6. *After this*, they put out Zedekiah's eyes (2 Kings 25:7). The critic cites only 2 Kings 25:7, but the fact that Zedekiah was brought to the king *before* he was blinded is directly stated one verse earlier (2 Kings 25:6). This again shows that the critic isn't interested in serious scholarship.

295. Where does God dwell? Psalm 9:11, 76:2, and Joel 3:17, 21 contradict Psalm 123:1 and Ecclesiastes 5:2.

Genre fallacy and bifurcation fallacy. First, the critic is attempting a hyper-literal reading of poetic passages — the genre fallacy. None of these are intended to give a physical location of God, as if God were a physical being. God is spirit — not a physical being with a specific and unique location in space (John 4:24; 1 Kings 8:27; 2 Chronicles 2:6). To the extent that God is anywhere in space, He is everywhere; He is *omnipresent* (Jeremiah 23:24; Psalm 139:7–10).

Yet, even if we take the verses listed by the critic as literal, they are still non-contradictory. Consider: God is everywhere. So, does God dwell in Zion? Yes — Zion is part of everywhere (Psalm 9:11, 76:2; Joel 3:17, 21). Does God dwell in heaven? Yes — heaven is part of everywhere (Psalm 123:1; Ecclesiastes 5:2). The critic has committed the bifurcation fallacy in suggesting that either God dwells in heaven or God dwells in Zion. But in reality, God is present everywhere.

296. How should adulterers be punished? Leviticus 20:10 contradicts John 8:3–8.

Sweeping Generalization fallacy and failure to read the text carefully. The Mosaic Law teaches that the penalty for adultery is death (Leviticus 20:10) *only* if there are two or more witnesses (Deuteronomy 17:6, 19:15) who are themselves innocent of the crime (Deuteronomy 19:15), in which case *both* the man and woman who committed adultery were to be punished (Leviticus 20:10). Moreover, the innocent witnesses were to throw the first stone (Deuteronomy 17:7). Jesus followed the Mosaic Law perfectly in John 8:3–11, for He required an innocent witness to throw the first stone (John 8:7), and apparently there were none (John 8:9). Far be it from contradicting the Mosaic Law, Jesus was insisting that it be followed to the letter.

YES OR NO?

In this chapter we examine claims that one verse of Scripture affirms what another denies. If one verse answers "yes" to a question, while another verse answers "no" to the same question at the same time and sense, then this would constitute a genuine contradiction. Such an instance cannot be a mere compatible difference, because yes and no are incompatible. A contradiction is *defined* as one premise denying what another affirms. This category of alleged contradiction is therefore the most serious — if the claims turn out to be legitimate.

297. Is it wrong to commit adultery? Exodus 20:14; Deuteronomy 5:18; and Hebrews 13:4 say that adultery is wrong, but Numbers 31:18 and Hosea 1:2, 3:1 teach that it is okay.

Failure to read the text. The Bible unilaterally denounces adultery as sin. Neither Numbers 31:18, nor Hosea 1:2, 3:1 say otherwise. Numbers 31:18 refers to virgin women that the Hebrew men would be allowed to marry — there is not the slightest hint of adultery. Nor does God endorse or approve of adultery anywhere in Hosea. Rather, God commands Hosea to marry an (at that time) unmarried woman (Gomer) who was or would become an adulteress. It's an unusual command, but it does not require Hosea to commit adultery, nor does it endorse the past or future adultery of Gomer. Even when Gomer is unfaithful to Hosea, God commands Hosea to love her and take her back (Hosea 3:1). Where is the supposed contradiction?

298. Did Jesus tell His disciples everything? John 15:15 says *yes*, but John 16:12 says *no*.

Failure to read the text carefully. In John 15:15, Jesus tells His disciples that He had made known to them *all things He had heard [i.e., at that time] from His Father* — that is, all those things pertaining to the Gospel and Christ's mission of redemption. The text does not say that He told them "everything" — as in every fact that God knows — which would be infinite. Nor does John 16:12 state this. In John 16:12, Jesus indicates that He has more to say to them, not with respect to the main doctrines of the Gospel which He had already disclosed to them (John 15:15), but on other issues. Neither John 15:15, nor John 16:12 indicate that Jesus told His disciples everything about everything.

299. Should you answer a fool according to his folly? Proverbs 26:5 says *yes*, but Proverbs 26:4 says *no*.

Failure to distinguish different senses. The sense is different between these two verses. Proverbs 26:4 indicates that a fool should not be answered according to his folly *in the sense of becoming like him*. That is, a person should not embrace the fool's standards. However, Proverbs 26:5 indicates that a fool should be answered in such a way to expose his folly, so that he cannot be wise in his own estimation. That is, the standards of the fool should be exposed as foolish.

The original Hebrew language uses a different form of the verb "answer" to make the distinction even clearer. In verse 4, the verb is in the imperfect form, indicating that it is descriptive. It describes the fact that we become like fools if we continually answer them by their standard. In verse 5, the verb "answer" is in the imperative; it commands us to answer the fool in such a way that he see his foolishness.

300. Did Asa remove the high places? Second Chronicles 14:3–5 says *yes*, but this contradicts 1 Kings 15:14 and 2 Chronicles 15:17.

Failure to read the text carefully. Second Chronicles 14:3–5 indicates that Asa removed the high places (altars) of the *foreign gods* from all the cities of Judah. However, these verses say nothing of high places that were set up to worship the living God (presumably before the temple was built). First Kings 15:14 and 2 Chronicles 15:17 confirm that not all the high places were removed; those dedicated to the worship of the living God remained.

301. Did Peter ask Jesus where he was going? John 13:36 says *yes*, but John 16:5 says *no*.

Failure to distinguish different times. When Jesus said "Where I am going, you cannot come" (John 13:33), Peter did ask where he was going (John 13:36). *Later*, when Jesus said, "I am going to Him who sent Me," neither Peter nor anyone else asked where He was going (John 16:5). There is no contradiction in a person asking a question at one time, and then not asking a question at a later time.

302. Did Jesus baptize anyone? John 3:22 says *yes*, but John 4:2 says *no*.

Failure to read the text carefully. Christ baptized through His disciples, but He did not baptize anyone Himself. That is, Christ's disciples baptized in Christ's name and by His authority. Had the critic bothered to read John 4:1–2, rather than just verse 2, this would have been obvious. John 4:1 states that the "Pharisees had heard that Jesus was making and baptizing more disciples than John" and verse 2 *clarifies* that "although Jesus Himself was not baptizing, but His disciples were."

303. Did Jesus tell His apostles to go barefoot and without a staff? Matthew 10:10 and Luke 9:3 say *yes*, but Mark 6:8–9 says *no*.

Failure to read the text carefully. No. Jesus told the disciples that they should not take *extra* supplies with them, because they would be provided with whatsoever they needed — "a worker is worthy of his support" (Matthew 10:9–10). Hence, they should not bring *two* tunics, *two* pairs of sandals, or *two* staves (Matthew 10:10). But it does *not* forbid wearing *one* pair of sandals, having *one* staff, and *one* tunic.

All three passages confirm this. Luke 9:3 says that they should not take "staves" — plural in the original Greek (in both the Matthew and Luke passage) — indicating that they should not have *two* staves, but one staff is acceptable. Mark 6:8 states that a "staff" (singular in the Greek), e.g., one staff, is acceptable. And Mark 6:9 indicates that they may wear sandals (but not carry an extra pair), but must not put on *two* tunics. So, all three passages are fully consistent.

304. Should we believe everything? First Corinthians 13:7 says *yes*, but Proverbs 14:15; Thessalonians 5:21; and 1 John 4:1 say *no*.

Failure to read the text in context. That love "believes all things" (1 Corinthians 13:7) in context indicates that the loving person accepts truth from God. All things *that God says* are true and are therefore to be believed (Romans 3:4; Matthew 4:4). However, words spoken by men should be carefully tested (Proverbs 14:15; 1 Thessalonians 5:21; 1 John 4:1) and rejected if they contradict God's Word (Galatians 1:8–9; Acts 17:11).

305. Can God do anything? Genesis 18:14; Job 42:1–2; Jeremiah 32:17, 27; Matthew 19:26; Mark 10:27; Luke 1:37, 18:27; and Revelation 19:6 all affirm that He can. But Judges 1:19; Mark 6:5; and Hebrews 6:18 mention things God cannot do.

Equivocation fallacy. "Anything" can mean any (actual) thing that is logically possible, or it can mean "anything" including hypothetical absurdities, contradictions, etc. God can do anything that is logically possible, anything that is in line with His self-consistent nature (Genesis 18:14; Job 42:1–2; Jeremiah 32:17, 27; Matthew 19:26; Mark 10:27; Luke 1:37, 18:27; Revelation 19:6). But He cannot do things that are logically absurd or contradictory, such as lie (Hebrews 6:18), or deny Himself (2 Timothy 2:13). This is why Jesus could do only a few miracles in His hometown (Mark 6:5). It is not because He lacked the power, but because it would be contrary to God's will to heal those who are unrepentant and unbelieving (Mark 6:6; Deuteronomy 28:58–61; Exodus 23:25). Note that the critic's mention of the Judges 1:19 passage is a red-herring fallacy. This passage speaks of what the *Israelites* were not able to do due to their fear and lack of faith, not what God allegedly was unable to do.

306. Is casting out devils a sign of a true Christian? Mark 16:17 says *yes*, but Mark 9:38 and Luke 9:49 say *no*.

Failure to read the text carefully, and fallacy of commutation of conditionals. One of the characteristics that would mark the early Christians and show God's approval of them is that they would cast out devils (Mark 16:17). Mark 9:38 and Luke 9:49 confirm this rather than contradicting it. Jesus affirmed that those who were casting out devils were with Him, not against Him; the critic would have realized this if he had continued to read the next verses (Mark 9:39–40; Luke 9:50).

The critic could have made a more persuasive case if he had listed Matthew 7:22–23 as a counterexample. Yet even this does not contradict the passages previously listed, for none of these passages teach that saving faith is a *requirement* for casting out devils. Therefore, although casting out devils is a characteristic that would follow believers in the early church, it is not proof that one is a true Christian.

307. Is it a good thing to be childish? Matthew 18:3, 19:14; Mark 10:15; and Luke 18:17 say *yes*, but 1 Corinthians 13:11, 14:20 and Ephesians 4:14 say *no*.

Equivocation fallacy. In English, childish can mean "immature" and may reflect the self-centered nature often associated with young children, as well as reflecting their lack of critical thinking skills. The Bible unilaterally teaches that we should not remain like this (1 Corinthians 13:11, 14:20; Ephesians 4:14). But "childlike" can also be associated with the positive, biblical qualities often found in children — such as unwavering faith. And it is a very *good* thing to have child-like *faith* — indeed, this is required for salvation (Mark 10:15–16; Luke 18:16–17). At times, children recognize their helpless state and this produces humility, which is also a positive trait that we should emulate (Matthew 18:3–4, 19:14).

Note that the context of these passages makes clear that the sense is different. We are not to be like children *in our thinking* (1 Corinthians 14:20) but we should be inexperienced (like children) when it comes to sin (*also* 1 Corinthians 14:20).

308. Is God the author of confusion? Genesis 11:7–9 and 1 Corinthians 1:27 indicate that He is, but 1 Corinthians 14:33 states that He is not.

Specious reasoning. No, God is a God of order and peace, not confusion (1 Corinthians 14:33). And God approves of order and peace, and is pleased to give these to those who obey Him. But does this mean that God is not able to bring confusion or destruction to those who rebel against Him? Clearly not. Just as the God of peace (Hebrews 13:20) can bring war and destruction upon those who are evil (Deuteronomy 28:15, 20, 25; Leviticus 18:25–28), the God of order can bring confusion upon the wicked (Deuteronomy 28:15, 20; Genesis 11:4–9).

309. Is it okay to covet? First Corinthians 12:31, 14:39 say *yes*, but Exodus 20:17; Deuteronomy 5:21; Romans 13:9; Ephesians 5:3; and Colossians 3:5 say *no*.

Equivocation fallacy. The Old English word "covet" meant to desire *earnestly*. It is commendable to earnestly desire those things of which God approves. Conversely, it is detestable to desire those things that God condemns. In modern English, "covet" has mainly the latter connotation — to desire *wrongfully*. So, God encourages His people to earnestly desire godly things, such as the gifts of the Spirit (1 Corinthians 12:31, 14:1, 39) or the salvation of loved ones (Romans

10:1; John 17:24). But God disapproves of wrongful desires, such as for a neighbor's property (Exodus 20:17; Deuteronomy 5:21; Romans 13:9) or greed (Ephesians 5:3; Colossians 3:5). Is it really that hard for a critic to understand that God approves of godly desires, and disapproves of wicked desires? How could that possibly be contradictory?

310. Is it okay to curse people? Romans 12:14 says *no*, but 1 Corinthians 16:22 says *yes*.

Sweeping generalization fallacy and equivocation. To "curse" can mean to "wish evil, calamity, injury, or destruction" on someone, it can also mean "to swear at" someone, or it can mean to "excommunicate." The critic has conflated these different uses in selecting two verses where the word is used in two different ways. Although God may authorize exceptions, Christians *generally* should not curse others (wish them misfortune), as a Christian should be characterized by grace and not by bitterness (Romans 12:14; James 3:9–11).

However, Christians are required to excommunicate people under certain circumstances. This is what 1 Corinthians 16:22 describes. Paul here is not instructing Christians to "wish evil upon" anyone, but rather is instructing the Church to excommunicate those who profess Christianity but who do not love the Lord. There is no contradiction because the word is used in a different sense.

311. How did David kill Goliath? First Samuel 17:49–50 says David killed Goliath without a sword, but 1 Samuel 17:51 says that he did so with a sword.

Specious reasoning. The order in which events are mentioned is not necessarily the order in which they occurred; that's true in English as well as Hebrew. First Samuel 17:49–50 indicates that David struck Goliath in the forehead with a stone, causing the giant to fall to the ground and assuring David's victory — and that this was all done without a sword in David's hand. Thus, David won the battle with no sword. But how was Goliath actually *killed*?

First Samuel 17:50 states that David "struck the Philistine and killed him" but it does *not* say that these two events were *simultaneous*. That is, David did not kill the giant in the instant that he struck him with the stone, but rather shortly afterward. First Samuel 17:51 clarifies that David actually ended the unconscious giant's life by cutting off Goliath's head with a sword. When the text is read carefully, it is fully self-consistent.

312. Did Adam die on the day he ate from the tree of knowledge of good and evil? Genesis 2:17 says *yes*, but Genesis 3:6, 5:5 says *no*.

Failure to read the text carefully. This is a common mistake. But the Bible does not actually state that Adam would die instantly or *on the day* that he ate of the fruit from the tree of knowledge of good and evil. Rather it says, "in the day that you eat of it you shall *surely* die." (Genesis 2:17). The word "surely" is an important qualifier, and is a good way to translate a difficult Hebrew phrase, which is most literally rendered "dying you shall die." Yes, the Hebrew word "die" is used twice, indicating the certainty of it. It's not that death would occur on that day, but rather death became *certain* and unavoidable *on that day*.

Before Adam ate from this fruit, he was immortal. His death was merely a hypothetical scenario. But when he ate from the forbidden fruit, his death went from a hypothetical possibility to a certainty — and this happened on that very day. The dying process began immediately, and though it took many years to culminate, Adam's death was assured on the day he ate. Perhaps a good paraphrase into modern English would be, "On the very day you eat of it, you will become mortal." Genesis 2:17 therefore indicates the certainty of (the future) death of Adam if he should eat from the forbidden fruit; and indeed Adam became mortal on the day he ate the fruit as Genesis 3:19 and 5:5 confirm.

313. Is death final? *Yes,* according to Joshua 23:14; Job 7:9, 14:10, 12, 20:7; Psalm 6:5, 31:17, 88:5, 115:17; Ecclesiastes 3:19, 9:5, 10; and Isaiah 26:14, 38:18. *No,* according to 1 Kings 17:22; 2 Kings 4:32–35, 13:21; Isaiah 26:19; Ezekiel 37:12; Daniel 12:1; Matthew 9:24–25, 25:46, 27:52–53; Mark 5:39–42; Luke 7:12–15, 9:30, 14:14, 20:37; John 5:28–29, 11:39–44; Acts 26:23; 1 Corinthians 15:16, 15:52; and Revelation 20:12–13.

Elephant hurling fallacy, and failure to read the text in context. Perhaps the critic thinks that by listing so many verses that we will not look them up, and simply take his word that these are contradictory — the "elephant hurling" fallacy. However, many of these verses do not say *anything* about whether physical death is final/permanent. These include Joshua 23:14; Job 14:10, 20:7; Psalm 6:5, 31:17, 88:5, 115:17; Ecclesiastes 3:19, 9:5, 10; Isaiah 38:18; Daniel 12:1; and Matthew 25:26. How could they contradict about the finality of death when they say nothing about the issue?

The following verses all teach that resurrection from the dead *is possible* and *has happened or will happen*: 1 Kings 17:22; 2 Kings 4:32, 13:21; Matthew 9:24–25, 27:52–53; Mark 5:39–42; Luke 7:12–15, 9:30, 14:14, 20:37–38; John 5:28–29, 11:39–44; Acts 26:23; 1 Corinthians 15:16, 52; Revelation 20:12–13. The following prophetic passages also foreshadow the resurrection: Isaiah 26:19; Ezekiel 37:12; Daniel 12:2. So, there is no doubt that the Bible teaches that physical death is not final; resurrection from the dead (1) is possible, (2) has happened for some, and (3) will happen for everyone (John 5:28–29).

All that remains then is to see if any of the other verses listed by the critic contradict by teaching that physical death is final/permanent, and that there is no resurrection. In Job 7:9, Job poetically states that the death of a man is like a cloud vanishing — men go to the grave and don't come up; but he does *not* say that this state persists *forever*. Indeed, Job later states that after his "skin is destroyed" (death), "yet from my flesh" (his resurrected living body) "I shall see God" (Job 19:26). Job expected to be resurrected after death. So, there is no contradiction. After all, clouds do — eventually — come back again.

In Job 14:12, Job again states that a "man lies down and does not rise . . ." but it does not say that this state persists *forever*. Indeed, the rest of the verse says, "*Till* the heavens are no more." This is a reference to judgment day, when the heavens pass away and are remade anew (2 Peter 3:10; Revelation 21:1). That is, Job says that the dead do not live again *until* the final day at the resurrection.

Isaiah 26:14 states that "The dead will not live, the departed spirits will not rise" (NASB). Does this contradict the resurrection? Not when we read the verse *in context*. The passage refers to the tyrannical kings who have oppressed God's people (Isaiah 26:13) being destroyed so thoroughly that they will never again rise *to power*. They will of course be resurrected and judged, but never again will they live *in this world*, nor will they ever oppress God's people again. The passage is poetic, and does not exclude the resurrection. Thus, having examined all the verses listed by the critic, and having read them in context, we see that there is no rational basis for claiming any contradiction.

314. Can the devil capture us at will? Second Timothy 2:26 says *yes*, but James 4:7 says *no*.

Failure to read the text carefully and to consider context. The devil can certainly ensnare those who are sinful and unrepentant — those who are *not submitted to God* (2 Timothy 2:25–26). But the devil must flee from those who resist him if they *are submitted to God* (James 4:7).

315. Is the devil free to roam? Second Peter 2:4 and Jude 6 say *no*, but 1 Peter 5:8 says *yes*.

Reification fallacy and failure to read the text carefully in context. Presumably, the critic thinks that since the angels who sinned are kept in eternal bonds in hell, that they are not "free to roam" — as if angels were physical beings being held in a physical location with physical chains. But the Bible teaches that angels are spirits (Hebrews 1:13–14), and therefore do not have physical bodies with flesh and bones (Luke 24:39). So, the "chains" with which angels are bound are not *physical* chains that prevent *physical* motion. Yet, the critic seems to have taken them to be physical — a reification fallacy. Rather, they indicate a *restriction of freedom*. But just as physical chains do not restrict all actions, likewise, the devil is still free to tempt people (Matthew 4:1), and to figuratively prowl around "like a roaring lion seeking someone to devour" (1 Peter 5:8; NASB). Nonetheless, there has been a restriction on his freedom, and that of his angels (2 Peter 2:4; Jude 6) — much as a criminal on parole does not have unlimited freedom to go where he wishes. All the Scriptures agree that, yes, the devil has limited freedom to "roam" but that his fate has already been determined.

316. Does God desire animal sacrifices? *Yes,* **according to Genesis 4:4, 8:20–21, 15:9–10; Exodus 20:24, 29:11–37; Leviticus 1:5, 23:12–18; Numbers 18:17–19; and Deuteronomy 12:27.** *No,* **according to Psalm 40:6, 50:13, 51:16; Isaiah 1:11, 66:3; Jeremiah 6:20; Micah 6:6–7; and Matthew 9:13, 12:7.**

Failure to read the text carefully and in context. God does not desire animal sacrifice *in itself* (Psalm 40:6, 50:12–13; Psalm 51:16). Rather, He delights in obedience and right motives (1 Samuel 15:22; Micah 6:6–8; Matthew 9:13, 12:7). God gave the Israelites ceremonial laws regarding animal sacrifice to teach them about blood atonement and to foreshadow Christ (Galatians 3:24; Hebrews 10:1, 3). God was pleased when His people sacrificed animals *with right motives in obedience to His Word* (Genesis 4:4, 8:20–21, 15:9–10; Exodus 20:24, 29:11–37; Leviticus 1:5, 23:12–18; Numbers 18:17–19; Deuteronomy 12:27). And God was displeased when His people sacrificed animals *with wrong motives, or in ways contrary to His Word* (Isaiah 1:11, 66:3; Jeremiah 6:19–20). How is there any contradiction here inasmuch as the sense is different?

317. Must everyone die? *No,* **according to Genesis 5:24; John 8:51, 11:26; and Hebrews 11:5.** *Yes,* **according to Romans 5:12 and Hebrews 9:27.**

Sweeping generalization fallacy and equivocation. First, let's deal with the egregious equivocation fallacy of the critic in conflating the two very different meanings of the word "death." The Bible distinguishes between two different types of death: physical death and the "second death" which is *spiritual* death — separation from God's grace in the lake of fire (Revelation 20:14). Physical death is temporary and will be undone by Christ for everyone on the last day (John 5:28–29, 6:40; Revelation 20:13). But the second death, the lake of fire, is the final and eternal destination for those who refuse to receive God's mercy and forgiveness (Matthew 25:41; Revelation 20:10, 15; John 5:29). The critic has failed to distinguish which type of death is being discussed — an equivocation fallacy.

Must everyone die *spiritually* — the second death? No. Christians will not experience the second death (Revelation 20:6; John 8:51, 11:26). Note that the two passages the critic cites in John clearly are speaking of this second death. Context makes this clear. If the critic had started reading just one verse earlier, he might have realized his mistake; John 11:25: "Jesus said to her, 'I am the resurrection and the life. He who believes in Me though he may die, he shall live' " (a reference to physical death and life — you will die, but you will live again); John 11:26: "And whoever lives and believes in Me shall never die" (spiritual life — the Christian never dies spiritually).

Must everyone die physically — yes *as a generalization*. Hebrews 9:27 states that "It is appointed for men to die once, but after this the judgment." The verse gives the generalization that men have an appointment with death (the ceasing to function of their earthly bodies) that they cannot avoid. The Bible does allow exceptions of a sort to this general principle, as Enoch (Genesis 5:24; Hebrews 11:5) and Elijah (2 Kings 2:11), and on one common interpretation those who are believers at the time of Christ's coming (1 Corinthians 15:51–52). And yet, these are not so much exceptions as a different kind of death. Normally death involves "sleep" — a period of time between the death of the person and his resurrection on the last day. Yet the persons mentioned above are also changed from corruptible mortal bodies to incorruptible ones, albeit instantaneously with no "sleep" in between. This consideration shows full agreement with both Hebrews 9:27 and 1 Corinthians 15:51–52.

318. Should believers discuss their faith with non-believers? First Peter 3:15 and Colossians 4:5–6 say *yes*, but 2 John 1:10; 1 Timothy 6:20–21; and 2 Timothy 2:16 say *no*.

Failure to read the text in context, and elephant hurling. Most of the verses listed by the critic do not deal with the appropriateness of discussing *faith* with non-believers at all. They cannot contradict each other on that issue, because they do not discuss that issue. First Peter 3:15 does not say that we should or should not discuss our faith with unbelievers, only that we should be *ready* to give a defense of our hope.

Colossians 4:5–6 says nothing about the content of our discussion, but rather deals with the quality of our words — that our speech should always be full of grace. Second John 1:10 deals with false teachers — those who continually promote false doctrine and refuse to repent — and teaches that we are not to receive them into our house or give them a greeting in the sense of a blessing. First Timothy 6:20–21 instructs us to avoid profane and vain babblings: discussions that are empty of meaning or that are blasphemous. These verses warn that some who have not heeded this advice have gone astray from Christian doctrine. Likewise, 2 Timothy 2:16 instructs us to avoid "worldly and empty chatter" — again referring to meaningless or derogatory speech. It's not clear why the critic thinks that these different passages somehow conflict.

319. Does anyone ever do anything good? *No,* according to Isaiah 64:6; Psalm 14:3, 53:3; Romans 3:12; and Ecclesiastes 7:20. *Yes,* according to John 5:29; 2 Corinthians 5:10; and 3 John 11.

Equivocation fallacy and bifurcation fallacy. "Good" in what sense, and with respect to what? In order to do something good — something that is *pleasing to God* — it must be done with the right motive, with the right goal, and in the right way. The biblical teaching is that our goal should always be to glorify God (Psalm 86:12; 1 Corinthians 6:20; 1 Peter 4:16), our motive to please God (Hebrews 13:16; Mark 1:11; 2 Timothy 2:15), and our way as faithful obedience to God's Word (Deuteronomy 27:10, 28:1, 30:8). Now that "good" has been defined scripturally, we can ask, does anyone do good? The answer is:

believers — with the enabling of the Holy Spirit — can do good, but unbelievers cannot.

Although unbelievers might do things that seem externally good and have positive consequences (Luke 11:11–13), they never do this with (1) the right goal — to glorify God, (2) the right motive — to please God, or (3) in the right way — in faith and in obedience to Scripture. Indeed, that which is not of faith is sin (Romans 14:23). So, unbelievers are unable to please God due to their sinful lack of faith; even their seemingly "good" works are done with wrong goals, motives, and methods (Isaiah 64:6; Psalm 14:3–4; 53:3–4; Romans 3:12–18; Ecclesiastes 7:20; Titus 3:3; Genesis 6:5; Job 15:14). Note that the context of the above verses makes clear that this is the natural state of man *before salvation*. Even believers would be unable to do good apart from the regenerating work of the Holy Spirit (Romans 7:18). But with the help of the Holy Spirit, believers can indeed do good works (Matthew 5:16; John 5:29; 2 Corinthians 5:10; 3 John 1:11; 1 John 5:2).

320. Did Jesus drink on the cross? John 19:29–30 says *yes*, but Mark 15:23 says *no*.

Failure to read the text carefully. Jesus was offered wine mixed with myrrh (Mark 15:23; Matthew 27:34), which He tasted but was unwilling to drink. This seems to have been offered to Him *before* He was put on the Cross (Mark 15:23–24; Matthew 27:34–35). During the crucifixion, Jesus said, "I am thirsty" and so they offered up to His mouth a sponge of vinegar or "sour wine," which Christ received. Note that the text uses a different Greek word for the vinegar that Christ received on the Cross, from the wine mixed with myrrh that Christ had refused before His crucifixion. It is possible that Christ refused the wine because it would have dulled the pain, diminishing the purpose of the crucifixion. In any case, it is not a contradiction to refuse one type of drink, and then receive another at a later time.

321. Will the earth last forever? *Yes,* according to Deuteronomy 4:40; Psalm 37:29, 78:69, 104:5; and Ecclesiastes 1:4. *No,* according to Psalm 102:25–26; Isaiah 65:17; Matthew 5:18, 24:35; Mark 13:31; Luke 21:33; Hebrews 1:10–11; 2 Peter 3:10, 3:13; and Revelation 21:1.

Equivocation fallacy. Will our physical bodies live forever? In one sense, no, since all will die (Hebrews 9:27). But in another sense, yes, since the dead bodies of believers will be resurrected and glorified and they will live again (John 11:25). There is both continuity and change, since our present bodies will have been transformed into imperishable bodies (1 Corinthians 15:42). Likewise, the earth will "die" (2 Peter 3:10) and will be resurrected as a perfect, restored, imperishable world (Acts 3:21; Isaiah 65:17, 66:22). So, will the earth last forever? Yes, but not in its current state (Psalm 78:69, 104:5; Ecclesiastes 1:4). It will be remade and changed (Psalm 102:25–26; Matthew 24:35; Mark 13:31; Luke 21:33; Hebrews 1:10–11; 2 Peter 3:10) into a "new" earth in which righteousness dwells (Isaiah 65:17; 2 Peter 3:13; Revelation 21:1).

Note also that Deuteronomy 4:40 says nothing about the issue of the earth's permanence, but indicates that the Israelites were to keep God's commandments forever. Likewise, Psalm 37:29 teaches only that the righteous will inherit the land and dwell in it forever; the passage says nothing about whether such land will be transformed into an imperishable land. Likewise, Matthew 5:18 does not directly address the issue, since it merely states that the smallest part of the law will not pass away before the earth does — whether such an event is real or hypothetical is not said in that specific passage. These red herrings shows that the critic is not serious in attempting to ascertain the meaning of these passages.

322. Did Lot's daughters think God had killed every man? *No,* according to Genesis 19:21–22, 30. *Yes,* according to Genesis 19:31.

Failure to read the text. Genesis 19:21–22, 30 says nothing about what Lot's daughters thought. So, how can it contradict another passage on this issue when it says nothing about the issue? Did the critic actually bother to read the text? In Genesis 19:31, the first daughter says that "there is no man on the earth to come in to us." The last part seems key; she felt that there were no men willing to sire their children. Whether she really thought this, the text does not say. Whether she was using hyperbole, the text does not say. All we know is that she said this, and there is no other verse in Scripture that contradicts it.

323. Does the gospel of Luke contain everything that Jesus did? Acts 1:1–2 says *yes*, but John 21:25 says *no*.

Semantic range fallacy. Presumably the critic thinks that Luke was claiming to have recorded everything that Jesus did. But that is absurd on the face of it. When Acts 1:1 states that Luke wrote "about all that Jesus began to do and teach," the Greek word translated "about" is *peri*. This word means "of" or "for" or "concerning" or "touching." Moreover, the Greek word translated "all" is *pas* and in this context is used collectively; it means "some of all types." Just as "all kinds of animals can be found at the zoo" does not mean that each and every kind of animal is found in a zoo. Rather it means that the zoo contains a large variety of animals, that every major category is represented. Likewise, Luke wrote about, or "touched on" a wide variety of examples of all that Jesus did and taught. He did not, of course, record every breath that Christ drew, or every thought that Jesus had. John 21:25 confirms that Christ did many things that were not recorded in the Gospels.

324. Did the 11 disciples believe the two men? *Yes*, according to Luke 24:33–34, but *no*, according to Mark 16:12–13.

Failure to read the text carefully. No, the rest of the 11 disciples did not initially believe the two that had seen him while walking to the country (probably to Emmaus) (Mark 16:12–14). Luke 24:33–34 does not contradict this at all. It says nothing about how the disciples responded to the claim that Christ had risen; instead it says that Christ appeared to them. It does strongly imply that they doubted the Resurrection, since Jesus asked them, "Why do doubts arise in your hearts?" (Luke 24:38). So, there is no inconsistency at all.

325. Was John the Baptist Elijah? Matthew 11:13–14, 17:12–13 and Mark 9:13 say *yes*, but John 1:21 says *no*.

Equivocation fallacy. Obviously, John the Baptist was not literally the same person as Elijah (John 1:21). But he came *in the spirit and power* of Elijah (Luke 1:17), and can be said to be Elijah in a metaphorical way, in the sense that he represents his prophetic role (Matthew 11:13–14, 17:12–13; Mark 9:13). Note that Luke 1:17 (which the critic did not list) explicitly explains this.

326. Did Enoch die? Hebrews 11:13 says *yes*, but Genesis 5:24 and Hebrews 11:5 say *no*.

Failure to distinguish different senses. "Die" in what sense? Enoch did not "see" death in the sense that he did not experience the pain and indignity normally associated with death since God directly translated him (Genesis 5:24; Hebrews 11:5). But he did die in the sense that he has passed on from this world, and is now glorified in the presence of God, and has no more knowledge of or share in the present world (Ecclesiastes 9:5–6; Philippians 1:21).

327. Will Ephraim return to Egypt? Hosea 8:11–13, 9:3 says *yes*, but Hosea 11:3–5 says *no*.

Failure to read the text in context. Hosea 8:11–13, 9:3 describe the consequences of the sin of the people of Ephraim — that they will "return to Egypt, and shall eat unclean things in Assyria" (9:3). The verse employs the Hebrew poetic device of synonymous parallelism, where the same concept is stated in two slightly different ways. Namely, Egypt and Assyria were, at various times, enemies to Israel, and thus the "return to Egypt" is meant to remind the Israelites of their earlier captivity before God delivered them. The passage indicates that God will remove some of His blessings from Ephraim. Of course, Ephraim would not literally return to Egypt, nor be able to seek help from Egypt against Assyria (Hosea 11:3–5), yet Ephraim would endure bondage as they had when they were formerly in Egypt (Hosea 8:11–13, 9:3). So, the passages are fully consistent in context.

328. Is everyone descended from Adam and Eve? Genesis 3:20 says *yes*, but Hebrews 7:3 says *no*.

Equivocation fallacy on the word "everyone." All *human beings* are descended from Adam and Eve (Genesis 3:20; Acts 17:26). God is not. Melchkizedek is a pre-incarnate appearing of Christ (Hebrews 7:1). Christ is God, and thus (before the incarnation) was not descended from Adam and Eve.

329. Is God the creator of evil? Second Kings 6:33; Isaiah 45:7; and Amos 3:6 say *yes*, but 1 John 4:8 says *no*.

Equivocation fallacy on the word "evil." "Evil" can mean "wicked" or "unrighteous." In that sense, God does not create evil because He is perfectly holy and righteous (Leviticus 11:44–45) and all His work is perfect (Deuteronomy 32:4). "Evil" can also refer to destruction or "calamity." And God does indeed create calamity and brings destruction upon the wicked (Isaiah 45:7; Amos 3:6) — which is perfectly just and righteous. Only this latter meaning fits the context of 2 Kings 6:33; Isaiah 45:7; and Amos 3:6.

330. Do evildoers prosper? *Yes*, according to Job 12:6; Psalm 73:3-7, 12; and Jeremiah 12:1, but *no*, according to Psalm 34:21.

Failure to distinguish different times. Evildoers sometimes prosper for a while in this world (Job 12:6; Psalm 73:3–7, 12; Jeremiah 12:1). But ultimately, unless they repent, they will die and be condemned for eternity (Psalm 35:20; John 5:29). Where is there any inconsistency in prospering at one time, and being condemned later?

331. Did Moses see God face to face? Exodus 33:11 and Deuteronomy 34:10 say *yes*, but Exodus 33:20–23 says *no*.

Equivocation fallacy on the word "face." The expression "face to face" in these passages means "in person." That is, God talked to Moses *directly*, rather than through an angel or through a prophet. This is made clear in Numbers 12:5–8. (Notice that the text does not say that Moses "saw God's face.") Moreover, "face" can also refer to the "full presence" of a person — in fact the same Hebrew word (*panim*) is used for both "face" and "presence." Sinful man cannot live in the *full* presence of God, and cannot therefore "see His face" and live (Exodus 33:20). Consequently, God revealed only part of His glory to Moses (Exodus 33:20–23). So, Moses did not see God's face, but did talk with God in person, i.e., face to face.

332. Is it possible to fall from grace? Galatians 5:4; Hebrews 6:4–6; and 2 Peter 2:20–21 say *yes*, but John 10:28 and Romans 8:38–39 say *no*.

Equivocation fallacy. It is certainly possible to fall from the *doctrine of grace*; but people who have been saved by grace do not fall but persevere. That is, people may intellectually understand that salvation is by God's grace (the doctrine of grace) and then revert back to believing in the unbiblical concept of salvation by works (Galatians 5:4). They may intellectually understand the Gospel and enjoy fellowship with God's people, while never experiencing saving faith and thereafter return to a lifestyle of sin (Hebrews 6:4–6; 2 Peter 3:13; Luke 8:13). But those who are genuinely saved by God's grace will not fall away since God has promised to complete the work He began in them (Philippians 1:6; John 10:28; Romans 8:38–39). So, people can fall away from *grace as a doctrine*, but not from the *substance* of God's eternal grace.

333. Is it okay to call your father (or anyone else) "father"? Matthew 23:9 says *no*, but Exodus 20:12; Deuteronomy 5:16; Ephesians 6:2; 2 Kings 2:12, 6:21; and 1 John 2:13–14 all indicate *yes*.

Failure to read the text in context. Of course it is perfectly acceptable to refer to our earthly fathers by the term "father." The critic has not read Matthew 23:9 *in context* and has misconstrued the meaning of the passage. In context (Matthew 23:1–11), Christ is telling His disciples not to be like the scribes and Pharisees, who are quick to give themselves titles of honor in order to exalt themselves over others. They acted as if they were spiritually superior to other men. This, specifically, is what Christ forbids.

In the Greek, the term "your" as in "your father" is in the plural, meaning that Jesus is indicating that there is no father over all believers except God alone. No man can be the one spiritual authority over another man's conscience (father / teacher / master) because we answer ultimately to God alone. This is made clear by the previous verse (Matthew 23:8) where Christ explains that sinful humans are all on the same level; we are spiritually "brothers" and therefore should not elevate one as a spiritually superior "father" to another. Obviously, this does not forbid referring to biological fathers as fathers. All the other verses listed by the critic refer to biological fathers.

334. Did Moses fear the king? Exodus 2:14–15 says *yes*, but Hebrews 11:27 says *no*.

Failure to recognize different times. When Moses was young, and when he slew the Egyptian, he experienced fear and fled for his life (Exodus 2:14–15). At a later time, because of his faith in God, Moses returned to Egypt to free the Israelites, at which point he did not fear the wrath of the king (Hebrews 11:27; Exodus 10:29).

335. Should we look for signs in the heavens? Luke 21:11 says *yes*, but Jeremiah 10:2 says *no*.

Failure to read the text carefully. God created the heavens to give us information about time (Genesis 1:14–19). So, there is no problem in using the heavens to understand time (Matthew 16:2–3; Luke 21:11). Jeremiah 10:2 does not contradict this at all. Rather it says that we should not be "terrified" or "dismayed" by the signs of the heaven. So, the Bible denounces astrology, but endorses astronomy.

336. Should we fear God? *Yes,* according to Leviticus 25:17; Deuteronomy 4:10, 6:2, 6:13, 24, 10:12, 20, 14:23, 28:68, 31:12–13; Joshua 4:24, 24:14; 1 Samuel 12:14, 24; 2 Kings 17:39; 1 Chronicles 16:25; Nehemiah 5:9; Job 28:28; Psalm 19:9, 25:14, 33:8, 18, 34:9, 47:11, 96:4, 103:11, 13, 17, 111:10, 112:1, 115:13, 128:1; Proverbs 1:7, 14:2, 22:4, 24:21; Ecclesiastes 5:7, 12:13; Isaiah 8:13; Hosea 3:5; Malachi 2:4–5; Jeremiah 5:22; Matthew 10:28; Luke 12:5, 1:50; Romans 3:10–18; 2 Corinthians 7:1; Ephesians 5:21; Colossians 3:22; Hebrews 10:31; 1 Peter 2:17; and Revelation 14:7, 15:4. *No,* according to 2 Timothy 1:7 and 1 John 4:8, 4:18.

Two equivocation fallacies. The critic fails to define what group of people "we" refers to (Christians or non-Christians), and also fails to define what type of "fear" is intended. "Fear" can refer to a state of terror, to be afraid, as in fearing for one's life. Or, fear can refer to a healthy *respect,* as a child fears (respects) his parents whom he loves. This latter reverential sense is more commonly used in Scripture.

The Bible unilaterally teaches that *Christians* should fear God *in the sense of respecting Him* (Leviticus 25:17; Deuteronomy 4:10, 6:2, 13, 24, 10:12, 20, 14:23, 31:12–13; Joshua 4:24, 24:14; 1 Samuel 12:14, 24; 2 Kings 17:39; 1 Chronicles 16:25; Nehemiah 5:9; Job 28:28; Psalm 19:9, 25:14, 33:8, 18, 34:9; Psalm 96:4, 103:11, 13, 17, 111:10, 112:1, 115:13, 128:1, 147:11; Proverbs 1:7, 14:2, 22:4, 24:21; Ecclesiastes 5:7, 12:13; Isaiah 8:13; Hosea 3:5; Malachi 2:4–5; 2 Corinthians 7:1; Ephesians 5:21; Colossians 3:22; 1 Peter 2:17; Revelation 14:7, 15:4), but should *not* fear God in the sense of being afraid to approach Him (Hebrews 4:16; 2 Timothy 1:7; 1 John 4:8, 18; Mark 10:14; Psalm 56:11).

And what about unbelievers? Those who have not repented of their sin should fear God in *both* senses of the word (Psalm 2:10–12; Matthew 10:28; Luke 1:50, 12:3; Deuteronomy 28:68; Jeremiah 5:22; Romans 3:10; Hebrews 10:31). Note that all the verses listed by the critic fall neatly into one of these categories, with no inconsistency at all.

337. Was Jesus the first to rise from the dead? Acts 26:23 says *yes*, but 1 Samuel 28:11, 14; 1 Kings 17:22; and 2 Kings 4:32–35 say *no*.

Failure to read the text carefully. No. A number of people were resurrected before Christ (1 Kings 17:22; 2 Kings 4:32–25; John 11:43–44) and no verse — including Acts 26:23 — contradicts this. The critic might have realized his mistake if he had read several English translations of Acts 26:23, such as the NAS. Christ was not the first person to be resurrected. However, He was the "first to proclaim light both to the Jewish people and to the Gentiles" by virtue of His Resurrection. Moreover, Christ was the first to be resurrected *immortal* and glorified. All people who were resurrected before Christ died once again.

(Note that 1 Samuel 28:11–14 is *not* a resurrection, but the temporary spiritual appearance of a deceased person.)

338. Will the righteous flourish? Psalm 92:12 says *yes*, but Isaiah 57:1 contradicts that view.

Failure to read the text carefully and specious reasoning. When read in context, Psalm 92:12 teaches that the righteous will flourish *eventually*, just as all the wicked will be scattered and perish (verse 9) but *not always immediately* (Jeremiah 12:1). The righteous also will have trouble at times (John 16:33). Isaiah 57:1–2 does not speak to this issue, but rather indicates that when the righteous man dies, he is at rest and at peace and is spared from the evil to come.

339. Is it okay to call someone a fool? *Yes,* according to Psalm 14:1, 53:1; Matthew 23:17, 19; Luke 11:40, 24:25; Romans 1:21–22; 1 Corinthians 15:36; and Galatians 3:1. *No,* according to Matthew 5:22.

Bifurcation fallacy. The Bible teaches that unbelievers are fools, and therefore may be referred to as such (Psalm 14:1, 53:1; Matthew 23:17, 19; Luke 11:40; Romans 1:21–22; 1 Corinthians 15:36). However, it would be inappropriate to call a *brother in Christ* a fool, since Christians are not (Matthew 5:22). Luke 24:25 and Galatians 3:1 might seem like exceptions in English translations. But these two verses do *not* use the (Greek equivalent of the) word "fool," but rather the Greek word *anoetos* which means "not understanding" or "unwise." So, there is no inconsistency.

340. Is it good to be foolish? First Corinthians 1:21, 3:18, 4:10 indicate *yes*, but Psalm 5:5 and Ephesians 5:15 say *no*.

Failure to read the text in context and failure to recognize non-literal usage of language (semantic range fallacy). No, obviously, it is not good to be *literally* foolish (Psalm 5:5; Ephesians 5:15; Jeremiah 4:22). In 1 Corinthians, Paul employs a non-literal play on words to make his point more emphatically, as context makes clear. Beginning in verse 18, Paul explains that the cross (a reference to the Gospel message) is "foolishness *to those who are perishing*, but to us who are being saved it is the power of God." In other words, unbelievers consider the Gospel to be foolish; it *appears* that way *to them* even though we know it is not actually foolish at all, but is an example of the power of God. Context makes clear that Paul is not claiming that the Gospel is actually, objectively foolish, but rather that it seems that way "to those who are perishing" (1 Corinthians 1:18).

Paul continues this theme in verse 21, explaining that God used what the secular world considers to be foolish, namely the preaching of the Gospel, to save those who believe. He goes on to say that the Greeks seek (what they consider to be) wisdom, and they consider the message of Christ crucified to be foolish (verse 22–23). This metaphor continues in verse 25, where Paul says that the foolishness of God is wiser than men — the usage is obviously non-literal, because God is all-wise and therefore has no literal foolishness at all.

Paul picks up the metaphor again in chapter 3 verse 18, where he says of those who think they are wise in this world, that they must become foolish — in the sense of embracing the Gospel which the secular world considers to be foolish — in order that he may become *genuinely* wise. The two verses that follow make this clear.

They indicate that what the world considers to be wisdom (secular thinking) is what we must reject, and what the world considers to be foolish (the Gospel) is what we must accept, if we are actually to be wise and not fools. Paul is well aware of the irony, and uses it masterfully to make his point. He continues the theme in chapter 4, verse 10 where Paul indicates that he is considered a fool by worldly standards for the sake of Christ; he has given up worldly honor and worldly comforts (verse 11) for the sake of God's kingdom. But it is not good to be actually foolish, in the sense of ignorant or unbiblical, as Paul makes clear in Galatians 3:1. So, there is no inconsistency when the passages are read in context.

341. Can God be found? *Yes,* **according to Proverbs 8:17; Matthew 7:8; and Luke 11:9–10.** *No,* **according to Psalm 18:41; Proverbs 1:28; Lamentations 3:8, 3:44; Amos 8:12; and Luke 13:24.**

Failure to distinguish different times. God extends an offer of grace to everyone; and is willing to save anyone who will repent and call upon His name (Proverbs 8:17; Matthew 7:8; Luke 11:9–10; Isaiah 55:7). But, He does *not* extend this offer *indefinitely.* Those who continually refuse God's offers of mercy and salvation, at some point, will no longer have an opportunity to "find" God even if they should wish to avoid condemnation (Proverbs 1:28; Amos 6:8–9, 8:12; Luke 13:24; Matthew 7:22–23, 23:37–38; Hebrews 12:16). Of course, those who refuse to repent will never find God (Psalm 18:41).

Isaiah 55:6 explains this directly. "Seek the LORD *while He may be found,* call upon Him *while He is near*" (emphasis added). The qualifiers imply that God gives people a limited amount of time to repent and "find" Him. At some point, the door of grace closes (Genesis 7:11–16). It's a pity the critic didn't bother to read this passage, or he might have realized that all the verses he listed are consistent with it.

We note that Lamentations 3:8, 44 does not refer to "finding God" in the sense of salvation, but rather in God choosing to not answer a prayer in the way that the person wanted.

342. Do humans have free will? *Yes,* **according to Deuteronomy 30:19 and Joshua 24:15.** *No,* **according to Acts 13:48; Romans 8:29–30, 9:11–22; Ephesians 1:4–5; 2 Thessalonians 2:11–12; 2 Timothy 1:9; and Jude 4.**

Equivocation fallacy. The term "free will" can mean one of several different things. It can refer to our ability to make choices freely — volition. The Bible confirms that human beings have volition and can make some choices without physical external compulsion (Deuteronomy 30:19; Joshua 24:15). On the other hand, "free will" can refer to the ability to repent and choose to have saving faith in God *without any help from God.* The Bible denies this type of "free will" and instead indicates that we can repent and have faith in God only if God enables us to do so (1 Corinthians 12:3; 2 Timothy 2:25; Acts 13:48; Romans 8:29–30, 9:11–22; Ephesians 1:4–5; 2 Timothy 1:9).

(We note that 2 Thessalonians 2:11–12 does not deal with free will, but rather God helping the wicked to further deceive themselves. Nor does Jude 4 touch on this issue. Unsurprisingly, the critic seems not to have read these passages carefully.)

343. Does God ever get furious? Isaiah 27:4 says that God has no wrath. However, Isaiah 34:2; Jeremiah 21:5, 30:23; Micah 5:15; Nahum 1:2; and Zechariah 8:2 say that He does.

Failure to read the text in context. Of course God can become angry. No Scripture teaches otherwise. Isaiah 27:4 does not state that "God never gets furious," but rather reports that God has no wrath *at that time against His "vineyard"* (see verses 2–3), which seems to represent His people (Matthew 20:1, 21:33, 41–43). It's not a blanket statement that God never gets angry at anything, as the critic would have realized if he had bothered to read Isaiah 27:2–4.

344. Does God ever lie? *No,* according to Numbers 23:19; 1 Samuel 15:29, 7:28; Titus 1:2; and Hebrews 6:18. *Yes,* according to 1 Kings 22:23; 2 Chronicles 18:22; Jeremiah 4:10, 20:7; Ezekiel 14:9; and 2 Thessalonians 2:11.

Failure to read the text carefully. No, God never lies, and no verse says otherwise. God is truth and cannot lie (Numbers 23:19; 1 Samuel 15:29; 2 Samuel 7:28; Titus 1:2; Hebrews 6:18; John 14:6). But He does allow *others* to lie, and on occasion He even sanctions deception to those who are wicked, though He Himself never lies (1 Kings 22:23; 2 Chronicles 18:22; Jeremiah 4:10, 20:7; Ezekiel 14:9; 2 Thessalonians 2:11). Where is there any inconsistency?

345. Does God love everyone? *Yes,* according to John 3:16, 4:8, 4:16. *No,* according to Leviticus 20:23; Psalm 5:5, 11:5; Proverbs 6:16, 19; Hosea 9:15; Malachi 1:3; and Romans 9:13.

Sweeping Generalization fallacy and failure to read the text carefully. Contrary to what many Christians think, God does *not* love everyone. Indeed, there are some whom God hates due to their wickedness (Psalm 5:5, 11:5; Proverbs 6:16, 19; Hosea 9:15; Malachi 1:3; Romans 9:13). John 3:16 teaches that God loved the world (e.g., the inhabitants of the world), but it does not say that God loved *each and every* person in the world. John 4:8 and 4:16 do not speak to the issue, but perhaps the critic meant to cite *1* John 4:8, 16, which teach that God is love. That is, God is characterized by love, and love stems from God's nature. But it would be a sweeping generalization fallacy to conclude that God must therefore love *everyone*. After all, God is also merciful and characterized by mercy, but that doesn't mean that He extends mercy to everyone (Romans 9:15).

346. Does God know what is in everyone's heart? *Yes,* according to Acts 1:24 and Psalm 44:21, 139:2–3. *No,* according to Deuteronomy 8:2, 13:3 and 2 Chronicles 32:31.

Equivocation fallacy on the word "know." To "know" something can either mean to have *intellectual* knowledge about it (as from reading a book on the topic), or *experiential* knowledge of it (learning firsthand from experience). Both in English and Hebrew, the word "know" can take on either meaning, depending on context. If someone said, "I know how to juggle" we would naturally take this to mean experiential knowledge — that the person has, in actual fact, juggled before and knows how by experience. We would be surprised if he had actually meant it in the academic sense — that he had read books on the topic but had never actually tried to do it. The Bible distinguishes between these two types of knowledge, but the critic seems oblivious to this.

God knows everything intellectually because His understanding is infinite (Psalm 147:5). Therefore, God knows what is in everyone's heart (Acts 1:24; Psalm 44:21, 139:2–4). But God does not *experience* the outward actions of a person's heart until the person performs the action (Deuteronomy 8:2, 13:3; 2 Chronicles 32:31). And so, with no contradiction, we can say that God knew Abraham's heart before testing Him; but Abraham's actions were not *experienced* until he performed them, at which point God rightly said through the angel, "Now I *know* [experientially] that you fear God, since you have not withheld your son, your only son, from Me."

347. Is anyone good? *No,* according to Isaiah 64:6 and Mark 10:18. *Yes,* according to Mark 5:45; Matthew 13:47–48, 22:10; and Luke 3:50.

Failure to distinguish different senses. The Bible unilaterally teaches that no one aside from God is good *of himself* (Isaiah 64:6; Mark 10:18; Romans 3:10). However, those who repent and trust in God are treated by God *as if* they were righteous because Christ's righteousness has been *imputed* to them (2 Corinthians 5:21; Romans 5:19; Isaiah 53:11; Revelation 7:9). Therefore, those who have faith in God are counted as righteous (Romans 4:3–5), not by their own works, but by Christ's (Titus 3:5). These are the righteous that Jesus mentions in Matthew 13:46–48, 22:10. (We again note the critic's sloppy lack of scholarship in listing verses that do not exist: Mark 5:45 and Luke 3:50. Perhaps he meant Matthew 5:45 and Luke 23:50, but again these refer to those who, by faith, receive Christ's imputed righteousness.)

348. Is it okay for men to have long hair? Numbers 6:5; Judges 13:5; and 1 Samuel 1:11 all indicate *yes*, but 1 Corinthians 11:14 says *no*.

Failure to read the text carefully. It is *not* a sin for men to have long hair for the purpose of fulfilling the Nazarite vow (Numbers 6:5; Judges 13:5; 1 Samuel 1:11). No verse teaches otherwise. Note that 1 Corinthians 11:14 is not contrary to this; it does *not* say that it is sinful for a man to have long hair. Rather it says that long hair on a man is a *dishonor* or *shame* to him. That seems to be the reason why the Nazarite vow included such a provision; it was a way of humbling oneself before God — an outward sign of humiliation.

349. Is it good to be happy? Proverbs 17:22 and Ecclesiastes 8:15 say *yes*, but Ecclesiastes 7:3–4 and Luke 6:25 say *no*.

Failure to distinguish different sense. Good in what sense? There are both positive and negative aspects to being happy. So, it is good in some senses, and not good in *other* senses, but there is no contradiction or inconsistency. Happiness can lead to increased health (Proverbs 17:22), which is good. And happiness is pleasurable and to be enjoyed (Ecclesiastes 8:15). On the other hand, happiness and contentment can lead to complacency, which does not draw a person closer to God, and that is not good. So, our personal growth and increase in wisdom is often greater during times of sorrow (Ecclesiastes 7:3–4).Luke 6:25 does not address the issue, but merely points out that circumstances can change.

350. Should we follow our own hearts? *Yes*, according to Ecclesiastes 11:9, but *no*, according to Numbers 15:39.

Equivocation fallacy. Which heart — unregenerate or regenerate? Should we follow the sinful, unregenerate heart of fallen man (Jeremiah 17:9)? No (Numbers 15:39; Proverbs 18:12). Should we follow the new regenerated heart that God gives us at salvation (Psalm 51:10; Ezekiel 18:31, 36:26) — a heart that desires to obey God's law (Jeremiah 31:33; Ezekiel 11:19–20)? Yes. (Ezekiel 11:19; Romans 2:29; Psalm 119:70; Ecclesiastes 11:9).

351. Does God help in times of need? *No*, according to 1 Samuel 8:18; Psalm 10:1, 22:1–2; Isaiah 1:15, 45:15; Ezekiel 20:3; Habakkuk 1:2; and Hosea 5:6. *Yes*, according to Psalm 22:24, 46:1, 145:18 and Nahum 1:7.

Failure to read the text carefully and to distinguish the referent and the sense. God helps those who obey Him (Psalm 22:24, 46:1, 145:18; Nahum 1:7), though not always at the time or in the way that they wish (Psalm 10:1, 22:1–2, 24; Habakkuk 1:2, 2:2–3). God does not always help those who have acted contrary to His approval (1 Samuel 8:18–19; Isaiah 1:15–16, 45:15; Ezekiel 20:3, 6–8; Hosea 5:6–7).

352. Does God approve of human sacrifice? *Yes*, according to Genesis 22:2; Exodus 22:29; Leviticus 27:28–29; Numbers 31:25–29; Judges 11:29–40; 2 Samuel 21:1, 8–9, 14; 1 Kings 13:2; 2 Kings 23:20; and 2 Chronicles 34:1–5. *No*, according to Leviticus 18:21, 20:2; Deuteronomy 18:10; and 2 Kings 21:6.

Incidental fallacy and failure to read the text carefully. The critic has made so many ridiculous errors here that it is hard to know where to begin. Obviously, God does not approve of human sacrifice in the sense of taking people who are innocent of a capital crime and executing them against their will for the sake of appeasing God's wrath. Such an action is despicably wicked, and forbidden by God (Leviticus 18:21). Christ might at first seem to be the only exception to this, but of course He was not an exception because He died *willingly* (John 10:15–18). After all, *self*-sacrifice is biblically permitted — John 15:13; 1 John 3:16. But to sacrifice an innocent person against his will is forbidden by God, and incurred the death penalty (Leviticus 18:21, 20:2–5; Jeremiah 7:31, 32:25; 2 Kings 16:3; 2 Chronicles 28:3; Ezekiel 16:20–21). None of the verses listed by the critic contradict this biblical principle. Let's examine each:

In Genesis 22:2, God command Abraham to offer Isaac as a burnt offering, which *at first* seems contrary to the biblical prohibition against human sacrifice. But, had the critic read the rest of the chapter, he would have realized that God was merely testing

Abraham, and had no intention of letting him actually sacrifice his son (Genesis 22:11–12). Moreover, God used this example to illustrate the concept of substitutionary atonement (Genesis 22:13).

Exodus 22:29 says nothing about human sacrifice. Rather, the firstborn sons were to be dedicated to God — not killed! The firstborn of animals were indeed to be sacrificed, but the firstborn of men were to be *redeemed by symbolic substitutionary atonement*, as Exodus 13:12–13 *explicitly* states. This is repeated in Exodus 34:20 and Numbers 18:15.

Leviticus 27:28 teaches that anything set apart for the Lord is holy and shall not be sold or redeemed (in the sense of exchanged) – including men who are dedicated to God. This says nothing about human sacrifice. Leviticus 27:29 refers to those who have been "cut off" (Hebrew: *charam*), indicating those men who have committed a capital offense. Their punishment may not be substituted, but they are to be executed. This is not a human sacrifice of an innocent person, but rather appropriate capital punishment for someone who deserves it.

Numbers 31:25–30 says nothing about sacrifice or *burnt* offerings at all. Rather, it was how to divide the spoils of war. One in five hundred of every man or animal captured was to be given to the Levites for their use as a type of offering (as the critic might have noticed if he had read just one more verse). The text does *not* say that these were to be burned.

In citing Judges 11:29–40, the critic commits the incidental fallacy — confusing what God approves of with what happened. Here Jephthah made a foolish vow, to offer as a burnt offering the first thing to come through his door, which turned out to be his own daughter. The Bible records Jephthah's foolishness, but it does not sanction it. *God does not approve of Jephthah's foolish vow.* So, there is no contradiction. Furthermore, Jephthah may have substituted an animal to redeem his daughter's life so that she would not be killed, but merely dedicated to Temple service for life, and not allowed to marry (Judges 11:37–40).

353. Is it okay to make images? *No,* **according to Exodus 20:4; Deuteronomy 5:8, 4:16–18, 23, 27:15; and 2 Kings 18:3–4.** *Yes,* **according to Exodus 25:18, 20 and Numbers 21:8.**

Sweeping generalization fallacy and failure to read the text carefully. In general, there is nothing wrong with making images (Exodus 25:18–20; Numbers 21:8). However, God forbids *worshiping* images, or making images *of God as part of a worship service* (Exodus 20:4–5; Deuteronomy 5:8–9, 4:15–18, 23, 27:15; 2 Kings 18:3).

354. Is incest forbidden? *Yes,* **according to Leviticus 18:9, 18:12, 20:17, 20:19 and Deuteronomy 27:22.** *No,* **according to Genesis 20:12, 17:16 and Exodus 6:20.**

Failure to distinguish different times and semantic range fallacy. "Incest" in the sense of sexual relations between a father and daughter, or mother and son, is indeed forbidden, and this has always been so (Leviticus 18:8; Deuteronomy 27:20; 1 Corinthians 5:1). However, marriage between other relatives is necessarily permitted, since all people are related (Acts 17:26; Genesis 3:20). The remaining question then is this: is marriage permitted for *very close* relatives? The answer is: initially it was permitted and was logically necessary, since the children of Adam and Eve were all siblings — (Genesis 4:17, 5:4, 17:15–16, 20:12; Exodus 6:20). At a *later* time (over 2,000 years later) God added a restriction against marriage between very close relatives (Leviticus 18:9, 12, 20:17, 19; Deuteronomy 27:22). There are good reasons for this additional law, but these aren't necessary to show that there is no contradiction between a particular action being permitted *at one time in one circumstance,* and then that action being forbidden *at a different time in a different circumstance.*

355. Are we punished for the sins of others? *Yes,* **according to Genesis 9:21–25, 20:18; Exodus 20:5, 34:7; Deuteronomy 5:9, 23:2, 28:18; Numbers 14:18; 1 Samuel 3:12–13; 2 Samuel 12:14, 21:6–9; 1 Kings 2:33, 11:11–12, 21:29; 2 Kings 5:27; Isaiah 14:21; Jeremiah 16:10–11, 29:32, 32:18; and Zephaniah 1:8.** *No,* **according to Deuteronomy 24:16; 2 Kings 14:6; Jeremiah 31:29–30; and Ezekiel 18:20.**

Naturalistic fallacy, equivocation, and failure to read the text carefully. "Punishment" can simply mean *suffering* as when a boxer "takes a lot of punishment." Or it can refer specifically to suffering that is intentionally inflicted as the *penalty* for a crime. Now, in the first sense of the word, there is no doubt that people suffer for the sins of others. The Bible teaches this in many ways but it is especially obvious in Romans 5:12. God *does allow* the actions of wicked men to adversely affect the righteous. The ultimate example of this is Christ, who was innocent of any crime, and yet suffered an excruciating death because of our sins (2 Corinthians 5:21).

Do people sometimes suffer because of a rightly inflicted *penalty* on another person? Again, the answer is yes. When a father murders someone, and is rightly executed for his crime, his children suffer because they are now fatherless. Likewise, when God punishes a person's sin, this punishment may extend to others (Genesis 20:7, 18; Exodus 34:7; Deuteronomy 23:2, 28:18; 1 Samuel 3:12–13; 2 Samuel 12:14; 1 Kings 11:11–12, 21:25, 29; 2 Kings 5:27; Jeremiah 29:32, 32:18), even the children — especially if the children willingly follow in their parent's wickedness (Exodus 20:5; Deuteronomy 5:9; Genesis 9:21–25; Numbers 14:18; Isaiah 14:21; Jeremiah 16:10–12).

Separately we might ask, "*Should* we intentionally inflict punishment on people for the sins of others?" The answer here is no. People should be punished for their own crimes. And while that punishment may, as a secondary result, adversely affect others who are innocent (e.g., children become fatherless because their father is rightly executed for his crimes), we should not intentionally punish those who are innocent. The critic committed the naturalistic fallacy in confusing what *is* the case (the innocent suffer) with what *should be* done (we should not intentionally inflict suffering on the innocent).

Consequently, does God sanction civil government to put to death one person for the crimes of another? No. The government may only invoke the death penalty on those who committed the crime — not their offspring (Deuteronomy 24:16; 2 Kings 14:6; Jeremiah 31:29–39; Ezekiel 18:20; 1 Kings 2:31–34; Zephaniah 1:6, 8). Second Samuel 21:6–9 is not an exception because the sons here were *also guilty* as indicated by 2 Samuel 21:1. God Himself is under no such restriction; He may take the life of a child on account of the parent's sin (2 Samuel 12:14) since all life belongs to Him anyway, but the state may not. And when it comes to ultimate, final judgment, God will judge individuals based on their own actions and whether they have repented and trusted Christ (Ezekiel 18:30–32). All the above verses consistently apply these principles with no contradiction.

356. Did Saul inquire of the Lord? First Samuel 28:6 says *yes*, but 1 Chronicles 10:13–14 says *no*.

Equivocation fallacy and failure to check the original language. Saul did inquire (Hebrew: *shawal*) *in the sense* of asking God for help (1 Samuel 28:6), but He did *not* inquire (Hebrew: *darash*) *in the sense of earnestly seeking God's direction* (1 Chronicles 10:13–14). Two different words are used in the original language with two somewhat different meanings.

357. Will God destroy those that intermarry? *Yes*, according to Exodus 34:16; Deuteronomy 7:3–4; and 1 Kings 11:1–2. *No*, according to Genesis 46:20 and Numbers 12:1, 9–10.

Bifurcation fallacy. God condemns believers marrying unbelievers (2 Corinthians 6:14). And thus, Israelites were not to marry *pagans* from the surrounding nations (Deuteronomy 7:3–4; Exodus 34:16; 1 Kings 11:1–4) *as long as the pagans remained pagans.* But God blesses marriages between two believers, regardless of their nationality (Ruth 4:13; Joshua 6:25; Matthew 1:5; Genesis 46:20; Numbers 12:1; Acts 10:34–35). One such example is Ruth, a Moabite convert, who married Boaz. All the verses above are consistent with this principle.

358. Was Jarius' daughter alive when Jesus was approached? Matthew 9:18 says *no*, but Mark 5:22–23 and Luke 8:41–42 say *yes*.

Failure to check original language and failure to read the text carefully. Jaruis' daughter was at the point of death, but apparently still (barely) alive when Jarius approached Jesus (Luke 8:41–42, 49). The report of her death came while Jesus was on the way to the house (Luke 8:49; Mark 5:35). Some English translations of Matthew 9:18 seem to suggest that she had already died, but the Greek text does not actually say this; its meaning is rather that she was "near death" or "at the point of death" or that "she has reached the end of her life." This comports with Mark 5:23 which states that she was "at the point of death."

The critic's error is doubly ridiculous because Matthew records what Jaruis *said*, whereas Luke reports what was actually the case. There would be no contradiction in Scripture even if Jarius meant to imply "she is at the point of death, and by this time must be dead." It would simply mean that he was mistaken, and the Bible infallibly records his statement.

359. Did Jehoshaphat remove the high places? Second Chronicles 17:5–6 says *yes*, but 1 Kings 22:42–43 and 2 Chronicles 20:31–33 say *no*.

Failure to read the text carefully and to distinguish sense. Jehoshaphat removed only the high places *that were dedicated to the worship of idols* (2 Chronicles 17:5–6). Here, the word *Asherim* (translated "groves" in some English versions) indicates the image of Astarte, the Canaanite goddess and consort of Baal. Jehoshaphat removed these. However, Jehoshaphat did not remove the high places dedicated to the worship of the true God (1 Kings 22:42–43; 2 Chronicles 20:31–33).

These too were inappropriate, because under the Mosaic administration, sacrifices were to be offered only in the tabernacle/Temple. But Jehoshaphat perhaps considered this a lesser sin, or perhaps he was simply unable to prevent the people from sacrificing to God at these high places.

360. Did Abraham know God's name? Genesis 22:14 says *yes*, but Exodus 6:3 says *no*.

Semantic range fallacy and failure to read the text carefully. Yes, Abraham knew God's name (Genesis 22:14), as did many others before Moses. Exodus 6:3 does not contradict this in any way; it does *not* say "no one knew my name before Moses." Rather, it says that *by His name*, YHWH, He did not make Himself known to them (Abraham, Isaac, and Jacob). That is, the *meaning* of the name YHWH was not experienced by Abraham, Isaac, and Jacob. The meaning of the name YHWH implies the eternally, self-existent One — the One whose existence is not derived from another but exists because He exists. The word *YHWH* is a form of the Hebrew verb "to be" HWH with a Y prefixed to indicate that the action of that verb is continuing, because God's "being" is always continuous. He is the one and only eternal Being. And to whom did God first reveal the nature of His name in saying, "I am that I am"? That's right; it was Moses.

361. Was Joseph the father of Jesus? *Yes*, according to Acts 2:30, 13:23; Romans 1:3; 2 Timothy 2:8; Hebrews 2:16; and Revelation 22:16. *No*, according to Matthew 1:18, 22:45; Mark 12:35–37; and Luke 1:31–35.

Bifurcation fallacy. Since Christ was supernaturally conceived, Joseph was legally, but not biologically, the father of Jesus (Acts 2:30, 13:23; Romans 1:3; 2 Timothy 2:8; Hebrews 2:16; Revelation 22:16; Matthew 1:18, 22:45; Mark 12:35–37; Luke 1:31). No verse states otherwise.

362. Did Jesus know everything? *Yes,* **according to John 16:30, 21:17 and Colossians 2:2–3.** *No,* **according to Mark 5:30, 13:32; Matthew 8:10; and Luke 7:9.**

Bifurcation fallacy and failure to distinguish sense. With respect to His divine nature, Jesus knows everything (John 16:30, 21:17; Colossians 2:2–3). With respect to His human nature in His earthly ministry, he did not know everything (Mark 13:32; Luke 2:40, 52; Philippians 2:5–8). Note that Mark 5:30 is silent on the issue; Jesus may have asked questions rhetorically to which He already knew the answer. Likewise, Matthew 8:10 and Luke 7:9 do not speak to the issue.

363. Did Jesus bear witness of Himself? **John 5:31 says** *no,* **but John 8:14, 18 say** *yes.*

Failure to read the text carefully and in context. Yes, Jesus bore witness of Himself, but not *by* Himself. That is, He was not the *only* one to bear witness, as the critic would have realized if he had simply read the next verse — John 5:31–32. John 8:14, 18 fully agrees: Christ bears witness of Himself, *and* the Father also bears witness of Him.

364. To judge or not to judge. Do *not* **judge: Matthew 7:1; Luke 6:37; Romans 14:10; and James 4:12.** *Judge:* **Leviticus 19:15; John 7:24; and 1 Corinthians 2:15, 5:12–13, 6:2–3.**

Failure to read the text carefully and distinguish the sense. We are supposed to judge rightly by biblical standards (John 7:24; Leviticus 19:15; 1 Corinthians 2:15; John 5:12–13, 6:2–3). We are not supposed to judge *hypocritically* or by *unbiblical standards* (John 7:24; Matthew 7:1–5; Luke 6:37, 41; Romans 14:1–10; James 4:10–12). John 7:24 makes this distinction very clear, so there is no excuse for the critic's blunder.

365. Does Jesus judge people? John 5:22, 5:26–27, 9:39; 2 Corinthians 5:10; and Revelation 19:11 say *yes*, but John 8:15, 12:47 say *no.*

Failure to distinguish different times. The purpose of Christ's earthly ministry was not to judge the world but to save the world; thus, He did not come to judge anyone *at that time* (John 3:17, 8:15, 12:47). However, when He comes again, He will judge all those who have rejected Him (John 5:22, 26–27, 9:39; 2 Corinthians 5:10; Revelation 20:13).

366. Has there ever been a just person? *No, according to Ecclesiastes 7:20.* But all the following verses mention just/righteous persons: Genesis 6:9; Psalm 37:12; Proverbs 3:33, 4:18, 9:9, 10:6–7, 20, 11:9, 12:13, 21, 17:15, 26, 20:7, 21:15, 24:16, 29:10, 27; Ecclesiastes 7:15, 8:14; Isaiah 26:7; Lamentations 4:13; Ezekiel 18:5–6, 9; Hosea 14:9; Amos 5:12; Habakkuk 2:4; Matthew 1:19, 5:45, 13:49; Mark 6:20; Luke 1:17, 2:25, 14:14, 15:7, 23:50; Acts 10:22, 24:15; Romans 1:17; Galatians 3:11; Hebrews 10:38; Titus 1:7–8; Hebrews 12:23; James 5:6; and 2 Peter 2:7.

Equivocation fallacy. (Same error as #165, #218, and #387) No one is "just" in the sense of never having sinned except God Himself (Ecclesiastes 7:20; Romans 3:10, 23; 1 John 1:8, 10; Psalm 53:3). But many have been made just by receiving Christ's imputed righteousness; they daily follow His law, though imperfectly (Philippians 3:9; Genesis 6:9; Psalm 37:12; Proverbs 3:33, 4:18, 9:9, 10:6–7, 20, 11:9, 12:13, 21, 17:15, 26, 20:7, 21:15, 24:16, 29:10, 27; Ecclesiastes 7:15, 8:14; Isaiah 26:7; Lamentations 4:13; Ezekiel 18:5–6, 9; Hosea 14:9; Amos 5:12; Habakkuk 2:4; Matthew 1:19, 5:45, 13:49; Mark 6:20; Luke 1:17; Galatians 3:11; Hebrews 10:38, 12:23; Titus 1:7–8; James 5:6; 2 Peter 2:7).

367. Is anyone justified? Matthew 12:37 says *yes*, but Psalm 143:2 says *no.*

Equivocation fallacy. (Same error as previous). Man can indeed be justified by receiving (through faith) Christ's righteousness (Galatians

3:6; Ephesians 2:8; Romans 10:9–10; Matthew 12:3). But no one is righteous by his own merit (Romans 3:23; Psalm 143:2; Galatians 3:11).

368. Does God know and see everything? *Yes,* **according to Job 42:2; Psalm 44:21, 139:7–8; Proverbs 15:3; Jeremiah 16:17, 23:24; and Acts 1:24.** *No,* **according to Genesis 3:8, 4:14, 16, 11:5, 18:9, 17, 20–21, 22:12, 32:27; Numbers 22:9; Deuteronomy 8:2, 13:3; 2 Chronicles 32:31; Job 1:7, 2:2; Hosea 8:4; and Jonah 1:3, 10.**

Failure to recognize anthropomorphic language (genre fallacy) and specious reasoning. Of course God "sees" and knows everything (Hebrews 4:13; Job 42:2; Psalm 44:21, 139:7–12; Proverbs 15:3; Jeremiah 16:17, 23:24; Acts 1:24). No verse teaches contrary to this. The Bible sometimes uses anthropomorphic language for our benefit, a figure of speech in which the non-material aspect of God is described using human terms — as in the "eyes of the Lord" referring to God's knowledge of everything, even though God does not have physical eyes. When God "hides His face" is another example in which God shows His disapproval of an individual, even though God does not have a physical face to hide. The withdrawing of God's presence is another example of God showing disfavor, even though God remains omni-present (His power is immediately available everywhere). And God asks questions for our benefit for the purpose of conversation, not because He doesn't already know the answer. With these points in mind, we can see that the critic has not read carefully or thought about the passages he lists.

In Genesis 3:8, Adam and Eve attempt to hide from the Lord — but this is an error on their part and does not indicate that they could have possibly succeeded since God sees and knows everything. In Genesis 4:14–16, Cain went out from the "presence of the Lord" and regrets that God will hide His face from him — both indications of God's disfavor. Yet neither implies that God literally cannot see or know about Cain.

In Genesis 11:5, God is anthropomorphically described as coming down to see the city, a phrase used for our benefit since God already knows and sees all things. God and the angels with Him ask Abraham a question in Genesis 18:9; this is for the purpose of conversation and does not remotely indicate that God didn't already know the answer. In Genesis 18:17, God asks a rhetorical question — again. He's not asking for information about something that He doesn't already know. In verses 20–21, God is said to go down to the city to see, but this language is for our benefit; God already knew what He would find.

Genesis 22:12 relates to *experiential* knowledge; even though God has knowledge of all things, not all things have been experienced. Nonetheless, God already knew how Abraham would respond. The critic has repeated his error in #346. God tests people for their benefit, to produce endurance (James 1:2–4), even though He knows how they will respond. This is seen in Deuteronomy 8:2, 13:3; 2 Chronicles 32:31.

In Jonah 1:3, 10 we read about Jonah attempting to flee from the presence of the Lord. But was he successful? Of course not. Indeed, one of the main points of that book is that it is impossible to flee from God's sight. Genesis 32:27 gives another example of God asking a question to promote conversation, and to segue to Jacob's new name; the passage does not even remotely suggest that God didn't already know the answer. This same conversational question is used in Numbers 22:9 and Job 1:7, 2:2.

Hosea 8:4 is a poetic passage using a Hebrew figure of speech known as *synonymous parallelism*, in which an idea is expressed twice, using different words. Namely, God indicates that Israel has appointed rulers (kings/princes) that do not meet God's approval. This is expressed as "not by Me" and "I did not know it." Therefore, this does not indicate a literal lack of knowledge of these rulers, but rather God's lack of *approval* of them. He did not "know" them in the sense of enjoying fellowship with them (Matthew 7:23).

369. Is it wrong to lie? *No,* **according to Joshua 2:4–6; James 2:25; Exodus 1:18–20; 1 Kings 22:21–22; and 2 Kings 8:10.** *Yes,* **according to Exodus 20:16, 23:1, 7; Leviticus 6:2–4, 19:11; Deuteronomy 5:20; Proverbs 12:22, 13:5, 24:28; Luke 3:14; Ephesians 4:25; Colossians 3:9; and Revelation 21:8, 27.**

Sweeping generalization fallacy. In general, it is inappropriate to lie (Leviticus 6:2–4, 19:11; Proverbs 12:22, 13:5, 24:28; Colossians 3:9; Ephesians 4:25; Revelation 21:8, 27), and specifically to bear false testimony as in court (Exodus 20:16, 23:1, 7; Deuteronomy 5:20; Luke 3:14). Intentional use of false or misleading information that is intended to dishonor God or to harm innocent humans is a form of sin. Notice that the ban on bearing false witness was qualified by the phrase "against your neighbor" (Exodus 20:16).

So, the Bible does not forbid all instances of lying, but instead gives the generalization that we should be characterized by truth. Nonetheless, the Lord gives certain qualifying exceptions where it is permissible to lie, such as to save someone's life (Joshua 2:4–6; James 2:25; Exodus 1:18–20). Or God might authorize a spirit to deceive the wicked to their own destruction (1 Kings 22:21–22). The Bible teaches these principles consistently, without any contradiction.

The critic also lists 2 Kings 8:10, but in fact this is not an exception to the generalization, but simply sloppy reading by the critic. Here Elisha instructs the wicked Hazael to tell his king that he will recover from his sickness, meaning he will not die *from this disease.* Nonetheless, Elisha knew that the king would die by Hazael's hand, which is exactly what happened. No lie was told since the king would indeed have recovered fully from his sickness, if Hazael had not murdered him (2 Kings 8:7–15).

370. Was Lot a righteous man? Second Peter 2:7–8 says *yes,* **but Genesis 19:8, 19:30–36 says** *no.*

Failure to read the text carefully and to distinguish sense. Does the critic mean "righteous" as in *sinless,* or righteous as in *justified* by Christ? The critic confuses these two very different types of righteousness, but the Bible does not. Like all believers Lot was not righteous in the sense of having never sinned (Genesis 19:30–36; Romans 3:23; 1 John 1:8–10), but he was righteous in the sense of being justified through faith (2 Peter 2:7–8; Romans 4:3,6). (Note that Genesis 19:8, which the critic lists, is not likely an example of sin, but an attempt to stall and distract the wicked men.)

371. Will everyone see the majesty of God? Isaiah 40:5 says *yes*, but Isaiah 26:10 says *no*.

Failure to distinguish different times. Isaiah 26:10 says that the wicked, at that time, do not perceive the majesty of the Lord. Isaiah 40:5 reports of a time in Isaiah's future when all flesh will see the glory of the Lord revealed.

372. Should Christians be concerned with material things? Matthew 6:31, 34 says *no*, but 1 Timothy 5:8 says *yes*.

Equivocation fallacy. "Concerned" in what sense? We should not be concerned in the sense of *worried,* because God takes care of those who seek His righteousness first (Matthew 6:31–34). Note that Matthew 6:33 (which the critic conveniently omitted) does *not* say that we should not seek material things, only that we should seek *first* the kingdom of God and His righteousness, and then these things will be given; thus we should not worry. But we should work to provide for our family (1 Timothy 5:8). Where is there any inconsistency at all?

373. Did the Israelites kill every male in Midian? Numbers 31:7, 16–17 says *yes*, but Judges 6:1–2, 5 says no.

Failure to read the text carefully, to distinguish different times, and specious reasoning. In the battle Moses led against Midian, the Israelites killed every male Midianite that was present in the battle, *and* Midian's kings (Numbers 31:7–8). None of the males were taken prisoner. That the text does not include males that were not present in battle as being slain is obvious from verse 8, which adds that the kings were *also* slain, an unnecessary addendum if Moses had intended to indicate in verse 7 that all males in Midian (even those who did not go to battle) were killed. Obviously, those who fled before the battle took place were not around to be killed. The events of Judges 6:1–5 took place many years later, at which point Midian had been repopulated. No verse contradicts these.

374. Was Moses in good mental and physical health at age 120? Deuteronomy 34:7 says *yes*, but Deuteronomy 31:2 says *no*.

Failure to read the text carefully. Moses still had good vision and strength at age 120 (Deuteronomy 34:7). Deuteronomy 31:2 does not state otherwise, only that Moses said that he was no longer able to come and go; though he does not say why. He does *not* say that his inability to come and go was due to deteriorating health. Rather, it may have been because God had decreed that Moses's ministry time was nearly over. In any case, there is no contradiction. Even if Moses's health did decline rapidly only days before his death, this would not contradict Deuteronomy 34:7, which indicates that he still had health and good vision at age 120 (at an earlier time in that year).

375. Was Moses a good speaker? Acts 7:22 says *yes*, but Exodus 4:10, 14–16, 6:12, 30 says *no*.

Failure to read the text carefully. None of these passages address the issue, and therefore cannot contradict it. Acts 7:22 does not say whether Moses was a "good speaker" or a "bad speaker" — only that he "was mighty in words and deeds." That is, his words and actions carried great weight and must be taken seriously. The other passages the critic lists indicate that *Moses* himself at least thought that he was "slow of speech" and "unskilled in speech." Whether this was actually so, or merely an excuse offered by Moses, the texts do not say. Perhaps Moses truly was slow of speech; yet his few words had power because they were endorsed by God.

376. If God likes you, will everyone else like you too? Proverbs 16:7 says *yes*, but 2 Timothy 3:12 says *no*.

Sweeping generalization fallacy. No. The Proverbs were given as divinely inspired and true generalizations. They were not intended to specify what always happens in every situation, but rather what generally happens, most of the time. Proverbs 16:7 teaches that when a person's ways are pleasing to God, even his enemies will tend to be at peace with him. But this doesn't mean that he will never, under any circumstances, face persecution. Second Timothy 3:12 is occasional, meaning it is addressing a specific situation occurring at that time. Paul warms Timothy that those, at that time, who desire to live godly lives in Christ will face some persecution. But how does that contradict the general principle given in the Proverbs? Even Proverbs does not say that believers will *not* face any persecution.

The critic should have remembered a basic principle of Bible interpretation: later-written Scriptures presuppose harmony with earlier-written Scriptures — likewise, later-written Scriptures presuppose that the reader will already know about earlier-written Scripture. Readers of Proverbs should already know that persecution of believers, by unbelievers, was an occurring reality as far back as Cain killing Abel, so Proverbs 16:7 should be read with this presupposed qualification in mind.

377. Is it okay to take oaths? *Yes,* according to Genesis 21:23–24, 24:2–3, 9, 31:53, 47:31; Leviticus 27:2, 10; Numbers 30:2; Deuteronomy 6:13, 10:20, 23:21; Psalm 63:11; Isaiah 45:23, 48:1, 65:16; Jeremiah 4:2, 12:16; Hebrews 6:13; and Revelation 10:5–6. *No,* according to Matthew 5:34 and James 5:12.

Failure to read the text in context. Yes, it is okay to take oaths — but not to break oaths. Therefore, if you do not have any intention of fulfilling your oath, then don't make it. The Pharisees had taught that it's not so bad to break an oath as long as you swore by something other than God. It is this misconception that Jesus corrects in Matthew 5:34, and James corrects in James 5:12. Matthew 5:37 makes clear that Christ's statement in verse 34 is not meant to be taken as forbidding *all* oaths, but rather forbids making oaths that will not be kept.

378. Are all those of God who believe that Jesus is the Christ? *Yes,* according to 1 John 4:2, 15, 5:1. *No,* according to Mark 1:23–24, 3:11 and James 2:19.

Equivocation fallacy and failure to read the text carefully. The question is worded rather awkwardly. Presumably, the critic means to ask if a person believes that Jesus is the Christ, does that make that person "of God?" The word "believe" can refer to an academic assent as in "Of course I believe in the president" (that the president actually exists). Or, it can refer to a foundational trust as in "I really believe in our president" (trust him, affirm confidence in him). Clearly, a person can assent to the existence of the president without believing in him in a trusting way. Yet, the critic has confused these two meanings.

Mere academic assent to the existence of God or the deity of Christ is *not* sufficient to be saved — to be called a child of God (Mark 1:23–24, 3:11; James 2:19). However, a genuine trust in Christ that comes from a repentant heart is sufficient to receive salvation (1 John 1:9, 4:2, 15; 5:1), and is evidenced by a desire to obey God (1 John 2:3–5). James 2:14–26 clearly and explicitly teaches the difference between these two types of faith — mere academic assent vs. the genuine trust which results in obedience. So, again there is just no excuse for the critic's obvious error.

379. Do Christians need to obey Old Testament laws? *Yes,* according to Genesis 17:19; Exodus 12:14, 17, 24; Leviticus 23:14, 21, 31; Deuteronomy 4:8–9, 7:9, 11:1, 11:26–28; 1 Chronicles 16:15; Psalm 119:151–2, 160; Malachi 4:4; Matthew 5:18–19; and Luke 16:17. *No,* according to Luke 16:16; Romans 6:14, 7:4, 6, 10:4; 2 Corinthians 3:14; Galatians 3:13, 24–25, 5:18; Ephesians 2:15; and Colossians 2:14.

Sweeping generalization fallacy. Christians are morally obligated to obey all *standing* laws of the Old Testament that apply to them

(Hebrews 8:10; Genesis 17:19; Exodus 12:14, 17, 24; Leviticus 23:14, 21, 31; Deuteronomy 4:2, 8–9, 7:9, 11:1, 26–28; 1 Chronicles 16:15; Psalm 119:151–152; Malachi 4:4; Matthew 5:17–19; Luke 16:17). Obviously, neither Christians nor anyone else are required to obey laws that God Himself has set aside by later revelation — such as the ceremonial laws of the Old Testament (Galatians 3:24–25, 4:10–11, 5:1–7; Ephesians 2:15) which included animal sacrifice (Hebrews 9–10). All of the verses listed by the critic agree with this principle, with no exceptions.

Some of the verses listed by the critic are utterly irrelevant to the issue, suggesting that he has not understood them. For example, Romans 6:14 indicates that those who are saved are no longer under the curse of the law — the penalty for disobedience (Galatians 3:10); it says nothing about being relieved of moral *obligation* to the law as the very next verse makes clear! Nor does Romans 7:4–6 encourage disobedience; it again deals with the believer's deliverance from the curse of the law, not obligation to the law. Romans 10:4 puts an end to unbiblical attempts to be righteous through obedience to the law — for salvation is by faith; but the passage does not free us from obedience to the law. Paul specifically explains this in Romans 6:1–2, 15.

Luke 16:17 indicates that the Old Testament Scriptures were proclaimed before John the Baptist, and has nothing to do with the issue of which laws are obligatory in the New Testament. And how could 2 Corinthians 3:14 possibly be taken as freedom to disobey the law? Being no longer "under the law" means that Christians are free from the curse, *not* free to sin (Galatians 5:18, cp. 13; Colossians 1:14). In Galatians 3:13, Paul explicitly and clearly explains that Christ frees the believer from the *curse* of the law — not from *obedience* to the law! When critics bungle the text as badly as this critic has done here, it reveals the truth of 1 Corinthians 2:14.

380. Is the law of God perfect? Psalm 18:30, 19:7 says *yes*, but Hebrews 8:6–7 says *no*.

Bluff, equivocation fallacy, and failure to read the text carefully. First, we note that neither Hebrews 8:6–7 nor Psalm 18:30 even mentions the *law of God*. This again shows that the critic isn't interested in the meaning of the texts at all, and isn't reading the texts carefully, but perhaps hopes that people will not bother to look up the passages.

Second, the word "perfect" has several distinct meanings; in Psalm 18:30 the word has the meaning of "without blemish." In other contexts "perfect" often means "complete." Obviously, the law of God is perfect, in the sense of without defect (Psalm 19:7), because everything God does is without flaw (Psalm 18:30).

Hebrews 8:6–7 discusses not the law of God, but the Old Covenant — the sacrificial system that God ordained to symbolically point forward to Christ. There was no error or mistake in this covenant; but it was never intended to be the *complete* revelation of God. The Old Testament was, by design, merely one installment of God's plan that pointed the way to the final installment — the New Testament. In Hebrews 8:8, the author quotes the Old Testament passage that teaches exactly this.

381. Can women be church leaders? *Yes*, according to Acts 18:26 and Romans 16:1, 7, but *no*, according to 1 Corinthians 14:34–35 and 1 Timothy 2:11–12.

Specious reasoning. Acts 18:26 says nothing about women being leaders of a church; rather it teaches of a married couple who gently and privately corrected a speaker about the way of God. In Romans 16:1, Paul commends a woman who is a servant in the church; the passage says nothing about church leadership. Nor does Romans 16:7 (has the critic even bothered to read these passages?) First Corinthians 14:34–35 instructs women not to disrupt a church service by asking questions, but to save those for home discussion. The context (1 Corinthians 14:26–40) makes clear that Paul is not forbidding women to speak in an absolute sense, or at appropriate times; rather, he forbids the disruption of an orderly worship service (verse 40). Note that 1 Corinthians 14 says nothing about women being church leaders. So, how could any of these passages possibly contradict on an issue that none of them even address?

First Timothy 2:11–12 also says nothing about women leadership in the church in general; but it does forbid a woman *exercising teaching authority over a man*. This might be considered a restriction on the types of leadership a woman may have in the church. But it does not deny, for example, a woman's freedom to lead a Sunday school class for women. In any case, there appears to be no inconsistency at all.

382. Should Christians pray in public? Matthew 6:5–6 says *no*, but 1 Timothy 2:8 says *yes*.

Hasty generalization fallacy and failure to read the text carefully. God isn't so concerned about *where* people pray as He is about *how* they pray, which is clearly the context of Matthew 6:5–6. Here, Jesus warns about praying hypocritically and for the purpose of being "seen by men" — self-glorification. It would be better to pray in private, than to pray aloud if the latter is for self-glorification. But this does not imply that public prayer is forbidden if done to the glory of God, as the critic would have realized if he had read the next several verses, where Jesus Himself prays in public (Matthew 6:9–13). So, Paul is perfectly consistent in wanting men in all parts of the world to pray within the church and without dissension (1 Timothy 2:8), so long as such prayer is not hypocritical and for self-glorification (Matthew 6:5).

383. Should we rejoice when we see our enemies suffer? Psalm 58:10 says *yes*, but Proverbs 24:17 says *no*.

Failure to read the text carefully and specious reasoning. No. The Book of Proverbs often uses the term "enemy" to refer to someone who is hostile but not actively attempting to murder — someone who is antagonistic but non-violent. When misfortune befalls such a person, Proverbs 24:17 indicates that we should not gloat. This Proverb forbids schadenfreude, but does not forbid rejoicing when God vanquishes the wicked in final judgment, as taught in Psalm 58:10. This is not rejoicing in their suffering, but rather rejoicing in the triumph of good. Obviously, there is a profound difference in rejoicing over victory in battle against murderous foes and petty gloating over the misfortune of an antagonist.

384. Is it okay for a divorced woman to remarry? Deuteronomy 24:1–2 says *yes*, but Luke 16:18 says *no*.

Failure to read the text carefully and specious reasoning. There are many nuances in understanding the biblical position on divorce, but these are not needed to expose the critic's sloppy reasoning in thinking that these two verses are somehow contradictory. First, the critic does not specify in what sense he uses the word "okay." Something might be okay in a *legal* sense, but *not* okay in a *moral* sense — such as the sin of coveting. Jesus is speaking to the moral issue in Luke 16:18, whereas Deuteronomy 24:1–2 appears to be dealing with what is legally tolerated. Moreover, Deuteronomy 24:1–4 appears to be a single unit, as worded in the NASB, NIV, and NKJV. So, it does *not* appear to teach anything about the acceptability of a divorced woman marrying another — only that *if* this happens, then the first husband may not remarry her. So, obviously, it cannot contradict another verse on an issue that it does not address.

385. Does God repent? *No*, according to Numbers 3:19; 1 Samuel 15:29; Ezekiel 24:14; Malachi 3:6; and James 1:17. *Yes*, according to Genesis 6:6; Exodus 32:14; Deuteronomy 32:36; 1 Samuel 15:11, 35; 2 Samuel 24:16; 1 Chronicles 21:15; Isaiah 38:1–5; Jeremiah 15:6, 18:8, 26:3, 13, 19, 42:10; Amos 7:3, 6; and Jonah 3:10.

Equivocation fallacy (*a very obvious one*). In Scripture, the word "repent" is used to mean three different things depending on context (which the critic has ignored). "Repent" can mean: (1) to feel anguish/sorrow, as in, "It repents me that people are so greedy." This usage was more common in Old-English than today, hence the KJV uses this more frequently than modern translations. (2) To change a *conditional* plan in light of the conditions: "I was considering punishing my son for stealing those cookies; but he owned up to it and has made restitution, so I have repented of that plan." (3) To regret an earlier injustice and change actual plans for the future or make amends, as in, "I used to cheat on my taxes, but I have repented of this." God can repent in the first two senses of the word, but not in the last sense because God has not done (and cannot do) anything wrong to regret (Deuteronomy 32:4).

It also should be noticed that the English word "repent" is used to translate different Hebrew words (*nacham* in niphal form, *nacham* in hithpaêl form, *shûb*) and different Greek words (*metanoeô, metamelomai*). So, the critic should be responsible in his criticism (by using a proper Bible concordance that differentiates between English words based on the actual words that they translate) to respect these differences of meaning.

Thus, God does "repent" in the Old-English sense of feeling sorrow (Genesis 6:6; 1 Samuel 15:11, 35; 2 Samuel 24:16; 1 Chronicles 21:15.) Some of God's promises are *conditional* (either explicitly or implicitly), and thus the promised outcome is enacted *only* if the conditions are met (Deuteronomy 28:1–14, 15–45; Jeremiah 18:8; Isaiah 38:1–5). For example, God often promises to punish the wicked *unless* they turn from their wickedness, but when they do turn, God "repents" of the stated conditional punishment (Jeremiah 26:13, 19, 42:10; Amos 7:2–3, 5–6; Jonah 3:10).

Of course, in all these cases God knew what the outcome would be and had planned it all along; so He didn't really change His mind. Rather, the people changed *their* minds, and such an action was a direct result of God's promise to punish them if they didn't (Jeremiah 15:6, 26:3–6, 13). A really interesting case of this is Exodus 32:10–14, where God's conditional plan to destroy Israel moves Moses to intercede on their behalf. God responds to such intercession and repents of the conditional plan to destroy Israel, even though God knew all along that Moses would intercede and that Israel would therefore be spared. God ordains not only the ends of His plan, but also the means.

But God never changes His unconditional plans and promises (Numbers 23:19; Isaiah 15:29; Ezekiel 24:14), or genuinely regrets any of His previous actions, since all His ways are perfect (Deuteronomy 32:4). Thus, God never "repents" in the penitent sense of the term, since He does not change (Malachi 3:6).

386. Does God respect anyone? *Yes,* **according to Genesis 4:4; Exodus 2:25; Leviticus 26:9; 2 Kings 13:23; and Psalm 138:6.** *No,* **according to Deuteronomy 10:17; 2 Chronicles 19:7; Acts 10:34; Romans 2:11; Galatians 2:6; Ephesians 6:9; Colossians 3:25; and 1 Peter 1:17.**

Equivocation fallacy. Here again, the critic picks an equivocal word which he never defines, and then criticizes Scripture for using the term rightly. The English word *respect* means "to show favor," but this can be done in at least two *very different* ways. 1. "Respect" can mean to hold a person or action in high esteem or honor — which God certainly does (Genesis 4:4; Exodus 2:25; Leviticus 26:9; 2 Kings 13:23). 2. Alternatively, "respect" can mean to show *unfair* favoritism that distorts justice*, to show partiality in judgment* — which God never does and forbids us to do (Deuteronomy 10:17; 2 Chronicles 19:7; Acts 10:34; Romans 2:11; Galatians 2:6; Ephesians 6:9; Colossians 3:25; 1 Peter 1:17; Proverbs 24:23, 28:21). So, the above verses show perfect agreement, because there is no contradiction in God honoring people, and yet showing perfect fairness in judgment. In fact, although these two very different meanings are both translated as "respect" in the King James Version of Scripture, the original language uses *different* words entirely, so the critic obviously has not done any study on this issue at all.

387. Has there ever been a righteous person? *No,* **according to Job 15:14; Isaiah 41:26, 64:6; and Romans 3:10.** *Yes,* **according to Genesis 7:1; 2 Samuel 22:25; Job 2:3; Psalm 1:5–6; Ecclesiastes 9:1; Ezekiel 14:14, 20; Matthew 5:20, 23:35, 25:46; Luke 1:6; Hebrews 11:4; James 5:16; and 2 Peters 2:5, 2:7–8.**

Equivocation fallacy and failure to read the text in context (see also #366). The critic uses the equivocal word "righteous" without specifying what he means by it. "Righteous" is used in at least three ways in Scripture:

(1) "Righteous" can refer to actual sinless perfection. Only God is perfect in this sense, although God's people will become such in the eternal state (1 John 3:2). After the Fall of Adam, no man besides Christ has ever been righteous in the sense of sinless and perfect (Ecclesiastes 7:20; Romans 3:10, 23; Job 15:14; Isaiah 41:26, 64:6). No verse contradicts this.

(2) "Righteous" can refer to positional perfection; this pertains to repentant people who have saving faith in God. God treats them *as if* they were sinless and righteous (Romans 4:3) since Christ paid for their sins (2 Corinthians 5:21; 1 John 1:7; Romans 4:7–8), while the people continue to struggle with besetting sins. All who are saved fall into this category (Genesis 7:1; Psalm 1:5–6; Ecclesiastes 9:1; Matthew 5:20, 23:35, 25:46; Hebrews 11:4; 2 Peter 2:5, 7–8).

(3) "Righteous" can refer to practical obedience — to those who love God and attempt to obey Him out of gratitude for salvation. Such people still sin from time to time, but are repentant, and are generally obedient as a way of life. These persons have already been made positionally righteous, and so this meaning overlaps greatly with the previous one (1 John 3:7). The heroes of the faith have this type of righteousness (Job 2:3; Hebrews 11:7; 2 Samuel 22:21, 25; Ezekiel 14:14, 20; Luke 1:6; James 5:16). So, there is no inconsistency when the texts are read in context.

388. Does righteousness come from following the Law? Luke 1:6 says *yes*, but Galatians 2:21 says *no*.

Equivocation fallacy (same as previous) and false-cause fallacy. Again, the critic equivocates on the word "righteousness," which is used in two different senses in the two passages he lists. "Righteousness" in the sense of sinless perfection cannot be attained by obedience to the law (Galatians 2:21), because no one obeys the law perfectly (Ecclesiastes 7:20). But "righteousness," in the sense of *general* obedience to God as a way of life in gratitude for salvation, is the lifestyle of all true believers — including John the Baptist's parents (Luke 1:6). Furthermore, obedience to the law is not the cause of righteousness, but rather the effect of righteousness (1 John 2:3–6).

389. Is it necessary to keep the Sabbath? *Yes,* according to Exodus 16:29, 20:8, 31:13–15, 34:21, 35:2; Leviticus 19:3, 30, 23:3; Numbers 15:32, 36; Deuteronomy 5:12; and Isaiah 56:2. *No,* according to Isaiah 1:13; Matthew 12:2; John 5:16; Romans 14:5; and Colossians 2:16.

Failure to distinguish different times, failure to read the text carefully, and specious reasoning. It is a commandment of God to keep the Sabbath day holy — to set aside one day a week to rest in reverence to God (Exodus 16:29, 20:8, 31:13–15, 34:21, 35:2; Leviticus 19:3, 30, 23:3; Numbers 15:30, 32, 26; Deuteronomy 5:12; Isaiah 56:2). The context for this commandment (Exodus 20:8–11) is in appreciation for God's actions as Creator of the universe. There are no verses that teach contrary to this — that encourage a violation of the Sabbath day rest. So, what about the verses the critic lists?

Isaiah 1:13 does *not* do away with the Sabbath; rather, it shows God's displeasure in Israel's failure to keep the Sabbath day *with the right attitude.* The people were bringing worthless offerings, not genuine worship with a repentant heart. And God was sick of that. But He didn't instruct them to stop observing the Sabbath day — only to stop their sinful way of observing it.

The remaining passages are all New Testament — and thus apply at a different *time.* So, even if these verses set aside the Sabbath day law (which they do not), this would not contradict the fact that the Sabbath day law applied in the Old Testament. After all, a contradiction is "A" and "not-A" *at the same time* and in the same sense.

In Matthew 12:2 and John 5:16, the Jews accuse Jesus of breaking the Sabbath, because He had healed on the Sabbath. But there is no biblical law against healing on the Sabbath. Nor is there any law that classifies healing as a type of work that cannot be performed on the Sabbath. Christ had violated no law (Hebrews 4:15).

Romans 14:5 says nothing about the Sabbath day; it certainly doesn't do away with it. Rather, it has to do with whether people celebrate certain festivals. Likewise, Colossians 2:16 says nothing about doing away with the Sabbath day — only that no one can act as your judge in matters regarding food, drink, festivals, and

Sabbaths. Moreover, the word *day* is not in the Greek text in this verse; thus, "Sabbath" likely refers to other Sabbath patterns, such as the Sabbath year. The Old Testament laws of Moses included many "Sabbaths."

390. Did the Samaritans receive Jesus? *No*, according to Luke 9:52–53, but *yes* according to John 4:39–40.

Failure to read the text carefully and to distinguish different times. Luke 9:52–53 indicates that one particular village of the Samaritans did not receive Jesus at one time when He was traveling *south* toward Jerusalem. Although, in verse 56 we read that a *different* village did receive Jesus at that time. John 4:39–40 speaks about *another* time when Jesus was traveling through Samaria, this time going *north* toward Galilee (John 4:3–4, 43). This time, the text states that some Samaritans from one city (Sychar — verse 5) received Jesus (John 4:39–40). How could there be any contradiction since these two texts record two different events that happened on two different visits to Samaria?

391. Should the gospel be preached to everyone? *No*, Jews only, according to Matthew 10:5–6, 15:24 and Acts 16:6. *Yes*, everyone, according to Matthew 28:19; Mark 16:15; Acts 8:25, 15:3, 22:21, 28:28.

Sweeping generalization fallacy, incidental fallacy, and failure to distinguish different times. The Scriptures teach that, in general, the gospel should be preached to all creation (Matthew 28:19; Mark 16:15); but they also give some instructions on how and *when* it should be presented.

First of all, the Gospel was to be given to the Jews first, then to the Gentiles (Romans 1:16). Thus, Jesus instructed His disciples to go to the Jews and not the Gentiles *initially* (Matthew 10:5–6). After the Jews were reached, then Jesus instructed His disciples to preach to the Samaritans and then to Gentiles as well (Acts 1:8). So, this is not an exception, but rather gives the *order* in which the gospel is to be preached to all creation. The same order is indicated in Matthew 15:24–28. Likewise, Paul was forbidden at one specific time from preaching in Asia (Acts 16:6), but this does not imply that the gospel should not be preached there at a later time.

Note that Acts 8:25 does not say one way or the other whether the gospel should "be preached to everyone"; it only indicates that the early Christians *did* in fact preach to many villages of the Samaritans. Nor do Acts 15:3, 22:21, and 28:28 explicitly teach what *should* be done; rather it states what *was* done. Though, in all these cases, what the Christians did was fully consistent with the biblical generalization to preach the gospel to all creation.

392. Did Sarah have faith that she would conceive? *Yes,* **according to Hebrews 11:11, but** *no,* **according to Genesis 18:10–15.**

Failure to distinguish different times. When Sarah first heard the news, it appears that she doubted (Genesis 18:10–15). At a later time, she came to believe the prophecy (Hebrews 11:11).

393. Were the Israelites to spare the trees in the countries they invaded? Second Kings 3:19 says *no,* **but 20:19 says** *yes.*

Bifurcation fallacy. The critic seems to think that either trees are not to be spared at all times in all battles, or they are to be spared at all times in all battles. But there is no logical reason to be restricted to merely those two options. In general, when a city was *besieged* and about to be *captured,* the Israelites were to spare fruit trees (Deuteronomy 20:19). This is obviously because they would need food once they occupied the city — and for future generations as well. In 2 Kings 3:19, the cities of the Moabites were not besieged, and were not to be captured, but were to be utterly destroyed. There was no intention of occupying the cities, and therefore no need to preserve the food supply. Thus, God commanded Israel to destroy such cities completely, including the trees.

394. Did Jesus have secret teachings? *Yes,* **according to Matthew 13:10–11, but** *no,* **according to John 18:20.**

Specious reasoning. Jesus taught openly (John 18:20). But He taught in such a way that the hard-hearted would not understand but that His followers would (Matthew 13:10). Where is there any inconsistency? Interestingly, the critic's poor understanding of the Bible and his specious reasoning from it is an illustration of the truth of Matthew 13:10–11.

395. Should we let others see our good works? Matthew 5:16 and 1 Peter 2:12 say *yes,* **but Matthew 6:1, 23:3, 5 says** *no.*

Failure to read the text in context and to distinguish different senses. Christians should do good even in the sight of others *in such a way that others give glory to God,* as Matthew 5:16 explicitly states. However, Christians should not do good in the sight of others for the purpose of glorifying themselves, for the purpose of being honored by men, as Matthew 6:1–2 states. Notice that that the context of both Matthew 6:1 and 23:3–5 is doing good "to be noticed by" men — for selfish reasons. But the context of Matthew 5:16 and 1 Peter 2:12 is doing good for the purpose of glorifying *God.* There is no contradiction in saying that we should do good openly for God-honoring reasons, but not for selfish reasons.

396. Can God be seen? *Yes,* **according to Genesis 12:7, 17:1, 18:1, 26:2, 24, 32:30, 35:9, 48:3; Exodus 3:16, 4:5, 6:3, 24:9–11, 33:11, 23; Numbers 14:14; Deuteronomy 5:4, 34:10; Judges 13:22; 1 Kings 22:19; Job 42:5; Psalm 63:2; Isaiah 6:1, 6:5; Ezekiel 1:27, 20:35; Amos 7:7, 9:1; Habakkuk 3:3–5; and Matthew 18:9.** *No,* **according to Exodus 33:20; John 1:18, 6:46; 1 Timothy 1:17, 6:16; and 1 John 4:12.**

Failure to distinguish different times, and different senses. God can be seen at some times and in some ways, but He cannot be seen at *other* times or in *other* ways. For example, God can be seen when He takes on human form or is metaphorically "seen" when He speaks through one of His angels, or through a representation such as cloud, fire, or whirlwind (Genesis 12:7, 17:1, 18:1, 26:2, 4, 32:30, 35:9, 48:3; Exodus 3:16, 4:5, 6:3, 24:9–11, 33:11, 23; Numbers 14:14; Deuteronomy 5:4, 34:10; Judges 13:20–22; Job 42:5; Psalm 63:2). Moreover, God can appear in visions or dreams (Isaiah 6:1, 5; Ezekiel 1:27–28; Amos 7:7, 9:1; Habakkuk 3:3–5). In all such cases, what is seen is a visible representation of the invisible God.

Though God can choose to manifest in visible form, He is not essentially visible (1 Timothy 1:17). He is not a physical being with a location within space/time that can be seen (1 Kings 8:27), except when He chooses to take on a physical nature. But no one has seen God's nonphysical essential form at any time (John 1:18) because God is not a physical being that can (normally) be seen.

There is a second sense in which we might ask "Can God be seen?" And that is, can we experience the full glory of God? God's glory is often represented by visual symbols, such as light (1 John 1:5) that are seen not literally, but spiritually. For example, God is perfectly pure and holy, expressed metaphorically as unapproachable light (1 Timothy 6:16). This indicates that sinful man cannot see God in that sense. The unveiled fullness of the glory of God (which is sometimes called His "face") cannot be seen by sinful man (Exodus 33:20; John 6:46; 1 John 4:12) — not in our present fallen state. But glorified men will enjoy the sight of God in the fullness of His glory, just as angels do (Matthew 18:10). Thus, there is no contradiction when the verses listed by the critic are exegeted in context.

(Note that Ezekiel 20:35 does not seem to refer to a visible representation of God, but rather the confrontational nature with which God will deal with His rebellious people — "face to face.")

397. Do bad things happen to good people? *Yes*, according to Habakkuk 1:4, 1:13 and Hebrews 12:6, but *no*, according to Proverbs 12:21, 19:23 and 1 Peter 3:13.

Failure to read the text in context, genre fallacy, and sweeping generalization fallacy. Of course, bad things happen to good people. The Gospel message on which the entire Bible is focused is about a truly horrible thing happening (death by crucifixion) to a perfectly righteous person (Christ). And there are those persons who are positionally righteous who nonetheless suffer at times in this world (Habakkuk 1:4, 13), as the entire Book of Job demonstrates.

Do Proverbs 12:21 and 19:23 contradict this? Hardly. The critic has ignored the genre principle. Proverbs are short sayings of generalizations — things that are true *most of the time*. Generally, when people obey God's law, things tend to work out for them most of the time. But there are exceptions. Yet the critic has committed the sweeping generalization fallacy in applying these generalizations as if they had no exceptions.

And what of 1 Peter 3:13? This too is stated as a generalization — that if you continually do what is good, people will not be inclined to hate or persecute you. The critic might have realized that this is a generalization if he had read the very next verse! First Peter 3:14 starts, "But even if you should suffer for righteousness' sake" — indicating that indeed, sometimes the righteous suffer bad things. The critic's sloppy lack of scholarship again shows that he is not seriously interested in getting to the truth of the matter.

The critic also listed Hebrews 12:6; but this verse does not pertain to this issue. Rather, Hebrews 12:6 discusses discipline. This would involve God disciplining a person who has acted inappropriately, just as a father punishes a son, so that the person will stop acting inappropriately. Hebrews 12:5–11 makes this abundantly clear.

398. Did Jesus perform many signs and wonders? *Yes,* according to Mark 16:20; John 3:2, 20:30; and Acts 2:22. *No,* according to Matthew 12:39, 16:4; Mark 8:12; and Luke 11:29.

Failure to read the text carefully and in context. Of course, Jesus performed many signs and wonders (Mark 16:20; John 3:2, 20:30; Acts 2:22). No verse contradicts this. The critic has taken out of context the accounts recorded in Matthew 12:39 and 16:4, which are repeated in Mark 8:12 and Luke 11:29. Here, Jesus does not say that He will give no signs, but rather that He will give no signs *to them*, except for one — the sign of Jonah (a reference to His upcoming Resurrection). So, the Pharisees would get only one sign from Jesus, and not the sign that they wanted to see. But all these texts agree that Jesus did give signs.

399. Do Christians sin? *Yes,* according to 1 Kings 8:46; 2 Chronicles 6:36; Proverbs 20:9; Ecclesiastes 7:20; Romans 3:23; and 1 John 1:8, 10. *No,* according to Romans 5:14; 1 John 3:6, 9, 5:18; and 3 John 11.

Failure to read the text carefully or in context. Of course, Christians sin at times, even after salvation (1 Kings 8:46; 2 Chronicles 6:36; Proverbs 20:9; Ecclesiastes 7:20; Romans 3:23; 1 John 1:9–10). We don't all sin in exactly the same way of course (Romans 5:14). But we do sin from time to time, and this is always wrong. Nonetheless, Christians do not *practice* sin, meaning we don't choose sin as a way of life or desire to become more sinful (1 John 3:6–9, 5:18, 3 John 11). Instead, those of us who are saved by grace practice *righteousness,* desiring to become more righteous in our character and actions though we are already righteous *in principle* (1 John 3:7).

A brief study in the original language confirms that all the above passages are perfectly consistent. Note that the word "sins" in 1 John 5:18 is in the present, active, indicative form, indicating *continued action.* That is, a Christian does not *willfully and consistently* engage in sin. This is the same verb tense used in Matthew 6:12 in reference to our continued forgiveness of others. We ask God to forgive our debts "as we forgive our debtors" (NKJV), e.g., we make a conscious and consistent choice to forgive others continually. A Christian will not therefore consciously, willfully, and consistently choose sin, even though the Christian continues to struggle against sin.

400. Does God sleep? *No,* according to Psalm 121:3–4, but *yes,* according to Psalm 44:23.

Failure to read the text in context, and genre fallacy. No, God — in the essence of His divinity — does not sleep (Psalm 121:3–4) and no verse states otherwise. Psalm 44:23 records a *song* of the sons of Korah where they ask why God "sleeps" as a metaphor for asking why God does not take action on their behalf. This is obvious given the context of both the preceding and following verses (Psalm 44:22, 24).

401. Was Jesus silent during His trial before Pilate? *Yes*, **according to Matthew 27:12–14, but** *no*, **according to John 18:33–38 and 1 Timothy 6:13.**

Failure to read the text in context. Note that the critic conveniently omitted Matthew 27:11, where Jesus verbally answers Pilate, in full agreement with John 18:33–38 and 1 Timothy 6:13. Matthew 27:12–14 indicates that Jesus remained silent *while He was "being accused by the chief priests and elders,"* that is, during *that part* of the trial. But Christ did answer some of Pilate's questions, and there is no Scripture that states otherwise.

402. Does God have a body? *Yes*, **according to Genesis 3:8; Exodus 33:11, 20, 22, 23, 34:5; Deuteronomy 23:12–13; Ezekiel 1:27, 8:2; and Habakkuk 3:3–4.** *No*, **according to Luke 24:39 and John 4:24.**

Sweeping generalization fallacy and genre fallacy. God, in the essence of His divinity, is spirit (John 4:24), and thus does not have a physical body (Luke 24:39). However, God is often *represented* in prophetic visions with a visible form (Ezekiel 1:27, 8:2). There is nothing illogical about a visible or physical thing representing something non-physical, such as the Statue of Liberty representing freedom.

Moreover, poetic and prophetic literature often describes God's power anthropomorphically (Habakuk 3:3–4; Isaiah 19:1), and such figures of speech will at times be used in historical narrative as well, such as Deuteronomy 23:14. (I can only assume that the critic meant verse 14, because Deuteronomy 23:12–13 have nothing to do with the issue). But visions and figures of speech do not contradict the fact that God is essentially spirit, not flesh.

That being said, God is an all-powerful spirit, and can certainly manifest physically in a body when He so pleases, and He has done so on a number of occasions (Genesis 3:8; Exodus 34:5). The most obvious and spectacular example of this is the incarnation of Christ

(John 1:1, 14). Jesus, the second member of the Trinity, now and forever has a human body in addition to His divine nature. God the Father, and God the Holy Spirit do not have a (permanent) body. Furthermore, when God spoke to Moses "face to face" in Exodus 33:11, this might mean that God took physical form, or it might simply indicate that the communication was direct, visible, and not mediated by an angel. In any case, the fullness of God's presence, His "face" was veiled (Exodus 33:20–23).

403. Is it wrong to steal? *No,* **according to Exodus 3:22, 12:35–36; Ezekiel 39:10; and Nahum 2:9.** *Yes,* **according to Exodus 20:15; Matthew 19:18; Leviticus 6:2–5, 19:11, 13; Deuteronomy 5:19; Psalm 37:21; Mark 10:19; Luke 18:20; Ephesians 4:28; and 1 Thessalonians 4:6.**

Failure to read the text carefully or think carefully (specious reasoning). Of course it is wrong to steal (Exodus 20:15; Matthew 19:18; Mark 10:19; Luke 18:20; Ephesians 4:28; Leviticus 6:2–5, 19:11, 13; Deuteronomy 5:19; Psalm 37:21). Everything ultimately belongs to God (Psalm 24:1), and He distributes it according to His pleasure. People are mere stewards of that which God has entrusted to them. Thus, it is morally wrong to *take without consent* a possession that God has entrusted to someone else. And by the same principle, it is morally right to take *back* something that was previously stolen. And of course, it is fine to ask for a gift, and it is morally commendable to give to others (Psalm 37:21). The passages listed by the critic are all examples of this — of *asking* for gifts (Exodus 3:22, 12:35), and of taking back what was previously stolen (Ezekiel 39:10; Nahum 2:9). Neither of these amounts to stealing.

404. Did Joshua remove the 12 stones from the Jordan River? *Yes,* **according to Joshua 4:20, but** *no,* **according to Joshua 4:9.**

Equivocation fallacy and failure to read the text carefully. Which 12 stones? *Two* sets of 12 stones were set up, as the critic would have realized if he had read verses 3–8. One set was brought from the Jordan River to the camp site (Joshua 4:1–8), and later to Gilgal (Joshua 4:20). The other set was set up by Joshua himself at the location where the priests crossed the Jordan River, and remained there.

405. Did the women immediately tell the disciples after finding the empty tomb? *Yes*, according to Matthew 28:8 and Luke 24:8–9, but *no*, according to Mark 16:8.

Failure to read the text carefully. Notice that *none* of these passages say that the women *immediately* told the disciples. They only state that the women *did* tell the disciples (Matthew 28:8; Luke 24:9; Mark 16:10). But this wasn't necessarily immediate. Apparently, they were *initially* afraid and needed some time to process what they had seen (Mark 16:8). When their joy overcame their fear, they *did* go and tell the disciples as Matthew 28:8; Luke 24:9; and Mark 16:10 all confirm in full agreement.

406. Can God be tempted? James 1:13 says *no*, which contradicts Exodus 17:2; Deuteronomy 6:16; Matthew 4:7; Luke 4:12; and Acts 15:10.

Equivocation fallacy. The word "tempted" is used in two different ways in Scripture. It can mean (1) to be tested or (2) to be enticed by lust. God can be tested (though it is wrong for us to test Him by any standard other than His own). But God cannot be enticed by lust. Context makes clear that the sense of "tempted" in James 1:13 is to be "enticed by lust" because the very next verse says just that! What a pity the critic didn't read verse 14. So, God cannot be enticed by lust because His nature is perfectly Holy.

But God can be tempted in the sense of being tested — people trying His patience (Exodus 17:2; Deuteronomy 6:16; Matthew 4:7; Luke 4:12; Acts 15:10). Note that Jesus was tempted in the sense of tested, and yet was never enticed to sin (Hebrews 4:15). Context makes all the difference, doesn't it?

407. Has God ever tempted anyone? James 1:13 says *no*, but Genesis 22:1; 2 Samuel 24:1; and Matthew 6:13 say *yes*.

Equivocation fallacy. (Same as #406). Since the word "tempt" can either mean "to test" or "to entice," we must ask which sense is used in the critic's question. Does God tempt people in the sense of enticing them to sin? Of course not (James 1:13–14); this would be inconsistent with His Holy character. He allows temptation at times, but is never the source of it. Rather, God delivers us from such temptation (Matthew 6:13). That this is the sense of James 1:13 is made obvious by James 1:14. People are enticed to sin by their own lust — never by God. Note that God sometimes allows Satan to tempt people often as a partial punishment for previous sin (2 Samuel 24:1 and 1 Chronicles 21:1).

But does God "tempt" people in the sense of "testing" their character? Of course — and this builds their faith and encourages others (Genesis 22:1–12; cp. Hebrews 11:17, 12:5–11).

408. Is it okay to test (or tempt) God? Judges 6:36–40; 1 Kings 18:36–38; and 2 Kings 20:8–11 say *yes*, but Deuteronomy 6:16; Matthew 4:7; and Luke 4:12 say *no*.

Failure to read the text carefully. No, it is not morally right to test God by any lesser standard (Deuteronomy 6:16; Matthew 4:7; Luke 4:12). God does give confirmation of His existence and power, but He does it *on His own terms* — through His Word, penned by His prophets as they were moved by His Spirit. It is inappropriate for us to create non-biblical tests by which we may judge who is God. The Scriptures are unified in this point.

So, in 1 Kings 18:36–38, the "test" was authorized by God — it was on His own terms that He would demonstrate His glory. Context makes this clear (1 Kings 18:1). This was not Elijah inventing a test for God because he doubted God; rather it was Elijah obeying God because he trusted God (1 Kings 18:1–2). Likewise, in 2 Kings 20:8–11, there is no indication that Hezekiah doubted God's Word, and no disgrace in His asking for a visible confirmation of it. Moreover, Hezekiah did not create a test for God; God set the terms of the sign (though He gave Hezekiah two options — 2 Kings 20:8–9).

The critic lists Judges 6:36–40 as a supposed counter-example; but Gideon is not testing God. Rather Gideon wanted to be sure that he was following God's voice, and not his own imagination. So, he appropriately and reverently asked the Lord for confirmation, which the Lord provided. Gideon did not put God to the test, because once he was certain that he had a promise from God, he acted in faithful obedience to it (Judges 7; Hebrews 11:32–34).

409. Can thieves go to heaven? Mark 15:27 and Luke 23:32–43 say *yes*, but 1 Corinthians 6:9–10 says *no*.

Failure to read the text carefully or in context. *Former* thieves can go to heaven if and only if they have repented of their sin and trusted in Christ (Mark 15:27; Luke 23:32–43). However, if they remain in sin and do not repent, then they will not inherit the kingdom of heaven (1 Corinthians 6:9–10). The critic conventionally stopped at verse 10; but if he had read on to verse 11 he would have seen that it says, "Such *were* some of you . . ." (1 Corinthians 6:11).

410. Was it okay to touch the risen Jesus before His ascension? John 20:17 says *no*, but Matthew 28:9; Luke 24:39; and John 20:26–27 all say *yes*.

Failure to study the original language or consult other translations. Of course there was no problem with Jesus being touched before His ascension, and many did so (Matthew 28:9; Luke 24:39; John 20:26–27). John 20:17 is perfectly consistent with this as the original language makes clear, and as the critic might have realized if he had consulted any translation besides the KJV. Jesus here says to Mary, "Do not cling to Me. . . ." So, He does not forbid being touched; rather, Mary was clinging to Christ as if to not let Him go, and He told her to stop because he wanted her to go and tell the brethren.

411. May Adam eat from any tree? *Yes,* **according to Genesis 1:29, but** *no,* **according to Genesis 2:17.**

Sweeping generalization fallacy and argument from silence. Many commandments given by God have qualifications, such that they can be stated as a generalization with one or more exceptions. That's also true of many man-made laws. For example, in the United States, *generally* you are required drive on the right side of the road. But there are legal exceptions — such as one-way streets. These exceptions need not be explicitly stated every time the generalization is mentioned — that would be tedious. One would think that this would be very obvious. But to our critic, apparently it is not.

Genesis 1:29 gives the generalization that Adam and Eve were permitted to eat of every tree on the surface of the earth. Genesis 2:16–17 gives a more detailed account, repeating the generalization and also stipulating one exception; the tree of knowledge of good and evil was to be off-limits. Now the fact that Genesis 1:29 does not explicitly mention this one exception does not mean that it wasn't given — that would be the fallacy of argument from silence.

412. Is there an unforgivable sin? *Yes,* **according to Matthew 12:31–32; Mark 3:29; and Luke 12:10, but** *no,* **according to Acts 13:39.**

Failure to read the text carefully and specious reasoning. Yes. When people continually reject the Holy Spirit's testimony that Christ is Lord, when they die without having trusted in Christ for salvation, that sin cannot be forgiven because it is only by believing in Christ that we can be freed from our bondage to sin (Matthew 12:31–32; Mark 3:39; Luke 12:10; Acts 13:39). Note that Acts 13:39 specifies that those *who believe in Christ* (and thus those who have not committed the unforgivable sin) are freed from all things. So, all the texts are fully consistent.

413. Is it okay to marry unbelievers? *Yes,* **according to 1 Corinthians 7:12–14, but** *no,* **according to 2 Corinthians 6:14–17.**

Failure to read the text carefully. It is not acceptable (it is sin) for Christians to marry someone whom they know is a non-Christian

(2 Corinthians 6:14–17). This is *not* the issue 1 Corinthians 7:12–14 is addressing. Rather, 1 Corinthians 7:12–14 describes a situation where a Christian is currently *already married* to a non-Christian. Perhaps this is because the Christian sinned, and violated 1 Corinthians 6:14–17. Or perhaps the person became a Christian *after* having already been married. Either way, the Bible indicates that it is not appropriate for the two to divorce, as long as the unbeliever consents to stay with [Greek: *suneudokeô* — literally meaning "together considers it good" or "together approves" the marriage with] the believer. The text really is pretty clear, and there is no inconsistency.

414. Does God ever tire? *No*, according to Isaiah 40:28, but *yes*, according to Exodus 31:17; Isaiah 1:14, 43:24; and Jeremiah 15:6.

Genre fallacy and equivocation fallacy. God does not literally tire, in the sense of *requiring rest* (Isaiah 40:28). But that doesn't imply that God doesn't "rest" in other ways. When God finished creating the universe, He "rested" in the sense of ceasing His activity of creating (Genesis 2:2; Exodus 31:17). But no text indicates that God was "tired" after creating the universe, in the sense of requiring rest. On the contrary, the Bible explicitly states that God's pattern of working for six days and resting for one was to be a pattern for us to emulate (Exodus 20:8–11). God's rest was for our benefit, not His (Mark 2:27).

Note that the Books of Isaiah and Jeremiah are prophetic literature, which make use of figures of speech such as anthropomorphism. Anthropomorphisms express an aspect of God using human characteristics — such as God's "arm" representing His power, even though God as a spirit doesn't literally have a physical arm. Thus, when Isaiah 1:14 speaks of God being "weary" of the festivals that had been emptied of genuine worship, we are not to take this as an indication that God required rest. Rather, it puts on human terms the disgust that God has with empty worship. Similarly, God being "wearied" by the sins of the people in Isaiah 43:24 isn't a reference to physical fatigue, and it would be ridiculous to take it as such. And once again, in Jeremiah 15:6, God is said to be "tired" or "weary" of continually withholding punishment from those who won't consistently follow Him. But He is not physically, or literally tired. I could equally well say that I am "sick and tired" of the critic making all these mistakes. But that doesn't imply that I need a nap or require medical treatment!

415. Does God destroy both the righteous and the wicked? *Yes,* according to Job 9:22; Ecclesiastes 7:15; and Ezekiel 21:3. *No,* according to Ezekiel 18:8–9, 19–20, 33:18–19.

Equivocation fallacy and failure to read the text carefully and in context. Both the wicked and the positionally righteous will experience physical death (which is a type of "destruction"); but the righteous will be resurrected unto eternal life and will never again die (John 11:25–26), whereas the wicked experience eternal death. The critic ignores this important distinction and conflates temporal punishment with eternal punishment. All people experience temporal death (Hebrews 9:27; Job 9:22; Ecclesiastes 7:15; Ezekiel 21:3). But only the unrepentant and wicked experience *eternal* death (Ezekiel 18:8–9, 19–21, 33:18; Revelation 20:14–15), as all the above verses teach without contradiction.

416. Do the wicked live long? *Yes,* according to Job 21:7, but *no,* according to Psalm 55:23; Proverbs 10:27, 24:20; Ecclesiastes 8:13; Jeremiah 23:19; and Nahum 1:3.

Sweeping Generalization fallacy and equivocation fallacy. The critic equivocates on the word "long," which is a relative word. The life of a man is long compared to a fly, but not long compared to a tree. As a general trend, the lives of the wicked are cut short; they do not live as long as they would have if they were righteous (Psalm 55:23; Proverbs 10:27, 24:20; Ecclesiastes 8:13; Jeremiah 23:19; Nahum 1:3). Passages like Proverbs 10:27 make this very clear — that the "years of the wicked will be shortened" from what they would have been otherwise. Many examples can be cited: Absalom and Judas died young as a result of their sins.

But that doesn't mean that their lives cannot be long relative to others. God does allow some wicked people to prosper to some extent and to grow old in this world before they are eternally condemned (Job 21:7–13; Psalm 73:3–4; Jeremiah 12:1–2). But this does not in any way contradict the general trend that the lives of the wicked are shortened by their wickedness.

417. Is God's will always done in heaven? *Yes*, according to Matthew 6:10, but *no*, according to Revelation 12:7.

Specious reasoning: false inference. Yes, God's will is always done in heaven and, in a sense, on earth too, since everything He plans is accomplished (Matthew 6:10, 28:18; Isaiah 46:10–11). Perhaps the critic merely *assumed* that God's plan does not include war, but this is false. It was by God's will that Satan was permitted to rebel and to be cast out of heaven (Revelation 12:7). So, there is no contradiction there. God does not always *approve* of what people (or fallen angels) do, yet even wicked actions are part of God's plan, and God can use even wicked actions to accomplish His will (Acts 2:23–24; Romans 11:11–12).

418. Is wisdom a good thing? *Yes* according to Proverbs 4:7, but *no*, according to Job 37:24 and 1 Corinthians 1:19.

Equivocation fallacy. Genuine wisdom — that which is from God — is good and to be desired more than gold (Proverbs 4:7, 3:13–14; James 3:17). Worldly "wisdom" that is contrary to God's word is foolishness to God (1 Corinthians 1:19–20; Job 37:24; James 3:15) and therefore not good but evil. Note that James 3:13–17 explicitly teaches the distinction between godly wisdom, which is good, and worldly wisdom, which is evil.

419. Does wisdom make people happy? Proverbs 3:13 says *yes*, but Ecclesiastes 1:18 says *no*.

Bifurcation fallacy. Yes, wisdom brings happiness (Proverbs 3:13). It also brings grief and pain (Ecclesiastes 1:18). Wisdom gives us a more accurate view of the world, a world that contains both good and evil. Wisdom makes a person more aware of the world. So, it stands to reason that increased wisdom results in increased capacity to experience both happiness and grief. It is just like how our eyes allow us to see things that are beautiful, and things that are ugly. There is no contradiction there.

420. Can only God work wonders? *Yes*, **according to Psalm 136:4, but** *no*, **according to 2 Thessalonians 2:9.**

Failure to read the text carefully or in context. First, we note that 2 Thessalonians 2:9 teaches that the man of lawlessness performs *"false wonders"* — that is, things that appear to be wonders but are *not*. So, this is fully consistent with Psalm 136:4, which teaches that God alone performs (true) great wonders. Second, we note that the context of Psalm 136:4 is God's acts of creation; see verses 5–9. It is these great wonders specifically that can be performed only by God.

CLOSING REMARKS

Rather than listing 420 genuine contradictions in the Scripture, the critic has actually given 420 examples of his own incompetence, lack of reading comprehension skills, and lack of critical thinking skills. In many cases, more than one fallacy is committed in a given example, so the true count is even higher. Of course, some of the examples could be classified in several different ways, so the exact breakdown may differ from my list below. Nonetheless, by my count, the critic has committed approximately 615 errors in reasoning, as broken down in the chart on the following page.

What is perhaps most surprising is which errors are the most common, and which are the least common. Naively, we might expect that the most common mistakes would involve a translational difficulty. After all, most Bible critics cannot read the Bible in its original language and are forced to use an (imperfect) English translation. They could be forgiven for misunderstanding a passage where there is some difficulty in translating a peculiar Hebrew or Greek expression into English (although it would still be incumbent upon the critic to check the original text before declaring the he had found a contradiction). But only 9 of the critic's 615 errors fall into this category — less than two percent.

The Critic's Errors	
195	Failure to read the text carefully or in context
89	Bifurcation fallacy
62	Equivocation fallacy
41	Failure to distinguish different times
40	Specious reasoning
33	Subset fallacy
26	Semantic range fallacy
22	Sweeping generalization fallacy
21	Bluff
18	Failure to distinguish different senses
11	Genre fallacy
10	Argument from silence
9	Failure to check original language
8	Failure to do textual transmission analysis
6	Semantic anachronism fallacy
5	False-cause fallacy
5	Incidental fallacy
3	Fallacy of elephant hurling
3	Hasty generalization fallacy
2	Arithmetic mistake
2	Question-begging epithet
1	Straw-man fallacy
1	Fallacy of commutation of conditionals
1	Reification fallacy
1	Fallacy of denying the antecedent
1	Naturalistic fallacy

What is the critic's most common error? Amazingly, it is a simple **failure to read the text carefully and in context**. This is the kind of error we expect from a six-year-old who is just beginning to read. But for an adult to make this kind of mistake so frequently is simply inexcusable. *Is this really what passes for scholarship among Bible critics?*

In the political arena, people will sometimes intentionally take their opponent's words out of context in a deliberate and unethical attempt to make their opponent look foolish. Is this what the Bible critic has done in his list? Or is the critic so eager in his attempt to mock Christianity that he is simply careless in his research? Either option does not speak well of the critic.

The second most common error the critic makes is the **bifurcation fallacy** — presenting two options as if they are the only two and are incompatible, when in reality a third option exists. Of these, most examples amount to compatible differences, akin to the statements "the car is fast" and "the car is red." The statements certainly differ. But there is no contradiction at all — no reason why both cannot be true. So, was Abraham justified by faith or by works? "Both" — of course — is the answer (see #139). Was Abiham's mother called "Micaiah" as in 2 Chronicles 13:2 or "Maachah" as in 1 Kings 15:2? "Both" again is the answer.

Equivocation was the third most common error — the conflation of different meanings for a word that has more than one meaning. Context determines meaning, and we've already seen from the critic's most common error that he really isn't interested in reading the text of Scripture in context. Many of his equivocation fallacies assumed that no two people have ever had the same name. Also, as #293 and #385 illustrate, there are many times when an English word is used to translate more than one Hebrew or Greek word. If these differences in original vocabulary are ignored (as a hasty conclusion of "inconsistency" is alleged) this constitutes an equivocation fallacy.

The **failure to distinguish different times** was the fourth most common of the critic's errors. Some things are true at one time, and false *at a different time*. This is not contradictory. Of course, the number of people from a particular family who returned from Babylon will be different at one time from another time. So, naturally, there will be some numerical differences between the list in Ezra chapter 2 and the list in Nehemiah chapter 7. That's hardly surprising, since the Nehemiah list was found a century later and therefore includes additions for late arrivals and deletions for those who moved away. One critic chose to list this as 17 separate alleged contradictions, perhaps to make his list look longer than it really is. He even distributed them among the other examples, perhaps hoping that no one would notice. If so, this would be the fallacy of elephant hurling — particularly since not one of these 17 examples is genuinely contradictory.

The above considerations prompt us to ask, "Do Bible critics do any legitimate research on these issues?" We can only conclude from this study that at least *most* critics do not. These oft-repeated examples are not carefully researched at all. It should be clear that most of the examples on the list were very obviously *not* contradictory at all when read in context. Only 9 (2%) required us to consult the original language to resolve any perceived problem. Only 8 required textual transmission analysis to resolve. If anyone did bother to check the list, he or she surely would have seen this. We must therefore conclude that these critics are not concerned about being honest. If this is the best that the critics have to offer, then the Christian worldview really has no serious competition at all.

The Biblical Basis for the Law of Non-Contradiction

But there is an even more profound irony in the critic's list of supposed Bible contradictions. The critic is providing this list presumably to convince people that the Bible is wrong. The argument is something like this:

1. Contradictions are always wrong.
2. The Bible has contradictions.
3. Therefore, the Bible is wrong.

But do you realize that premise #1 in the above argument is a biblical truth! In other words, the claim that contradictions are always wrong can only be rationally defended if the Bible is true. Think about it: how could anyone know for certain that contradictions are always wrong?

Most people simply dismiss such a question with the retort, "Well we all know that. We all know that two contradictory statements cannot both be true at the same time and in the same sense. It's obvious!" But if it's so obvious, *prove it!* That is something that most people cannot do. And yet, rationality requires us to have a good reason for our beliefs, and to relinquish beliefs that do not have good supporting reasons. So, what reason do we have for believing that truth must always be self-consistent and non-contradictory?

This question is easy to answer for the Christian. The self-consistent nature of truth stems from the self-consistent nature of God. God cannot deny (contradict) Himself (2 Timothy 2:13). And all truth is in God (John 14:6; Colossians 2:2–3). Therefore, truth will never deny/contradict truth. We know that this will be true at all times, because God does not change with time (Malachi 3:6; Psalm 110:4). We know that this will be true for all locations in the universe, because God is omni-present (Jeremiah 23:24).

But how would a person — apart from God's revelation — know that contradictions are always wrong? He can't appeal to his experience because his experience is not universal. That is, he can't say "Well, I've never experienced true contradictions, so I assume I never will." But that would be like saying, "Well, I've never died before, so I assume I never will." If you cannot conclude that you are immortal on the basis that you have never died before, then neither can you conclude that contradictions are never true simply on the basis that you've never experienced a true contradiction.

Nor can the unbeliever appeal to the collective past experience of humanity, because the experiences of all humanity are not universal. And the past experiences of humanity (by themselves) do not prove what is possible in the future. For example, it would be ridiculous to argue "it is impossible to go to Mars" on the basis that no one has gone there before. No one had gone to the moon before 1969, but that didn't make it impossible.

So, the unbeliever is really in quite a bind. On the one hand, he wants to argue against the Bible on the basis that it has what he believes to be contradictions. On the other hand, apart from the truth of the Bible there would be no basis for arguing that contradictions are always wrong — which is the first premise in his argument against the Bible.

To rationally resolve this issue, the unbeliever would have to either (1) embrace the truth of the Bible in order to get justification for the law of non-contradiction — in which case he cannot then reject the Bible for containing alleged contradictions, or (2) he would have to reject the premise that contradictions are always false, in which case he would then not be able to cogently argue that the Bible is wrong for allegedly having them. Either way, his argument above is unsound.

Conclusions

Far from disproving the Bible, the critic has actually confirmed what the Bible teaches in Romans 1:18–25. God has revealed Himself inescapably to all people (Romans 1:18–19) such that there is literally no legitimate excuse for denying biblical truth (Romans 1:20). That's why all people inherently know God's law of non-contradiction — because they all know God. The problem with unbelievers is not that they genuinely, sincerely have not been given enough information to know that the Bible is true. Rather, they suppress what they know to be true (Romans 1:18). They know God and therefore are able to have knowledge of other things as well by using God's laws of logic, by relying on the fact that God made our minds with the capacity to learn and to be rational, and by relying on the fact that God upholds the universe in a consistent way. But they don't thank God for His revelation; instead they replace their knowledge of God with foolish speculations, choosing to believe a lie rather than the truth (Romans 1:21–25).

Those who obstinately refuse the offers of grace and mercy extended by the Lord will repeatedly distort the Word of God to their own destruction (2 Peter 3:16). We have seen this principle demonstrated beyond any doubt in the above list. The critic did not perform a fair and objective analysis of the text. Rather, he relentlessly pulled the verses out of context, drawing unwarranted and incorrect inferences. Clearly, the critic is not interested in the truth. He has an ax to grind. He doesn't *like* the Bible. And he is not above distorting the text of Scripture in an attempt to persuade others that the problem is in the text. But this really shows that the problem lies with the critic. The fact that this list and others just like it are commonly used by atheists as evidence against the Bible reveals that this lack of scholarship is a common characteristic of critics.

The Christian can rest assured that the Bible really is the Word of God. People have attempted to disprove, destroy, and discredit the text. But they only succeed in destroying their own position. The Word of the Lord endures forever (1 Peter 1:25).

Scripture Index

recognize and refute

evolutionist arguments in a way that both honors God and lines up with the truth of His Word. (Eph. 5:1)

$13.99
978-0-89051-568-6

$10.99
978-0-89051-594-5

A Comprehensive Guide to the Heavens

"This book is meant to be an introduction only — a starting point to a biblical view of the universe. . . . Who knows what amazing truths are waiting to be discovered if only the shackles of secular thinking are removed. Now is the time of discovery. . . ."

7 x 9 • Hardcover
128 pages • $16.99
Full color interior
ISBN: 978-089051-471-9

Available at local Christian booksellers nationwide or at www.nlpg.com.

With a doctorate in astrophysics from the University of Colorado, Dr. Jason Lisle is your guide to the universe beyond our world in this remarkable book.

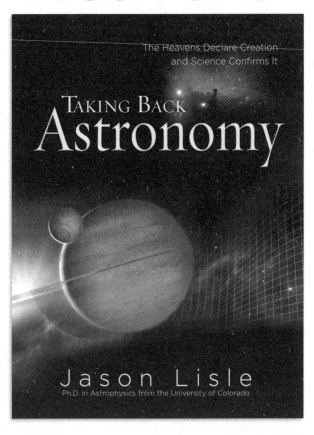

The Heavens Declare Creation and Science Confirms It

TAKING BACK Astronomy

Jason Lisle
Ph.D. in Astrophysics from the University of Colorado

Taking Back Astronomy is filled with facts that challenge secular theories and models of the universe — how it began and how it continues to amaze the scientific community. This book explores numerous evidences that point to a young universe: magnetic poles of planets, the spiral shape of galaxies, comets, and more. It explains the scale and size of the universe — something that is hard for our minds to imagine. With over 50 color photos of rarely seen stars, nebulas, and galaxies, Dr. Lisle guides you out among the stars to experience the awesome power of God's vast creation.